NEURAL NETWORKS
A Tutorial

Michael Chester

PTR Prentice Hall
Englewood Cliffs, New Jersey 07632

Library of Congress Cataloging-in-Publication Data

Chester, Michael.
   Neural networks : a tutorial / Michael Chester.
      p. cm.
   Includes bibliographical references and index.
   ISBN 0-13-368903-4
   1. Neural networks (Computer science) I. Title.
QA76.87.C45 1993
006.3—dc20   93-26
                                   CIP

Editorial/production supervision: bookworks
Manufacturing buyer: Mary McCartney
Cover designer: Lundgren Graphics

Published by PTR Prentice-Hall, Inc.
A Simon & Schuster Company
Englewood Cliffs, New Jersey 07632

The publisher offers discounts on this book when ordered
in bulk quantities. For more information, contact:

   Corporate Sales Department
   PTR Prentice Hall
   113 Sylvan Avenue
   Englewood Cliffs, New Jersey 07632
   Phone: 201-592-2863
   Fax: 201-592-2249

Printed in the United States of America
10 9 8 7 6 5 4 3 2 1

ISBN 0-13-368903-4

Prentice-Hall International (UK) Limited, *London*
Prentice-Hall of Australia Pty. Limited, *Sydney*
Prentice-Hall Canada Inc., *Toronto*
Prentice-Hall Hispanoamericana, S. A., *Mexico*
Prentice-Hall of India Private Limited, *New Delhi*
Prentice-Hall of Japan, Inc., *Tokyo*
Simon & Schuster Asia Pte. Ltd., *Singapore*
Editora Prentice-Hall do Brasil, Ltda., *Rio de Janeiro*

PREFACE

Artificial neural networks are analytical systems that address problems whose solutions have not been explicitly formulated. They contrast to classical computers and computer programs, which are designed to solve problems whose solutions—although they may be extremely complex—have been made explicit.

The topology of neural networks is a logical (and sometimes physical) structure in which multiple nodes communicate with each other through synapses that interconnect them. This topology is imitative of the structure of biological nervous systems. In the electronic case, the nodes, in general, are operational amplifiers and the synapses are variable resistors. In the optical case, the nodes are light transceivers and the synapses are optical media of variable transmissivity. In either case, the long-term knowledge stored in the network is represented in the states of the synaptic interconnections. Short-term knowledge is temporarily stored in the on-off states of the nodes. Both kinds of stored information determine how the network will respond to inputs.

To exercise the network, you introduce input voltages (or light intensities) into some or all of the nodes. The state of the nodes, when the network subsequently reaches equilibrium, is its response. It is fascinating to consider that this behavior seems a plausible model for how biological cells, forming into the first multicelled life forms, would communicate with each other.

In this book the emphasis is on the various mathematical paradigms by which different researchers have chosen to represent the logic of artificial neural networks. The treatment is at an intermediate level, designed for a technical audience without a specific previous background in artificial neural networks.

However, the coverage is not exclusively related to the neural paradigms.

CONTENTS

General concepts relating to the field are presented, especially in Chapter 1 ("Structure of an Artificial Neural Network"), Chapter 7 ("Learning Laws and Continued Taxonomy"), and Chapter 14 ("The Evolution of Intelligence"). Historical background is presented, along with analytical concepts, in Chapter 3 ("The Early Years"). Application examples are to be found throughout the text. Two chapters concentrate on hardware implementations: Chapter 12, "Integrated Circuits," and Chapter 13, "Optical Neural Nets."

Fuzzy systems, which, like neural networks, address problems with unformulated solutions, are also treated here, mostly in Chapter 11 ("Fuzzy Theory"). These systems utilize a logic based on the indefinite nature of sets to which elements are assigned.

The significance of the neural and fuzzy concepts comes from their unusual relationship to tacit knowledge. They have the ability to deal with aspects of perception, such as the recognition of topographies, that are best handled implicitly rather than explicitly—the things that we ourselves do not formulate.

Before neural networks became prominent, Michael Polanyi, a scientific philosopher, looked into the processes (such as recognizing faces) in which people employ tacit knowledge rather than explicit rules (Polanyi, 1966). One of his major conclusions is that knowledge has a hierarchical or layered structure. For instance, the manufacture of bricks depends on the molecular structure of the cements and clays that are the material of the bricks. However, there is nothing in molecular theory that defines bricks—neither their shapes, nor sizes, nor colors, nor the molds that form them.

Furthermore, although the building of brick walls, patios, or chimneys depends on the shape and strength of the individual bricks, there is nothing in the detailed physical description of a brick that says anything at all about those structures. Going up another level, the structures of walls and other surfaces say nothing about the master plan of an architect that will incorporate such structures. Yet, once again, the higher level concept depends on and utilizes the properties of the level just below it.

Polanyi sees this layered evolution of awareness as an aspect of tacit knowledge. Any given nth layer of knowledge, he points out, contains open boundaries to higher layers—potentialities for utilization by the next higher $(n + 1)$st layer that could not be arrived at through application of explicit nth layer principles, no matter how exhaustive.

Polanyi's analysis is reminiscent of Gödel's principle, which proves that a mathematical system includes among its theorems some theorems that, though true, cannot be proved within that system—but whose proofs must take place within a higher level, a metasystem. Gödel showed that this limitation holds true over a very broad class of systems, including our familiar integer arithmetic (Gödel, 1931).

Polanyi's ideas also suggest a later concept—the layered communications networks such as the OSI (Open Systems Interconnect) model developed by the

International Standards Organization. There, the "data link layer," which establishes the bit-packet structure to be used by the network, depends on the lower "physical layer," which establishes bit-level voltages, durations, and connections.

Going upward from the data link layer, there are higher layers (for a total of seven altogether), going through such conventions as network structures and message routing, all the way up to the "application layer," where the user defines an application. IBM's Systems Network Architecture (SNA) is a similar seven-layered structure, based on a somewhat different set of conventions.

If, as Polanyi and Gödel demonstrate, and as the OSI and SNA models exemplify, knowledge is hierarchical stuff with intrinsically tacit aspects at any given layer, then systems operating in tacit modes become singularly appropriate to the building of intelligence. Neural networks and fuzzy theory appear to be main contenders in the art of tacit representation. Both theories have already given rise to distinctive varieties of perceptive machines. And both have the potential to play major parts in our future efforts to understand and create the mysterious property of intelligence.

Acknowledgements

My talks and correspondence with many people in the fields of artificial neural networks and fuzzy theory have been crucial to my writing this book. I want to acknowledge especially John Caulfield, Bart Kosko, Rod Taber, and Fred Watkins for the extra time that each spent with me in valuable exchanges relating to these topics.

Michael Chester
Westlake Village, California

STRUCTURE OF AN ARTIFICIAL NEURAL NETWORK

The topology of interconnection and the rules employed by any neural network are generally lumped together as the *paradigm* (the model or pattern) of the network.   成 団

Artificial neural networks—or ANNs, as they are sometimes abbreviated—come in many different paradigms. Some of these require topologies with total interconnection among nodes (Figure 1-1a), and others require arrangement in layers (Figure 1-1b), with internodal connections between (but not within) layers. Figure 1-1c presents a topology in which there is bidirectional linkage between two layers, as well as communication between some of the nodes within a single layer. There are many other possibilities as well. The selected topology and the rules of operation are interrelated and are chosen by the theoretician or experimenter to implement a particular paradigm.

Artificial Neurons

Figure 1-2 shows the structure of a single node or neuron from an arbitrary network. The neuron in the figure, designated the jth neuron, occupies a position in its network that is quite general; that is, this neuron both accepts inputs from other neurons and sends its outputs to other neurons. Any neuron in a totally interconnected network has this generality. In a layered network, however, some neurons are specialized for either input or output; in such a network, it is only the interior or hidden nodes that maintain generality.

The generalized neuron gets its inputs from interconnections leading from

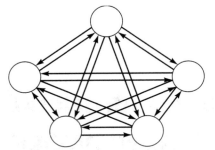 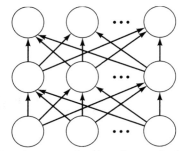

(a) A totally connected network   (b) A three-layer network with total connection between
                                          layers (in this case a feedforward network with
                                          no feedback from higher to lower layers)

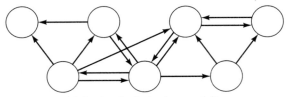

(c) A network of mixed connectivity

Figure 1-1: A neural network consists of interconnected nodes or "neurons." Nodes
present their output signals, typically in the form of voltage levels, to other nodes. In the
figure, the arrows indicate the direction of the signal flow. Many topologies are possible:
1-1(a) shows a totally connected network, in which every node outputs to every other
node; in 1-1(b) there are three layers of nodes, with total connection between layers (this
case showing a feedforward network, with no feedback from higher to lower layers);
1-1(c) shows a network of mixed connectivity.

the outputs of other neurons. Following the biological terminology for the connections between nerve cells, these interconnections are also known as *synapses*.

The synaptic connections are weighted. That is, when the *i*th neuron sends a
signal to the *j*th neuron, that signal is multiplied by the weighting on the *i,j*
synapse. This weighting can be symbolized as w_{ij}. If the output of the *i*th neuron is
designated as x_i, then the input to the *j*th neuron from the *i*th neuron is $x_i w_{ij}$.
Summing the weighted inputs to the *j*th neuron:

$$\mu_j = \sum_i x_i w_{ij} - \theta_j \tag{1.1}$$

where θ_j is a bias term.

This summing of the weighted inputs is carried out by a processor within the
neuron. The sum that is obtained is called the *activation* of the neuron. This activation can be positive, zero, or negative, because the synaptic weightings and the
inputs can be either positive or negative. Any weighted input that makes a positive
contribution to the activation represents a *stimulus* (tending to turn the *j*th neuron
on), whereas one making a negative contribution represents an *inhibition* (tending
to turn the *j*th neuron off).

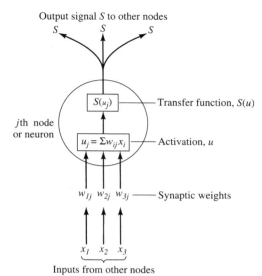

Output signal S to other nodes

jth node
or neuron

Transfer function, $S(u)$

$S(u_j)$

$u_j = \Sigma w_{ij}x_i$ — Activation, u

w_{1j} w_{2j} w_{3j} — Synaptic weights

x_1 x_2 x_3

Inputs from other nodes

Figure 1-2: This is a diagram of a generalized node in an artificial neural network. The jth node receives inputs (x_i) from other nodes. Each of these is multiplied by the corresponding synaptic weight, (w_{ij}), and the resulting products are summed within the jth node to produce the activation, u_j. The activation is transformed to produce the node's output signal, $S(u_j)$.

The activation is a purely internal state of the neuron. That is particularly true for biological neurons: neither the experimenter nor adjoining neurons in the biological nervous system have access to the internal state of any neuron. All that they see is the signal that emerges, and this represents a transformation of the internal state. In the case of artificial neurons, the experimenter has more flexibility. The internal state of a neuron can be displayed just as easily as its output signal. By definition, however, its fellow neurons in the network see only its output signal.

After summing its inputs to determine its activation, then, the neuron's next job is to apply a signal transfer function to that activation, to determine an output. There are various possibilities for what this transfer function should be (see Figure 1-3). For example, it could be a simple step function—a hard limiting threshold that puts the neuron into an *on* state whenever the activation is greater than 0 and otherwise puts the neuron into an *off* state. Many paradigms use this sort of logic. Or it could be a linear threshold function with an output that is low at a constant value until an initial activation threshold and then increases as a linear function of the activation, becoming constant again after a second threshold point is reached.

A very common formula for determining a neuron's output signal is through the use of a logistic function:

$$S = 1/(1 + e^{-u}) \tag{1.2}$$

where u is the activation. This function belongs to the class of S-shaped or sigmoidal functions, and has characteristics that are advantageous within the context of many paradigms. These characteristics include the fact that it is continuous, that it has a derivative at all points, and that it is monotonically increasing, asymptotic to 0 and $+1$, as its arguments go to $-\infty$ and $+\infty$, respectively. (Any signal trans-

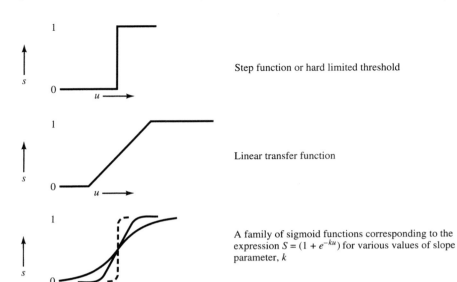

Step function or hard limited threshold

Linear transfer function

A family of sigmoid functions corresponding to the expression $S = (1 + e^{-ku})$ for various values of slope parameter, k

Figure 1-3: Various functions can be used to transform a neuron's internal activation, u, into its output, S. Shown here are a step function, a linear transfer function, and a family of sigmoid (S-shaped) curves. The equation shown in the figure is that of a logistic function, but there are also other functions that are used to generate sigmoidal shapes. Whatever the function that generates them, at their extremes the sigmoids can approximate step or linear functions.

The sigmoid transformations belong to a class often called *squashing functions*, because they accept inputs over a theoretically infinite range and compress or "squash" them to produce an output over a finite range—typically 0 to 1, or −1 to +1.

formation that accepts inputs having an infinite range to produce outputs over a finite range is also known as a *squashing function*.) As can be seen in the figure, limiting cases of a sigmoid can be approximated by a step function.

Of course, the processes happening inside biological neurons are not known in this kind of detail. Nevertheless, there are a number of ways in which the electronic model of the neuron approximates the behavior of neural cells. As shown in Figure 1-4, a living neuron receives multiple inputs from other neurons via branching input (afferent) paths called *dendrites*. The combined stimuli from these input signals activate a region called an *axon hillock*, where an outgoing (efferent) tendril called an *axon* connects to the cell body. The axon then transmits the neuron's output to still other neurons through their dendrites. Or, in some cases, the output that the neuron transmits along its axon goes directly to muscle or gland cells in order to activate or inhibit the functions that those cells perform.

The gap between an output axon of one neuron and the input dendrites of another is the location of the synapses. Information transfer across a synapse is controlled by biochemical agents—a process that is modeled in electronic neurons by the changing of synaptic weights.

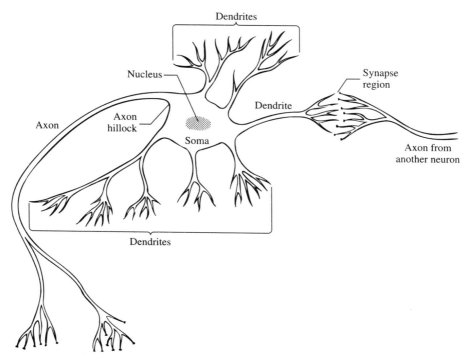

Figure 1-4: Artificial neurons are modeled on biological neurons. A biological neuron receives signals through synaptic regions at its dendrites; the input signal is carried by the incoming (afferent) dendrite to the body of the neuron, and the signal levels are combined at the axon hillock to transmit an output along the outgoing (efferent) axon to the dendrites of other neurons.

Aside from their function in receiving and transmitting nerve impulses, neurons are more or less like other cells of the body. Unlike other body cells, however, most neurons do not reproduce (maybe because the demands of their dedicated task do not allow them the diversion). Similarly, their metabolic functions are largely taken care of by attendant *glial* cells that transport nutriments and waste products to and from the neurons, regulate their chemical environment, and remove and digest the neurons when they are dead or damaged (see, e.g., Albus, 1981, pp. 22–23).

As for the site of "intelligence" within the brain—the increasing belief of people involved in this field is that intelligence resides, not within the interiors of the neurons, but diffusely throughout the rich network of interconnections. The multiplicity of neurons and interconnections in a human brain far exceeds that of any artificial neural network. It is estimated that the brain contains on the order of $(10)^{11}$ neurons, comparable to the number of stars in our galaxy, and $(10)^{14}$ to $(10)^{16}$ synaptic interconnections among these.

The vastness of these numbers seems appropriate to the richness of the human mind and would appear to correlate well with the vast panoramas of our imaginations, memories, and emotions. It is not surprising that artificial neural networks fall far short of matching our own capabilities. What is impressive is that neural networks have been conceived and built, and that they are advancing as rapidly as they are.

Nor can neural networks come close to matching the number of interconnections per second that the brain can create or change. Even though the individual neurons and synapses are far slower than their electronic counterparts, the parallelism of the brain is so considerable that great numbers of synaptic changes can take place concurrently.

Figures 1-5 and 1-6 present measures of neural network capabilities for the biological and electronic cases, respectively. It is heartening to see that, according to this source, neural networks have surpassed leeches and worms, are challenging the housefly, and are gaining on cockroaches and bees. It is also a nice reminder of the magnificence of nature.

Taxonomies

There are various possible taxonomies for classifying neural networks. One of these, based on Kosko (March, 1990), is shown in Figure 1-7, on page 8, and is referred to throughout this book. It breaks neural networks down in terms of how they are encoded (how they store knowledge) and how they are decoded (how, once knowledgeable, they process new input data). In its encoding property, a network can be either supervised or unsupervised; in its decoding, it can be either a feedforward or feedback (closed-loop) type.

Most of the emphasis in neural applications has been in quadrants I (supervised feedforward) and III (unsupervised feedback), involving two contrasting approaches to the field. However, quadrant II (unsupervised feedforward) contains some important examples, and quadrant IV has seen interesting fusions of contrasting approaches, in "recurrent backpropagation," described at the end of Chapter 6, and an unusual "homuncular system" described in Chapter 14.

In general, the boundaries between the quadrants of this taxonomy are somewhat indefinite, and there are instances of network paradigms that refuse to be contained within any single quadrant.

A supervised network is one in which, during training, the network is "taught" what response it should make to each input that it receives. At the same time that this taught response is being fed in, the network is outputting its own natural response, which is a function of its initial synaptic weights and its past training. The network compares its actual response with the taught response and then adjusts its weights in such a way as to move it gradually in the direction of what it is being taught.

Once the network has been trained, the teacher is removed and new, unknown patterns are presented. Then, in its nonlearning or "recall" mode, the net-

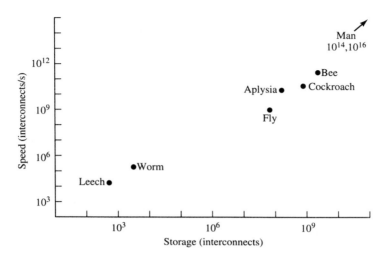

Figure 1-5: The computational capabilities of various life forms are estimated here in terms of speed and storage capabilities. Human capability is estimated at 10^{14} interconnects per second and storage of 10^{16} interconnects. An *interconnect* is a synapse between neurons, and the speed refers to the rate at which synapses can be changed. [DARPA Neural Network Study, October 1987–February 1988, AFCEA International Press, 1988.]

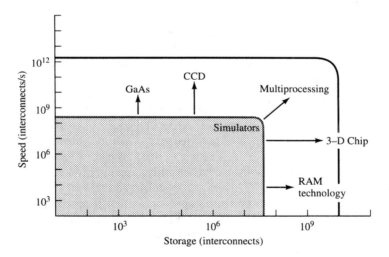

Figure 1-6: Estimates made in the late 1980s show (when this figure is used in combination with Figure 1-5) that technology available to artificial neural networks makes it possible to surpass leeches and worms in storage and rate parameters. The gray area of the diagram shows the past, established technology, while the outer contour shows the boundary toward which the technology is moving. [DARPA Neural Network Study, October 1987–February 1988, AFCEA International Press, 1988.]

Decoding

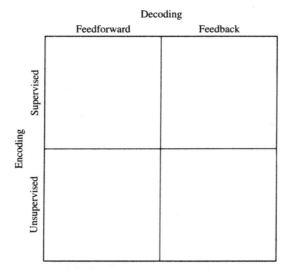

Figure 1-7: This neural network taxonomy, introduced by Bart Kosko of the University of Southern California, classifies networks by how they are encoded and how they are decoded. Although the taxonomy provides a useful organizing principle, actual networks do not always fit neatly into quadrants, but tend to overlap the boundaries. (Kosko, 1990b.)

work categorizes or responds to these patterns on the basis of the adaptations that it made during its learning phase.

The ability to learn is not restricted to networks with teachers. Unsupervised networks can also learn, using built-in rules for self-modification. Such networks change their synaptic weightings in response to the inputs they receive in their training phase, without any intervention by an external teacher. This remarkable self-organizing capability is prominent in the lower left quadrant of the Figure 1-7 chart, among the unsupervised feedforward networks, and is expanded on in Chapter 5. These paradigms also involve the convergence of synaptic values, corresponding to the gradual storage of knowledge. (As will be shown in Chapter 9, however, this quadrant also includes networks that, instead of learning, are constructed from the outset to be able to solve specific classes of problems.)

During the decoding, a feedforward model, regardless of how it was encoded, presents a fixed structure to the new inputs that it processes. It can be looked at as a logical tree, in which inputs are categorized through migrating to the tips of the final twigs or leaves. This signifies that the network is frozen, its operations now those of a deterministic mechanism.

On the other hand, a feedback network, which inhabits the lower right quadrant, is a dynamic system during the recall phase. Because of its cyclic property, in which output nodes not only are fed *by* input nodes, but also feed back *to* those input nodes, the state of the network reverberates until it reaches global stability—a stability defined by the states of the nodes. When it has reached stability, the acti-

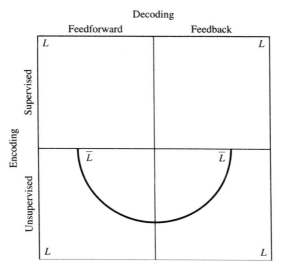

Figure 1-8: The taxonomy of the previous figure is shown here with an additional boundary—between networks that learn (L) and those that do not ($\bar{L}$). There are no non-learning regions under supervised encoding, because the supervision, by definition, governs a learning process. (Adapted from Kosko, 1990b.)

vation levels of the nodes become fixed or oscillate locally about a set of fixed values.

Although the dynamic behavior of feedback neural networks is interesting during decoding, they do not necessarily learn during encoding. In many cases, the synapses are constructed initially from the sets of patterns and responses that the network is to use as its exemplars. Then, during application, it reverberates to a solution in response to new inputs that it receives.

There also exist feedback networks that undergo learning—that is, synaptic changes. Both learning and nonlearning types of feedback networks are discussed in detail in later chapters.

As a point of philosophical interest, the construction of a feedback network from its exemplars (nonlearning case) could be considered as a kind of "batch learning"—a parallel process of learning all at once, rather than a serial process of learning from sequential experiences. It is as if the universe that is to be recognized is flung into the network at the time of the network's creation. Or it could be considered as "learning" in the sense that the genetic code that an organism receives is a kind of species-based learning. In any case, a neural network attains its knowledge through exposure to a training set—even if that exposure occurs during its initial creation.

The more specific sense of learning, however, in which we can watch a network adjust its synapses as it is presented with new inputs, is what will be meant here by a *learning* network, and those networks that do not do that will be categorized as nonlearning. (These attributes are added to the taxonomy in Figure 1-8.) That dichotomy fits both the terminology used in the professional field and our everyday idea of what learning is. Furthermore, it is a kind of process that allows us to simulate the learning behaviors of living organisms.

The most general commonality, pervading all neural networks, is this: a set of input signals causes a series of changes of state as different neurons turn on and off. The state of the network, when these changes have stopped and a steady state has been attained, is the network's response to the input.

Furthermore, the rapidly shifting activation states of neurons are analogous to short-term memory (STM). The weightings on the synapses, subject to gradual modification during training, are analogous to long-term memory (LTM).

It is interesting to observe that most feedback networks use only locally available information during learning (for those that learn); and most neural networks, regardless of category, use only local information during their recall phases. This means that the information available to any node is found only in its present state of activation and in new data entering through its own input synapses, weighted by the synaptic values. And a synapse is enlightened only by its own present states and the states of the two adjoining neurons. Even though the states of remote neurons and synapses play a tacit part in shaping these local conditions, no direct information from any nonlocal source needs to be taken into account at any neuron or synapse to determine its next state.

This local self-sufficiency is compatible with models of biological nervous systems. It also has some important benefits in any system. The autonomy of nodes and synapses means that a neural network is intrinsically fault tolerant—that it can continue to operate, with some loss of efficiency, after sustaining partial damage. There is no central processor or other vital component on which the whole system is dependent.

The mathematical structure that is the handiest in describing neural networks is the matrix. As Figure 1-9 illustrates, the row and column heads represent the neurons, and the entries within the matrix represent the synapses between neurons—that is, the weightings. The input patterns that address the network and the output patterns that the network issues are represented as vectors.

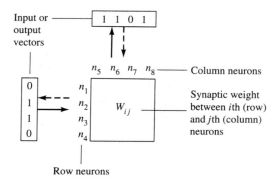

Figure 1-9: The matrix is shown as a mathematical descriptor of neural networks. Neurons are associated with rows and columns, and synaptic weights with matrix entries.

The topology and modes of operation of neural networks lend themselves to hardware implementations. The natural physical structure of a neural network is an array of processors interconnected by variable resistive paths. Then, if the output signal from any neuron is a voltage, V, and if the input synapse weight between that neuron and the next one is a conductance, $1/R$, the weighted input to the next neuron is a current, $I = V/R$.

Neural Network Logic

Neural networks produce results by selectively generating characteristic output patterns in response to various classes of input patterns. For example, a network designed to recognize handwritten symbols would learn how to output standard patterns representing letters or numerals in response to data extracted from script samples and provided at its input nodes.

Or, in a data processing application, the network might accept alphanumeric data concerning the past behavior of a stock and the business conditions for the company issuing that stock. The network's outputs, based on exposure to a training set, would relate these inputs to the probable future value of the stock.

The user, in cases such as these, would not generally be able to assign cause and effect relationships between the multiple attributes of the correlated patterns, nor discover those relationships in the internal parameters of the network. Acting in place of any such deductive link, the paradigm of the network establishes the mechanisms of synaptic and nodal change by which each class of inputs evokes a corresponding class of outputs.

2

APPLICATIONS

The more readily a problem can be explicitly formulated and the more readily the steps toward its solution can be explicitly formulated, the less likely it is that anyone would approach it with a neural network. In such cases, the master tool of the explicit approach is on hand; one puts the problem on a digital computer.

Many of the most complex problems in such areas as particle physics, the structures of organic molecules, spacecraft control, telemetry, and other advanced areas are well handled by computers—when the problems can be formulated. But when a problem is open ended or too elusive to formulate explicitly, or where the explicit formulation results in a loss of sensitivity due to coarse approximations or shortcuts, or when a noisy or harsh environment introduces extreme perturbations, then neural networks come into their own.

It is difficult to predict the extent to which neural networks, fuzzy theory, and other tacit approaches to logic will transform our lives decades in the future—just as the pervasive presence of computers and their implicit effects upon us were not foreseeable in the time of the first electronic computer, ENIAC, in 1946. So it is not clear whether we will eventually have neural or fuzzy autopilots for our cars—so that the driver need only climb into the car and tell it the destination; the neural- or fuzzy-guided car would take care of route selection as well as collision avoidance. Or will these techniques make automated language translators commonplace? Then one could speak English into a telephone to a listener who would hear the Japanese translation of the speech, or vice versa, over a wide range of languages.

The degree to which such transformations will occur, over the next two or three decades, is not yet clear. But the fact that such potentialities exist (where once they would have been sheer science fiction) is in itself remarkable.

Returning to the nearer future, Robert Hecht-Nielsen, a longtime contributor to the field, sees the application of neural networks over the next several years to be concentrated in three main areas. In order of their prevalence, he lists (1) data analysis, (2) pattern recognition, and (3) control functions. He goes on to describe subareas within each of these categories that are most likely to benefit from the neural approach.

Within data analysis, fields of potential application include the processing of loan applications; analysis of commodity trading; time series forecasts; crop pre-lictions; meteorology; marketing analysis; patterns of consumer activity; patterns if activity in public records; and law enforcement, involving the search of criminal ecords.

All of these analyses, in their more complex levels, involve the processing of ·ge data bases in which it may not be obvious how the elements interrelate. Some these, though eluding explicit solution by classical computer techniques, may be isceptible to solution by neural networks. Others, such as the prediction of long-:rm weather patterns, may be subject to chaotic factors and may be outside the cope of neural networks as well.

In pattern recognition, optical character recognition ranks high as a neural pplication—especially when it involves hand-addressed mail or hand-written hecks. Industrial inspection is another environment where complex pattern recog-ition problems exist. For example, in silicon wafer inspection, there are unexpect-:d defects that are not easily classified; a neural-network-based novelty filter then ecomes a likely tool, with the neural network perceiving, as a human observer night, that "this one looks different."

Other pattern recognition problems that do not lend themselves to exhaustive ɔrmulation include speech recognition (especially in the multiple-speaker, con-ected-speech domain); seismic sensing; and the analysis of radar or sonar echoes, whose signatures provide information concerning the nature of illuminated targets.

Control applications suitable for neural networks include such functions as the operation of machine tools. For example, a tool that is rigid enough to hog out metal blocks becomes susceptible to breakage at high speeds of operation. Sensors that detected vibrations and stresses could provide real-time clues to where the boundaries of operation lay—with a neural net trained to recognize the multi-dimensional boundaries. The result of that kind of intelligent supervision would be a significant rise in productivity.

Similarly, with sensors to detect vibrations of car wheels, axles, and springs, a neural-controlled active suspension system could be installed in cars to make them ride much more smoothly. Possibly closer than this on the application hori-zon are ANNs to control the engines of spacecraft in descent and landing opera-tions.

Neural autopilots have been demonstrated. For example, Neural Systems Inc. (Vancouver, British Columbia, Canada) developed the Genesis autopilot and ran it in conjunction with a National Aeronautics and Space Administration (NASA) flight simulator. The NASA system, simulating high-performance aircraft, generates signals corresponding to inputs from sensors that measure as many as 120 kinematic and dynamic variables—including linear and angular accelerations and velocities; pitch, roll, and yaw; and aerodynamic drag. Genesis, using a modified version of the backpropagation paradigm (see Chapter 6) was able, for example, to reduce altitude errors to ±3 ft—in contrast to ±30 ft attained by conventional autopilots.

Pattern recognition plays an important part in many Asian languages, which contain thousands of written symbols depicting words. These languages present a much more formidable problem in optical recognition than what is faced by an optical character reader that needs to recognize only 26 letters, 10 digits, and a handful of punctuation marks. Although classical computer techniques suffice for recognizing the Western alphanumerics, the intricacies of Asian ideographs would appear to call for a more implicit method of solution.

Nestor Inc. (Providence, Rhode Island) has developed a Kanji character recognizer for translating Japanese handwritten characters into English (see Figure. 2-1). At one stage of its development (not necessarily its present state), it could recognize approximately 2,500 Kanji characters with a reliability of 92%. This compares with the ability of the average Japanese reader to recognize between 1,800 and 3,000 characters, or of an intellectual Japanese reader to recognize about 10,000. The generalized logic in the translator network can just as well handle Cyrillic, Hebrew, and other alphabetic symbols.

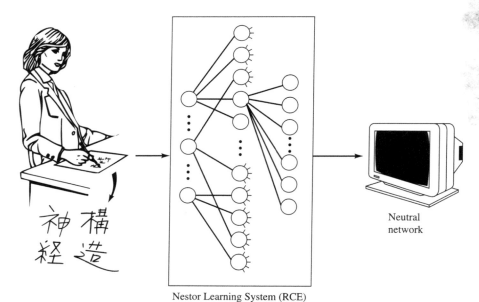

Nestor Learning System (RCE)

Figure 2-1: A Kanji character recognizer developed by Nestor Inc. demonstrated the capability of recognizing approximately 2,500 characters with a reliability of 92%. [DARPA Neural Network Study, October 1987– February 1988, AFCEA International Press, 1988.]

Language recognition by neural networks is being pursued on a voice level as well as in written symbols. As one of many examples of research in the voice area, Richard Lippmann of the Lincoln Laboratory at the Massachusetts Institute of Technology (MIT) has constructed a two-layer neural network, using supervised learning, that can recognize vowel sounds. Figure 2-2 shows how the network divides the vowel sounds into decision regions.

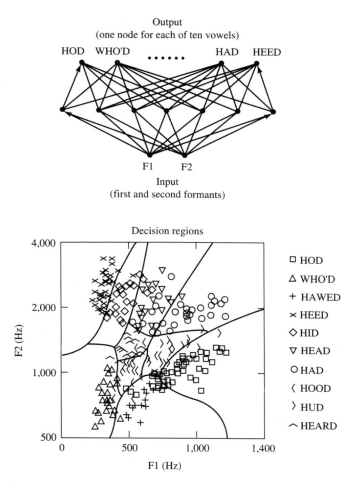

Figure 2-2:   Richard Lippmann of MIT Lincoln Laboratory used a feedforward neural network to recognize vowel sounds, assigning them to decision regions. [DARPA Neural Network Study, October 1987– February 1988, AFCEA International Press, 1988.]

Robots

An example of a robotic application can be seen in robot arm control software from Neural Systems Inc. Custom software from Neural Systems addresses the problem of controlling robotic arms—no trivial exercise when carried out by conventional software. The complexity of the problem is evident from the fact that the placement of the robot's "hand" at a particular location is not a single-solution problem—various combinations of joint angles can get the hand to the same location. This is something that you can demonstrate by grasping a doorknob and then, while still holding the knob, putting your shoulder, elbow, and wrist joints into various orientations.

But to train a neural network to control a robotic arm is conceptually simple. The user simply inputs an end state (the location of an object to be grasped) and any set of joint angles that will put the arm into that end state. The same thing is done for another end state.

Altogether, for an arm having n degrees of freedom, the user presents the network with $n + 1$ examples of this kind. From then on, the arm will generate the trajectory to take itself through any sequence of endpoints the user specifies. In other words, from the examples it has been given, it maps the geometry of the space.

The evolution of robots with neural capabilities has a history that goes back to 1969. Kaoru Nakano of the University of Tokyo has been experimenting with ANN-based robots since that time, and his work is still underway. Many of Nakano's robots are equipped with arms and legs (Johnson, 1989). But, rather than being programmed to do things like throwing balls and walking, they find out on their own. They do their learning using neural-network brains, with reward and punishment cues that make them "prefer" the motions that pay off—that is, those that lead to longer trajectories of thrown objects or faster forward locomotion.

These robots sometimes evolve motions that are more or less conventional—the kinds of motions that a human experimenter might have logically programmed them to do. In many cases, however, the robots evolve unique and unforeseen motions—snakelike or shambling or hopping locomotion, or grotesque windups for throwing things—because their learnings are opportunistic and not governed by their inventor.

Nakano has also constructed robots that can, with some help from other robots, repair themselves; robots that can track moving objects and draw pictures of those objects; and robots that evolve speech in order to signal to each other—here, developing a language that is incomprehensible to their inventor, but that has the desired effects in stimulating other robots to take specified actions.

Nakano's work is valuable on at least two levels. It may lead eventually to the production of very useful intelligent robots. And it provides a model of evolutionary processes.

The foregoing are only a few examples of applications in neural networks that are in existence or under development. There are many other such applications under way. As of now, the total number of these and the total financial investment in them is minuscule compared with the mature world of computer applications. Because of the complementary nature of the two technologies, however, there is good reason to believe that they will divide the applications space more evenly between them in the coming years.

The potential worth of what may evolve from neural networks is exemplified in a project that is underway to provide permanent communications between a person's nervous system and a paralyzed or artificial limb. An implanted ANN would enable the previously disabled person to move the limb at will, as well as to receive sensory inputs from it (Wan, Kovacs, Rosen, and Widrow, 1990).

Implementations

Simple neural networks were initially constructed from discrete components. Subsequent developments have led to neural networks on silicon chips as well as to optical neural nets. As these evolve, neural networks continue to be simulated in software running on computers.

As was indicated in Chapter 1, artificial neural networks usually depend on paradigms in which signals are multiplied by weights, with the resulting products being summed to determine activations. Therefore, systems designed to simulate ANNs at least need to be efficient in carrying out the summations of product terms.

Boards and computer systems, based on optimized special-purpose processors, have been used to simulate neural networks. Despite the fact these neural boards and systems are optimized to run ANN paradigms at very high speeds and efficiencies compared to how a general purpose computer would run them, they do not meet the performance levels that chip-level networks can attain in dedicated silicon. Furthermore, they are under increasing market pressure from ever-improving software simulations that run on standard computers. Nevertheless, they have provided an important transition capability.

ANN boards and systems are generally specified in terms of how many nodes and interconnections they can simulate and, in the case of a learning paradigm, how many simulated interconnection weights can be changed per second. High-end specifications denote the presence of millions of nodes and interconnections, with millions of synaptic changes occurring per second.

An example of an application performed using a board-level product can be seen in HNC's graded learning network, which initially ran on an early model of the company's Anza series of neural computers. This was developed as a technique for process control and made available as a proprietary tool for client applications.

Graded learning is a form of supervised learning. However, rather than providing a target output signal and a correction term representing the difference between target and actual outputs, a graded learning network merely punishes the network with a negative response when it fails and rewards it when it succeeds.

To illustrate this principle, HNC trained the system to balance a broom on end, using a stepper mechanism. The broom was mounted on a single degree of

freedom pivot on a cart (Figure 2-3). The controls of the cart determined accelera-
tion in either direction along the track. Success was defined as the pivot balancing
the broom for 15 seconds; failure was defined as the falling of the broomstick or
the collision of the cart against either of the two blocks that marked the endpoints
of its travel along the track. An optical sensor provided input to the network as to
the instantaneous position and velocity vectors of a point on the broomstick.

Given the optical input along with a punishment signal for every failure, the
network quickly learned to balance the broom with virtually no tilting motions taking place. This capability obviously has implications for servo control operations.

BROOM BALANCER WITH VISION FEEDBACK

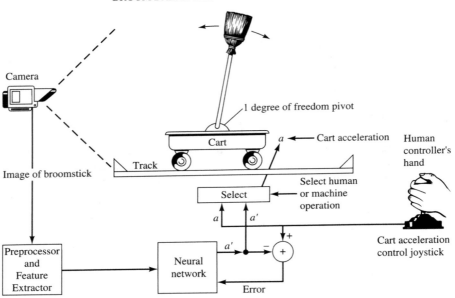

Figure 2-3: Graded learning (a form of supervised learning) is used to train a cart to
move in such a way as to balance a broom. Synaptic weights in the controlling ANN are
adjusted on the basis of how well it performs in maintaining the balance. [Courtesy of
HNC, Inc., San Diego, CA.]

3

THE EARLY YEARS

In the 1940s, Warren S. McCulloch, a neurophysiologist, and Walter Pitts, a mathematician, set out to establish a mathematical model of a nerve cell. Declaring that "neural events and the relationship among them can be treated by means of propositional logic" (McCulloch and Pitts, 1943), they went on to define what has since been known as the *McCulloch-Pitts neuron*. The neuron that they defined performed logical operations on two or more inputs to produce an output.

This conceptual neuron was static in that it did not include changing input weights. But it dealt with variable inputs, which were multiplied by the fixed synaptic weights, with the products being summed. If the sum exceeded the neuron's threshold, the neuron turned (or stayed) on. If the sum was below threshold or if a negative (inhibitory) pulse was received, the neuron turned (or stayed) off. That is, an inhibitory pulse was absolute in switching the neuron off.

The McCulloch-Pitts neuron is the ultimate ancestor of all artificial neural networks, even though its use of an absolute inhibition signal is not reflected in modern versions. The diagram shown in Figure 1-2 of Chapter 1 not only illustrates neurons as they are implemented in networks, but fits the McCulloch-Pitts model as well. This model also survives pervasively in the form of the Boolean logic gates of electronics, with their AND, NOT, OR, XOR, NAND, and NOR operations, which can all be expressed as special cases of McCulloch-Pitts.

The Perceptron

A few years after McCulloch and Pitts presented their neural model, Donald Hebb (1949) formulated a concept of how a synapse changes as a function of the activity across it (see Chapter 7 for elaboration on this). But Hebb's work, although it was important in the theory of learning, did not include any concept of observing the effects of combining multiple inputs to a single neuron.

In 1958 Frank Rosenblatt of the Cornell Aeronautical Laboratory put together a learning machine, the *perceptron*, that was destined to be the forerunner of the neural networks of the 1980s and 1990s. It combined the McCulloch-Pitts and Hebb models, and it did so in a functioning piece of hardware. Rosenblatt's machine was complicated and bulky (by more recent standards), using motor-driven potentiometers to represent variable synapses.

Figure 3-1 illustrates the perceptron as it was implemented in 1958. The *S-units*, as Rosenblatt called them, are *sensors* (photoreceptors). Behind these lie a bank of logic elements called *associators* or *A-units*. Each S-unit is connected to a random subset of the A-units (as in Figure 3-1).

Then comes an additional bank of elements, the *responders*, or *R-units*. The output from each A-unit goes to just one of the R-units. An R-unit, however, in addition to producing a primary output (to turn on an indicator), sends inhibiting feedback signals to a random set of A-units. But the single A-unit that is stimulating the R-unit receives a positive feedback signal. All this is shown in the figure.

When an input in the form of an illumination pattern is introduced to the S-units, some of the A-units—those whose thresholds are exceeded by summed inputs from the S-units—turn on and others turn off. When the *i*th A-unit turns on, so does the *i*th R-unit. However, the *i*th R-unit sends inhibiting signals back to each *j*th A-unit, for various *j* not equal to *i*. As a result, the whole arrangement goes through a series of iterations, with elements turning on and off, until the system stabilizes.

The term *perceptron* has become somewhat ambiguous. Sometimes it is used to refer to a network of multiple nodes, as described previously. In that context, when inhibiting signals are returned to the A-units from the R-units, the perceptron employs feedback.

In many (perhaps most) discussions, however, the individual R-units are called perceptrons. These are trained through the use of a supervised feedforward paradigm.

To train a perceptron, Rosenblatt developed a procedure for changing the synaptic weights (potentiometer settings) leading into an A-unit, or A-node, as it will be called here. The procedure, for a single A-node, is expressed as follows:

At time t, the output from an A-node is:

$$y(t) = \operatorname{sgn} \sum_i [x_i(t)w_i(t) - \theta]. \tag{3.1}$$

The sgn function is defined as equaling +1 if its argument is positive and −1 if its argument is nonpositive. The terms inside the brackets are: $x_i(t)$, the *i*th input signal; $w_i(t)$, the synaptic weight on the *i*th input to the node; and θ, the threshold for that node. The w_i can be excitatory (positive) or inhibitory (negative).

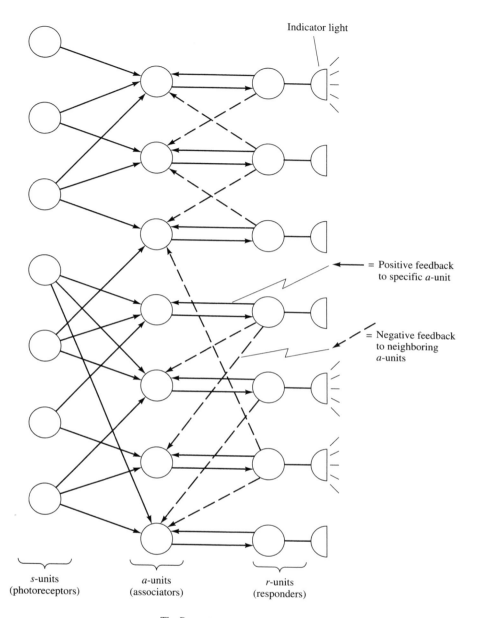

Indicator light

⟵——— = Positive feedback
to specific *a*-unit

⟵– – – = Negative feedback
to neighboring
a-units

s-units	*a*-units	*r*-units
(photoreceptors)	(associators)	(responders)

The Perceptron

Figure 3-1: Organization of a perceptron. The diagram shows the perceptron as Frank Rosenblatt designed it. Synapses between the input units (*A-units* or *associators*) and the trainable neurons (*R-units* or *responders*) are trained through supervised learning. The learning technique, based on the algebraic sign of the neuron's activation, changing only those synapses associated with an incorrect response, and having no internal ("hidden") neurons, proved to be limited to a narrow class of problems.

This figure shows the perceptron as consisting of multiple nodes, and includes a feedback feature, as R-units in the *on* state inhibit the inputs to their competitors. More commonly, the term *perceptron* is applied to a single neuron trained by the perceptron paradigm (see Figure 3-2).

If the sum of the weighted inputs, $x_i w_i$ in (3.1) exceeds the threshold, then $y(t) = 1$. Otherwise, $y(t) = -1$.

At the start of an experiment, the $w_i(0)$ and θ are set to small random values. Then the training of the network begins, with the objective of teaching it to differentiate two classes of inputs, I and II. Specifically, the goal is to have the node's output, $y(t)$, equal +1 if the input is of class I, and to have $y(t)$ equal -1 if the input is of class II.

The experimenter is free to choose any arbitrary set of inputs, x_i, and to designate them as being of class I or II (although, as shall be seen, there are choices of I and II that will defeat the effort of the perceptron to learn).

If the node happens to output a +1 signal when given a class I input pattern, the weights, w_i, are not changed. Similarly, no change is made if $y(t) = -1$ in response to a class II input pattern. (The perceptron works on a logic of "if it ain't broke, don't fix it.")

However, if the node outputs a wrong answer—$y(t) = -1$ for a I input pattern or $y(t) = +1$ for a II pattern—then the synapses are changed according to this rule:

$$w_i(t + 1) = w_i(t) + \eta[d(t) - y(t)] \, x_i(t). \tag{3.2}$$

The function $d(t)$ is the desired or target output; it is what y is supposed to be, so it equals 1 for a I input pattern and -1 for a II.

Since d and y assume only the values 1 and -1, their difference, if non-zero, can only equal ± 2. So, if they differ, then (from equation 3.2), a correction of $\pm 2\eta \, x_i(t)$ is made to the ith synapse. The symbol η represents a positive learning rate constant, generally no greater than .1 or .2; this allows smooth rather than wildly oscillating synaptic changes.

Consider the primitive case illustrated in Figure 3-2. Here a perceptron is shown consisting of only a single node and having only two inputs. The arbitrary initial values for this perceptron include input synaptic weights of .5 and .2, a bias of 1, and a learning constant of .1.

Suppose, as a simple exercise, that the perceptron is to distinguish patterns whose two inputs are each less than 1/3 (to be called class L for "low") from patterns whose two inputs are each greater than 2/3 (class H for "high"). The pattern (.3,.2) would be an example of class L, and the pattern (.7,.9) an example of class H. Also assume that this particular problem doesn't involve other patterns, such as (.5,.5), which belong to neither of these classes.

Start out by entering the L-like input (0,0). When the two zeros are substituted for x_1 and x_2 in (3.1), y becomes -1, which is what we want, so no corrections are made. But when the H-like input (1,1) is entered, y is again -1, which is an unwanted response because this time we want an output of 1. Therefore, the perceptron's weights are adjusted.

The table in Figure 3-2 shows the behavior of this perceptron to successive input pairs, with weights being adjusted whenever the output represents an incorrect classification of the input pattern. Gradually, the perceptron is trained to divide classes *L* and *H*. There are various combinations of weights that would provide solutions to this classification problem. Based on its particular history, however, this perceptron settles at weights in the vicinity of $W_1 = 1.0$ and $W_2 = .68$. At this point, as is shown in the table, the perceptron is precise enough to assign inputs that are close to the class boundary—such as (.7,.7) or (.3,.3)—to the correct categories.

Rosenblatt was able to demonstrate the capabilities of the perceptron to learn categories. Furthermore, he could take a pair of wire cutters and cut a bunch of arbitrarily selected wires in a densely interconnected multinode perceptron, and it would still work, though with some degradation.

But the paradise of the perceptron was in for a rude awakening. In 1969, Marvin Minsky and Seymour Papert of MIT published an analysis, demonstrating

Bias	Learning rate	Synaptic weights		Inputs		Argument	sgn function	Target	Correction factor	Corrections	
θ	η	w_1	w_2	x_1	x_2	α	y	d	$\eta(d-y)$	Δw_1	Δw_2
1	.1	.5	.2	0	0	−1	−1	−1	0	0	0
—	—	—	—	1	1	−.3	−1	+1	.2	.2	.2
—	—	.7	.4	1	1	.1	+1	+1	0	0	0
—	—	—	—	.8	.7	−.16	−1	+1	.2	.16	.14
—	—	.86	.54	.3	.3	−.58	−1	−1	0	0	0
—	—	—	—	.7	.7	−.02	−1	+1	.2	.14	.14
—	—	1.0	.68	.7	.7	.176	+1	+1	0	0	0
—	—	—	—	.3	.3	−.496	−1	−1	0	0	0

$$y(t) = \text{sgn} \sum_i \underbrace{[x_i(t)\, w_i(t) - \theta]}_{\alpha}$$

$$w_i(t+1) = w_i(t) + \underbrace{\eta\,[d(t) - y(t)]\, x_i(t)}_{\Delta w_i}$$

Initial: $w_1 = .5$, $w_2 = .2$, $\theta = 1$, $\eta = .1$, inputs $x_1(t)$, $x_2(t)$, output y

Final: $w_1 = 1.0$, $w_2 = .68$, output y

Figure 3-2: The structure and behavior of a perceptron are detailed here, with the perceptron as a single node having two inputs. It is trained to distinguish a pair of high inputs from a pair of low inputs. However, it would not be able to distinguish mixed pairs (one input high, the other low) from unmixed pairs (both inputs high or both low). That is, the perceptron cannot resolve an exclusive-OR (XOR) problem.

(in conclusive mathematics) that the classes of inputs a perceptron could distinguish were very limited. Only if the two classes were linearly separable (Figure 3-3) could the perceptron learn to distinguish them.

Suppose, once more taking a simple two-dimensional case, that the perceptron was asked to accept within a single category (category M for mixed) such mixed pairs as (.8,.1) or (.2,.7), in which one of the two inputs is higher than 2/3 and the other is lower than 1/3. Both high pairs like (.8,.9) and low pairs like (.2,.2) would go in a second category (U for unmixed).

It turns out that, when confronted by this classification problem, the perceptron would break down.

The ability to output a common response to mixed pairs (high–low or low–high) is exemplified by the exclusive OR (XOR) function of digital logic. A perceptron, because it is limited to linearly separable classes, cannot perform an XOR.

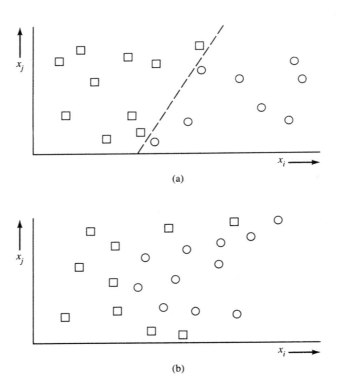

(a)

(b)

Figure 3-3: Quantities having components x_i, x_j can be separated into classes by a linear paradigm, such as that of the perceptron. This works in Figure 3-3a but not in Figure 3-3b. In an n-dimensional problem, the perceptron can sort only those sets that are separable by an $(n - 1)$–dimensional hyperplane.

Faced with patterns that are not linearly separable, such as the types deline-
ated in Figure 3-3b, the perceptron would adjust its weights up and down, but
never in such a way as to distinguish the two classes.

The Minsky-Papert analysis challenged the incipient neural theory by establishing criteria for what a particular network could and could not do. The attack
was clinical and precise—but was undoubtedly overinterpreted in the field as being
a nullification of all neural network approaches. The effect was devastating, and
almost everyone involved in the quest for machine intelligence abandoned neural
networks. Instead, nurtured largely by Minsky, rule-based expert systems and the
entire field of artificial intelligence (AI) became the dominant area of investiga-
tion, throughout the 1970s and early 1980s.

A well-known example of an early artificial intelligence system can be seen
in MYCIN, developed in the 1970s at Stanford University, stemming from the
Ph. D. dissertation of Edward Shortliffe. The function of MYCIN was to diagnose
bacterial disease from a patient's symptoms and recommend treatment.

Intended as a prototype for subsequent expert systems, MYCIN included a
knowledge base that stored information provided by specialists in various branches
of medicine. A doctor needing to make a decision regarding the treatment of a
patient would be able to engage the knowledge base through a program known as
an *inference engine*, which would respond to inquiries by consulting information
(rules) in the knowledge base. Doctors could selectively interrogate this extensive
body of data to act quickly on the basis of partial information in order to start treatment on patients.

Subsequently, a generic version of MYCIN, which included its inference
engine and shell but not its knowledge base, was made available for the development of expert systems involving other topics. In this form, it was known as
EMYCIN or "empty MYCIN."

The principles upon which MYCIN operated are typical of those that have
been used in other expert systems. These systems, characterized by rules formaliz-
ing cause-and-effect relationships between statements, represent an explicit form
of intelligence. The steps in the reasoning process of an expert system are steps in
a program, based on sequential logic, and rooted in the syntax of a computer
language.

A system such as MYCIN was capable of solving highly complex problems
by drawing upon a structure of logical syllogisms. It stood in direct contrast to
neural networks, whose potential lay in dealing with problems that could not be
posed in precise analytic terms.

Thus, it was an explicit form of machine intelligence that occupied the center
of the stage after the perceptron fell.

The truth was that Rosenblatt had come up with a remarkable invention. It
did not appear in absolute vacuum, in view of the earlier analytical models that had
preceded it. What Rosenblatt had done was a work of synthesis, bringing together
the earlier works.

The perceptron fell as a result of inadequacies in the model. The rule for training a perceptron, with its dependence on the sgn function and correction only of nodes that erred in classification, was not sufficiently rigorous.

It was to be 19 years after the Minsky-Papert analysis before an IEEE International Conference on Neural Networks would hear Marvin Minsky speak. Unfortunately, the transcript of that speech has been lost. But people have quoted him as starting off with words something like, "I know that I must be thought of as the devil himself in this audience . . ." Minsky then went on to acknowledge the enormous growth that had taken place in neural network technology. But he did so without apology, still taking a position of constructive criticism with regard to a technology that was clearly far beyond the perceptron.

The LMS Law

In between the birth and fall of the perceptron, there was another invention in machine intelligence, as Bernard Widrow and Marcian Hoff of Stanford University announced the "Adaline." Its name was originally an acronym for Adaptive Linear Neuron, changed later to Adaptive Linear Element. A later development, the Madaline, was a network of multiple Adalines.

The Adaline was essentially a perceptron that used a slightly modified version of Rosenblatt's equations. In place of equation (3.1), Widrow and Hoff employed an expression that did not use the sgn function. Instead, the output was just the argument that Rosenblatt used within his sgn function:

$$y(t) = \sum_i [x_i(t)w_i(t) - \theta] \qquad (3.3)$$

And, although the Adaline used the same correction equation that Rosenblatt did, it was applied differently. So the learning rule of (3.2) is repeated here:

$$w_i(t + 1) = w_i(t) + \eta[d(t) - y(t)]x_i(t). \qquad (3.2)$$

But (with 1 and -1 still being the target outputs for the classes A and B that are to be distinguished) the correction is applied continually, no matter how small the difference is between d and y.

This results in a stricter convergence of the synaptic weights to their correct limits. When compared to the perceptron, this paradigm has the intrinsic advantage of retaining all the information in the argument, in contrast to the sgn function, which (like rounding off) discards part of that information.

The learning rule for the change in synaptic weight,

$$\Delta w_i = \eta[d(t) - y(t)]x_i(t), \qquad (3.4)$$

applied in the continual fashion that the Stanford experimenters developed, became known as the Widrow-Hoff law or the *delta rule*.

Widrow and Hoff showed mathematically that the configuration of weights that the system generates will tend to minimize the sum of the squares of the errors between the test inputs and the responses, with the efficiency of this minimization being a function of how closely the test and training sets match. This property led to a generic name for the paradigm: the LMS (least mean squares) law.

As a finer instrument than the perceptron, the LMS law was destined to play a significant part in the evolution of supervised neural networks—especially, as is discussed in Chapter 6, in relation to the backpropagation paradigm.

This law is an example of a "gradient descent" paradigm. In this class of paradigms, each correction that is made improves the network accuracy through descent along the gradient of an error surface (see Chapter 6) defined over all synaptic weights and the distribution of the data field.

4

THE HOPFIELD NET

In 1982 John Hopfield of the California Institute of Technology designed a neural network that revived the technology, bringing it out of the neural dark ages of the 1970s.

Hopfield devised an array of neurons that were fully interconnected, with each neuron feeding its output to all others. The concept was that all the neurons would transmit signals back and forth to each other in a closed feedback loop until their states became stable. The Hopfield topology is illustrated in Figure 4-1.

This concept did not make use of the feedforward mechanism of adjusting synaptic input weights of nodes in order to tune the outputs of those nodes, as is seen in the perceptron. Instead, Hopfield made feedback the central feature of the network.

In the discrete Hopfield model, a set of n-dimensional binary vectors, $\mathbf{a}\{0,1\}^n$, are to be stored as synaptic weights in the network, which consists of n neurons and their $n(n - 1)$ two-way interconnections. This storage process is represented mathematically by an $n \times n$ square symmetric matrix having a zero main diagonal (no neuron feeding into itself). The vectors thus stored are the exemplar patterns that the network will use as its comparators in processing unknown input vectors.

Figure 4-2 provides some examples of a Hopfield network with nine neurons or nodes, A–I. Following Hopfield's procedure, the weights on the synapses of these neurons are to be generated through logical operations on the binary vectors that are to be stored. In this case, assume that there are three 9-dimensional vectors, α, β, and γ. These are arbitrarily defined as follows, with their bits arranged in clusters of three for readability:

$$\alpha = 101\ 010\ 101, \quad \beta = 110\ 011\ 001, \quad \gamma = 010\ 010\ 010.$$

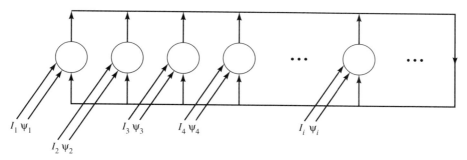

I_i = external input
ψ_i = bias

Figure 4-1: Hopfield network topology. The network is a fully connected single layer of nodes, each of which provides inputs to and receives inputs from every other node, as well as to and from the outside world. In practice, however, each neuron's feedback to itself is commonly "zeroed." This reduces any tendency of the synaptic matrix to act as the identity operator does.

The substitution of -1 for each 0 in these vectors transforms them into bipolar forms α', β', and γ':

$$
\begin{array}{rrrrrrrrrr}
\alpha' = & 1 & -1 & 1 & -1 & 1 & -1 & 1 & -1 & 1 \\
\beta' = & 1 & 1 & -1 & -1 & 1 & 1 & -1 & -1 & 1 \\
\gamma' = -1 & 1 & -1 & -1 & 1 & -1 & -1 & 1 & -1
\end{array}
$$

Each vector is multiplied by itself as an outer product to form a 9×9 matrix whose entries are 1s and -1s, and the resulting three matrices are added together to form a weight matrix, $\mathbf{W}$:

$$\mathbf{W} = \alpha'\alpha' + \beta'\beta' + \gamma'\gamma'. \tag{4.1}$$

When the main diagonal is zeroed, this becomes the matrix shown in Figure 4-2. The entries in the matrix represent synaptic weights. Specifically, each entry represents the synaptic weighting applied to a signal transmitted from the neuron on the vertical axis to the neuron on the horizontal axis. Thus, the signal from node C to node B is weighted by -3, and that from node F to node D by $+1$.

A binary input vector presented to the network sets the neurons' states to the 0s and 1s of the input vector. This initiates a cascade of changing states in the neurons, until they stabilize. Their values at that point represent the output vector generated by that particular input.

Hopfield emphasized random, asynchronous update to model a primitive level of behavior. This comes closer to the kind of organization that might be expected from the neurons in an evolving biological nervous system, not equipped with the luxury of orderly, synchronized signals. As a practical bonus, the use of asynchronous updates in an artificial neural network demonstrates the convergence of the network quickly and easily.

		to							
		A	B	C	D	E	F	G	H	I

		A	B	C	D	E	F	G	H	I
	A	0	-1	1	-1	1	1	1	-3	3
	B	-1	0	-3	-1	1	1	-3	1	-1
	C	1	-3	0	1	-1	-1	3	-1	1
From	D	-1	-1	1	0	-3	1	1	1	-1
	E	1	1	-1	-3	0	-1	-1	-1	1
	F	1	1	-1	1	-1	0	-1	-1	1
	G	1	-3	3	1	-1	-1	0	-1	1
	H	-3	1	-1	-1	-1	-1	-1	0	-3
	I	3	-1	1	-1	1	1	1	-3	0

Synaptic weight
matrix, nodes *A–I*

Start	*a*	*b*
$A = 1$	$A = 1$	$A = 1$
$B = 1$	$B \to 0$	$B = 0$
$C = 1$	$C = 1$	$C = 1$
$D = 1$	$D \to 0$	$D = 0$
$E = 1$	$E \to 0$	$E \to 1$
$F = 1$	$F \to 0$	$F = 0$
$G = 1$	$G = 1$	$G = 1$
$H = 1$	$H \to 0$	$H = 0$
$I = 1$	$I = 1$	$I = 1$

Example 1

Start	*a*
$A = 1$	$A = 1$
$B = 1$	$B = 1$
$C = 0$	$C = 0$
$D = 0$	$D = 0$
$E = 1$	$E = 1$
$F = 1$	$F = 1$
$G = 0$	$G = 0$
$H = 0$	$H = 0$
$I = 0$	$I \to 1$

Example 2

Start	*a*	*b*
$A = 1$	$A = 1$	$A = 1$
$B = 0$	$B = 0$	$B = 0$
$C = 0$	$C \to 1$	$C = 1$
$D = 1$	$D = 1$	$D = 1$
$E = 0$	$E = 0$	$E = 0$
$F = 0$	$F \to 1$	$F = 1$
$G = 1$	$G = 1$	$G = 1$
$H = 0$	$H = 0$	$H = 0$
$I = 0$	$I \to 1$	$I = 1$

Example 3

Figure 4-2: The matrix shows the synaptic weights between neurons. Each example shows an initial state for the neurons (representing an input vector). State transitions are shown by arrows, as individual nodes are updated one at a time in response to the changing states of the other nodes. In examples 1 and 2, the network output converges to a stored vector. In example 3, the stable output is a spontaneous attractor, identical to none of the three stored vectors. The density of 1-bits in the stored vectors is relatively high and the vectors share enough 1s in common bit locations to put them far from orthogonality— all of which may make the matrix somewhat quirky, perhaps contributing to its convergence toward the spontaneous attractor in example 3.

Sample Calculation

Assume that a node in the *on* state has an output of 1 and a node in the *off* state an output of 0. Suppose, furthermore, that a nonnegative summed input switches (or leaves) a node on, and that a negative summed input switches (or leaves) a node off.

Suppose that all nine nodes in example 1 of Figure 4-2 are initially set into an on state by an external input vector (111 111 111) that sends a 1 to each node. Also, let's temporarily drop the random requirement and examine the inputs to nodes in alphabetical order. Node *A* receives the sum of all weights in the first column, each of which is multiplied by the 1 state of the sending node. Thus, node *A* receives a summed input of 2, so it stays in the 1 state (on). Node *B*, on the other hand, gets a negative summed input (-6), so it switches off.

With *B* out of action, node *C* then experiences inputs only from nodes other than *B* and itself, for a total input of 3, and it stays on.

By similar logic, nodes *G* and *I* stay on, while nodes *D*, *E*, *F*, and *H* turn off. The items listed under the heading *a* show these outcomes, with an arrow indicating a transition in state and an equal sign indicating the perpetuation of the existing state. In the next cycle, node *E* switches on again, to produce the output vector listed under heading *b*.

It so happens that this output vector is identical to stored vector α = 101 010 101. The output vector is now applied to the inputs, and sequential calculations show that the output continues to be α. In other words, the network has classified the input as being α-like, rather than β- or γ-like.

The network's conclusion is not obvious ahead of time. That is, the all-1 input is equidistant (in Hamming distance) from stored vectors α and β. In this case, it has gravitated toward α. The element of unpredictability is common among neural networks. They are capable of doing worse than this—of finding false solutions nonidentical to any of the stored exemplar vectors. (More will be said about these issues later in this chapter.)

Given an input that is identical to one of the stored vectors, the network is reliable in returning that same vector as its output. Thus, each of the three vectors stored in the Figure 4-2 matrix will pass through the matrix untransformed. This is not a very informative result. But if the network, when exposed to a noisy version of one of these stored vectors, outputs the stored vector itself, then a noise-filtering process has occurred.

In the second example of Figure 4-2, the input vector is 110 011 000, a corrupted relative of β, with only the last bit in error. When it is processed asynchronously (again in alphabetical sequence by node) it generates an output identical to β—a good example of filtering.

On the other hand, the third example in Figure 4-2 does not lead to one of the three stored exemplars. The input vector, 100 100 100, stabilizes at the output vector 101 101 101, an induced solution not deliberately stored in the network.

In any of these cases, updating the nodes in random order can be shown to lead to the same results as in the sequential case—fulfilling the requirement for random, asynchronous updating.

Symbolic Operations

The matrix operations that were used in the Figure 4-2 example can be expressed more compactly. In symbolic form, the generation of a Hopfield network proceeds as follows:

1. Perform a bipolar transformation of the vectors, $\mathbf{a}^i$, that are to be stored, replacing every binary value, v, by $(2v - 1)$. Call the transformed vectors $\mathbf{x}^i$.
2. Perform an outer product of each vector, $\mathbf{x}^i$, with its transpose, $(\mathbf{x}^i)^T$, to form an $n \times n$ matrix:

$$\mathbf{W}^i = (\mathbf{x}^i)^T \mathbf{x}^i$$

3. Add the matrices thus formed, their sum being the matrix $\mathbf{W}'$:

$$\mathbf{W}' = \sum_i \mathbf{W}^i$$

4. Zero the main diagonal of $\mathbf{W}'$, resulting in matrix $\mathbf{W}$, with elements W_{ij}, where $W_{ij} = 0$ for $i = j$.

The matrix $\mathbf{W}$ represents the weights that are to be established on the synapses. The symmetry of the matrix means that the input weight from the ith to the jth node is equal to the input weight from the jth to the ith node.

Presentation of an unknown input vector, $\mathbf{b}$, to the network (Figure 4-3) is mathematically equivalent to multiplying matrix $\mathbf{W}$ by that vector, to yield vector output $\mathbf{c}$, having components c_j:

$$c_j = \Sigma \ W_{ij}b_j \tag{4.2}$$

or, equivalently,

$$\mathbf{c} = \mathbf{bW}.$$

A thresholding rule converts all nonnegative components of $\mathbf{c}$ to 1 and all negative components to 0, converting the output vector to binary form, $\mathbf{c}^1$.

In general, $\mathbf{c}^1$ will not equal $\mathbf{b}$, nor will it equal any of the stored exemplars. However, if $\mathbf{c}^1$ is then input back into the matrix, to yield (after another cycle of multiplication and thresholding) $\mathbf{c}^2$, and this process is reiterated to yield $\mathbf{c}^3$, $\mathbf{c}^4$, and so forth, the output converges. The typical end to the sequence will be that $\mathbf{c}^{n+1} = \mathbf{c}^n$. Ideally, the stable output will then match the stored exemplar that is closest in Hamming distance to $\mathbf{b}$. This is a restatement of the noise filtering or autocorrelation function performed by the network.

The equilibrium that is reached may not be represented by a single state of the network. It may be a dynamic equilibrium, in which the network settles into a rhythmic repetition among two or more states.

In the example of Figure 4-3, the input vector generates, not one of the two exemplars, but the complement to an exemplar. The result is indicative of the limited dimensionality of the network.

As the caption to Figure 4-3 denotes, Hopfield networks are not always implemented asynchronously. For example, a synchronous implementation based on optical techniques was performed in 1985 by Farhat, Psaltis, Prata, and Pack. Three 32-dimensional exemplar vectors were used to generate the weight matrix, providing adequate dimensionality for the number of vectors stored. Corrupted versions of those stored vectors that differed from their originals by Hamming distances up to 11 (37.5% of the bits in error) were always correctly filtered to match their originals. Hamming distances between 12 and 22 produced less certain results, tending in some cases to oscillate among solutions that did not include the stored vectors.

For Hamming distances $\geq$ 22, the input vectors produced the complements

$$a^1 = (1\ 0\ 0\ 1\ 0\ 0)$$
$$a^2 = (0\ 0\ 1\ 1\ 0\ 0)$$
$\left.\right\}$ Exemplar vectors

$$x^1 = (1\ -1\ -1\ 1\ -1\ -1)$$
$$x^2 = (-1\ -1\ 1\ 1\ -1\ -1)$$
$\left.\right\}$ Bipolar transforms of exemplars

$$W = (x^i)^T x^i$$
$$W' = \sum W^i$$

Set $W_{ij} = 0$ in W' for $i = j$,

to yield synaptic weight matrix W:

$$\begin{bmatrix} 0 & 0 & -2 & 0 & 0 & 0 \\ 0 & 0 & 0 & -2 & 2 & 2 \\ -2 & 0 & 0 & 0 & 0 & 0 \\ 0 & -2 & 0 & 0 & -2 & -2 \\ 0 & 2 & 0 & -2 & 0 & 2 \\ 0 & 2 & 0 & -2 & 2 & 0 \end{bmatrix}$$

Input vector b multiplies W to generate c, which thresholds to c(th).

$$b = 1\ \ 1\ \ 0\ \ 1\ \ 0\ \ 0$$
$$c_j = b_i\,W_{ij} = 0\ \ -2\ \ -2\ \ -2\ \ 0\ \ 0 \quad \text{cycle 1}$$
$$c(\text{th}) = 1\ \ 0\ \ 0\ \ 0\ \ 1\ \ 1$$

$$c_j = c_i(\text{th})\,W_{ij} = 0\ \ 4\ \ -2\ \ -4\ \ 2\ \ 2 \quad \text{cycle 2}$$
$$c(\text{stable}) = 1\ \ 1\ \ 0\ \ 0\ \ 1\ \ 1$$

Figure 4-3: This figure, illustrating symbolic Hopfield operations, uses synchronous update. Unlike Figure 4-2, where the more typical asynchronous process was represented, all nodes are updated cyclically and in unison. This is a rudimentary case in which two stored vectors generate a 6-dimensional matrix. With the vector 110011 generated at the end of two cycles, the network reaches stability. This vector, applied to the network, generates itself. It is a spontaneous attractor, equal to the complement of one of the stored vectors. (See the text for further discussion of this result.)

of the stored vectors. The authors point out that this is an expected result because of the fact that complementary bipolar matrices generate identical matrices when they are multiplied by their transposes (see step 2 in the preceding symbolic operations). Furthermore, the shifting of bits to Hamming distances this large approximates inputting the stored vectors' complements.

The generation of the complement in Figure 4-3 is interesting in the light of this—although why it occurs in that case is not immediately apparent.

Network Capacity and False Exemplars

In order to store multiple independent exemplars and be able to converge accurately to the one nearest the input stimulus, the dimensionality of the network (and its corresponding matrix) must be comfortably larger than the number of stored exemplars.

Hopfield estimated that the practical upper limit on the number of stored exemplar n-dimensional vectors was about $.15n$. So, in generating a matrix from 100-dimensional vectors, one could hope to store a maximum of about 15 such vectors.

Another statistical estimate would limit the storage to $n^{.5}$, allowing ten 1×100 vectors to be stored. With sparse coding, in which vectors contain few 1s relative to the number of 0s, it has been shown that many more vectors can be stored (Willshaw and Longuet-Higgins, 1970; Willshaw, 1971; Palm, 1980). The optimum number of 1s in an n-by-1 vector is shown to be $\log_2 n$. This constraint allows the network to store as many as $(n/\log_2 n)^2$ sparse exemplars (McEliece, Posner, Rodemich, and Venkatesh, 1987; Thakoor, Moopenn, Lambe, and Khanna, 1987).

There are other estimates for the capacity of networks similar in type to the Hopfield (see Chapter 9). All such estimates are subject to statistical interpretation, and they agree in principle that the matrices function best when they are lightly populated with stored patterns. The fewer exemplars a matrix stores relative to its dimensionality, and the sparser those exemplars, the fewer aberrations occur.

What are those aberrations, and when they do happen? The most pervasive is the existence of false exemplars—that is, stable endpoints (potential wells) that do not correspond to any stored exemplar. If any vector, whether it is newly input to the network (like **b** in the preceding discussion) or a thresholded result of such an input (like c^1), immediately recalls itself, then it is a de facto exemplar. Sparseness of storage reduces the frequency of such pitfalls but does not guarantee their total nonexistence. Even matrix dimensionalities much larger than required by the $.15n$ rule of thumb contain false wells.

On the other hand, the induced exemplars are not necessarily all bad. Some researchers see them as interesting spontaneous associations to the stored patterns. Anil Thakoor of the Jet Propulsion Library calls them "inspired states," noting that they correlate well with the network's exemplar patterns. Thakoor sees, in these states, despite their undesirability in associative recall applications, possible uses in the processes of inference—states inferred by the network from its exemplars (Thakoor, 1986).

The probability that the input will produce the ideal result—evoking the stored exemplar that is nearest to it in Hamming distance—depends on a few conditions. This outcome becomes more likely when the exemplars differ considerably from one another, when the input vector is quite close to one of the exemplars, and when the coding is diffuse. The limiting case occurs when all exemplars are orthogonal to one another (no two of them containing a 1 in a common component) and when the input is identical to one of the exemplars. In this case, the input vector will generate itself in a single cycle of multiplication.

The Lyapunov Condition

The state of a Hopfield network can be described by a Lyapunov function. This is a function that becomes smaller for any change in the state of the network, until a stable state is reached. When a stable state has been reached, then, by definition, neither the state of the network nor the Lyapunov function undergoes any further change.

The fact that Lyapunov functions exist for Hopfield networks (and, in fact, for all feedback networks) provides such networks with a characteristic that is equivalent to energy. In the context of the energy model, any stable state represents a potential well. An input vector introduced into the network represents an initial condition, which will lead to the selection of a particular potential well.

Hopfield demonstrated the existence of a Lyapunov function for his networks as follows:

First, he defined the energy state of the network as

$$E = -1/2 \sum_{i \neq j} \sum W_{ij} v_i v_j - \sum_i I_i v_i + \sum_i \psi_i v_i, \tag{4.3}$$

where W_{ij} is the synaptic matrix through which the jth neuron delivers its output to the ith neuron, v_i and v_j are the output signals from the ith and jth neurons, I_i is an external input to the ith neuron, and ψ_i is the threshold level (in amperes) of the ith neuron.

An increment in this energy function is:

$$\Delta E = -\left[\sum_{j \neq i} W_{ij} v_j + I_i - \psi_i \right] \Delta v_i, \tag{4.4}$$

in which the state of the ith neuron is changed by Δv_i.

By the definition of neural paradigms—see equation (1.1) in the first chapter—the expression in brackets in (4.4) drives the magnitude and sign of Δv_i—and therefore the bracketed expression and Δv_i are always of like sign. So the quantity ΔE is always negative or (at a stable point) zero. Thus the quantity E fulfills the Lyapunov requirement.

A Continuous Model

In the early 1980s the field of neural networks was evolving rapidly. A major contributor was Stephen Grossberg of the University of Boston, who was continuing his long-term research into learning laws and neural models (see Chapters 5 and 8). One of the fronts along which Grossberg and his associates were proceeding was in the development of continuous neural models—networks that, instead of being restricted to discrete inputs and signal functions, could handle continu-ously changing values.

Meanwhile, John Hopfield was pursuing a parallel course. In 1984, about two years after announcing his discrete model, he announced a continuous version of the network.

In the continuous Hopfield model, a circuit is defined whose terms are equivalent to the terms within the brackets in (4.4). The Hopfield circuit is governed by the following equation:

$$C_i (du_i/dt) = \sum_j W_{ij} v_j - u_i/R_i + I_i. \tag{4.5}$$

In Hopfield's biophysical interpretation of equation (4.5), C_i is the input capacitance of the ith neuron's cell membrane, and R_i is the transmembranic resistance. The term u_i is the activation level of the ith node, and v_j is the output signal from the jth node, distributed as input to all nodes, proportional to the synaptic weight W_{ij}.

The initial input vector, $\mathbf{v}$, that addresses the network provides the initial values of the components v_j, the inputs to the neurons. Then, as the network reverberates through its states, the outputs of the neurons provide the new and changing values of v_j.

It can be observed that equation (4.5) is a generalization of equation (4.2). When the continuously changing network is at equilibrium (as it is at the conclusion of each cycle in the discrete case), the neuronal outputs are not changing. Therefore, du_i/dt becomes 0. The term I_i represents a fixed bias current going into the ith neuron; suppose this is also 0. What remains is an equation for the activation of the ith neuron, in terms of the signal, v_j, delivered to it by the jth neuron via the interconnection matrix, W_{ij},

$$u_i/R_i = \sum_j W_{ij} V_j$$

—which has the required equivalence to (4.2).

Hopfield's symbol definitions, along with dimensional analysis, show that all terms of (4.5) are in amperes. Both u_i and v_j can be interpreted as potentials, and W_{ij} then becomes a conductance. The product of C_i (coulombs/volt) and du_i/dt (volts/sec) is also in amperes.

The activation u_i lags behind its stimulus v_j, which is why du_i/dt is retarded in equation (4.5) by the capacitance factor, by the resistance (R), and by the impedance implicit in the finite value of the conductance matrix. The negative term proportional to u_i represents an exponential decay of an existing activation—especially apparent when the other terms in the right-hand side of equation (4.5) are zero (see Chapter 7 for more on this decay).

When a Hopfield net accepting continuous inputs comes to equilibrium, the du/dt term in equation (4.5) becomes 0. At this point, the stable u value indicated on an output display defines the potential well corresponding to an input vector $\mathbf{v}$. Any other vector that is sufficiently close to $\mathbf{v}$ will evoke the same output, whereas an input vector $\mathbf{a}$ that is relatively distant from $\mathbf{v}$ will generally evoke a different output, associating the input with a different energy well.

Hopfield expressed the Lyapunov equation for the continuous case as:

$$E = -1/2 \sum_j \sum_i W_{ij} v_j v_i + \sum_i 1/R_i \int_0^{v_i} u_i dv_i. \qquad (4.6)$$

The first of these two terms is the energy expression for the discrete Hopfield net, with the external inputs and the thresholds set to zero at all nodes. The second term represents the contribution of the continuous form of the paradigm. This term is analogous to the first term, in that it also involves the product of two potentials and a conductance.

The energy that is expressed in the second term is the internal energy in the (now) continuous transformation of neuronal activations into output signals. The more energy is continuously involved in this process, the more the potential well represented by the network's overall state is diluted. This can be seen in the fact that the negative energy term in (4.6) is made less negative by the addition of the positive second term.

Hopfield further transforms equation (4.6) by introducing a transfer function, $v = g_i(u)$, from activation u to output signal v. Next, introducing a scaling factor, λ, he redefines the transfer function as $v = g_i(\lambda u)$. When, for example, the transfer function is sigmoidal, the parameter λ defines a family of sigmoids from very steep step functions ($\lambda \gg 1$) through typical sigmoids ($\lambda = 1$) to very gradual ramps ($\lambda \ll 1$).

Then, the inverse function (the transfer from output signal v to activation u, for the ith neuron) looks like this:

$$u = (1/\lambda)g_i^{-1}(v).$$

When this inverse transformation is substituted into (4.6), the second term in the equation becomes:

$$1/\lambda \sum_i 1/R_i \int_0^{v_i} g_i^{-1}(v)dv.$$

For $\lambda \gg 1$, this term disappears, and we are operating on an energy surface equivalent to that of the discrete case. In the discrete case, all states of the network correspond to the vertices of a hypercube in state space, whose coordinates in n dimensions are specified by the 0s and 1s of binary vectors. Those vertices whose vectors generate local minima in the energy equation are the stable points of the network. If λ is gradually lessened, the states of the network will spread into the general vicinities of the vertices and along the edges of the hypercube. Finally, back in the vicinity of $\lambda = 1$, network states, including equilibrium states, will map themselves throughout the interior of the hypercube, and we are once again in the continuous case.

Hopfield Network Applications

Hopfield networks are applicable not only to pattern matching, but to optimization problems as well. The latter was addressed by Hopfield in a paper coauthored with David Tank (1985) on the classical traveling salesperson problem (TSP), which long predates neural networks. A salesperson wants to visit n cities, once each, along a path that ends at the initial city. The problem is to perform this loop in such a way as to minimize the total mileage.

This goal spills over into many analogous practical problems—such as the optimum routing of traces on a printed circuit board, or what path a robot arm should follow in the performance of a function, or how resources should be distributed to their destinations from supply depots.

The TSP becomes computationally vast as the number of cities increases. For n cities, there are $n!$ possible arrangements. But, because the solution is a closed loop, it doesn't matter which city is chosen as the starting point (this divides the number of independent solutions by n), nor does the direction of traversing the loop matter (which divides the number of solutions by 2). Thus, the number of independent solutions becomes $n!/2n = (n - 1)!/2$. As n increases, the number of possible solutions becomes formidable in terms of the amount of number crunching that a computer would have to do to solve it.

If we assign the problem to a Hopfield network, an n-city TSP requires an array of n^2 neurons. For a four-city problem, for example, each row of the array represents a single city and each position in the row represents the order in which that city is visited. Figure 4-4 shows the logical state of the 4-by-4 neuron array corresponding to the route CABD. (Because 16 neurons would be involved in a four-city case, the weight matrix would be 16 by 16.)

All of the neurons are connected to each other (as is expected in a Hopfield network), their synaptic weights being a function of the mileage between cities. The four neurons shown to be active in the figure indicate the order in which each city is visited.

In their initial work, Hopfield and Tank applied the paradigm to the 10-city case and the 30-city case.

Because each city is to be visited exactly once, there is only one selected (active) neuron per row. Also, two or more cities cannot share the same place in the sequence—so therefore, only one selected neuron can exist in a column. And no city and no order of visit can be omitted from the solution. This resolves itself to an array with one and only one selection in each row and in each column.

Hopfield and Tank established an energy function that restricted the network to these one-per-row and one-per-column conditions through lateral competition among the neurons in each row or column. The energy function is also proportional to the sum of distances between cities on a selected route. When the network is triggered, it converges to a solution that tends to minimize the sum.

The network is started out at a good but not optimized set of conditions for

Order of
visit

	1	2	3	4
A	0	1	0	0
C B	0	0	1	0
i t y C	1	0	0	0
D	0	0	0	1

Figure 4-4: The TSP (traveling salesperson problem) is illustrated here for a four-city example. The trivial four-city case would require an array of 16 neurons and a corresponding matrix of 16^2 synapses.

the synapses. The input vector is constructed with a small constant value at all nodes to avoid biasing the results in any particular direction. However, absolutely identical values at each node tend to freeze the network into a static condition, so a small random noise value is added to each component. This noise, although it enables the paradigm to proceed, introduces a small bias into the results.

The input vector, with its small, noisy components, establishes nonbinary levels at each node—which is all right, even though Hopfield networks usually operate with binary levels. In any case, the TSP nodal levels converge toward binary values, as required by the nature of the problem.

In the 10-city case, there are over 180,000 distinct paths. In about 50% of the trials carried out by Hopfield and Tank, one of the two shortest possible paths was chosen. That represents selection of the best 10^{-5} (.001%) of all paths.

For a 30-city case, with $4.4(10)^{30}$ paths, statistical analysis showed that the network selected the best 10^{-22} to 10^{-23} of paths. For the particular set of cities used, Hopfield and Tank believed the minimum path to be 4.26 units long. Evaluation of 10^5 random paths indicated an average length of 12.5, with none less than 9.5. But the network usually converged to paths of less than 7 units long, and occasionally to paths of less than 6.

Despite these partially positive outcomes, the Hopfield network is not the universal balm for the TSP. The bad news is that the paradigm breaks down rapidly in the TSP situation as the number of cities increases above 30, and is no better than a random selector for the 100-city case.

The neural network literature abounds with other uses for the Hopfield paradigm. In a machine vision application reminiscent of the TSP, the network was used to determine the degree of bilateral symmetry of a visual object (Chang and Tong, 1990). The object was represented by line segments, and the Hopfield network was used to pair segments according to the degree of mirror symmetry that they showed relative to a vertical axis passing through a field of such segments. A node of the network is assigned to each possible pair of segments. Synaptic weights entering each node relate to the position and orientation of the two segments specific to that node. With each segment in the field represented by a column and a row, any pairing of mirror image segments is represented by the selection of one node in each row and one in each column—and is, thus, an optimization problem of the TSP type. Once the best pairing is established over the field of segments (minimizing an energy function that relates to deviations from symmetry between members of selected pairs), a measure of the lowest discoverable energy for the field becomes a measure of the symmetry of the perceived object.

Examples of other optimization problems dealt with by the Hopfield network include very large-scale integration (VLSI) cell placement (Caviglia, Bisio, and Curatelli, 1989), electric power load distribution (Matsuda and Akimoto, 1989), and the tracking of 40 simultaneous targets by an imaging system (Elsley, 1988). Another Hopfield example, in the category of pattern recognition, makes use of sonar data for autonomous guidance of a robotic vehicle, along with giving the

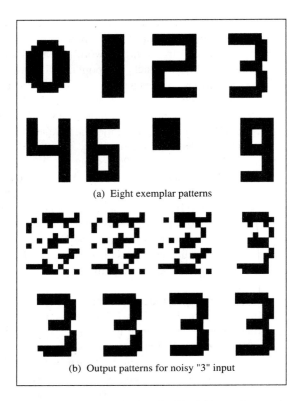

(a) Eight exemplar patterns

(b) Output patterns for noisy "3" input

Figure 4-5: An example of the behavior of a Hopfield net when used as a content-addressable memory. A 120-node net was trained using the eight exemplars shown in (A). The pattern for the digit "3" was corrupted by randomly reversing each bit with a probability of .25. The corrupted pattern is then applied to the net at time zero. Outputs at time zero and after the first seven iterations are shown in (B). [From Richard P. Lippman, "An Introduction to Computing with Neural Nets," *IEEE ASSP Magazine*, 1987.]

vehicle the ability to navigate around obstacles and to anticipate terrain features in a new environment (Jorgensen, 1988).

Figure 4-5, in the associative recall mode of the Hopfield, presents an example of noise filtering through the use of a network containing 120 nodes and therefore 14,400 weights (Lippmann, 1987). From a noisy binary input of the numeral 3, the network succeeded in extracting an exact match to the stored 3 after seven iterations.

The project designed to enable a person to receive sensory impressions from an artificial or paralyzed limb and to move that limb, mentioned at the end of Chapter 2, is based on the Hopfield network. Nerve endings are coupled with an implanted Hopfield network on a chip. The subject tries to make various motions, but, because the initial coupling geometry can only be arbitrary, the motion that occurs generally will not correspond to what the subject tried to do. The synapses of the network are adjusted electronically, and the patient tries the motion again. Gradually, the network is adjusted until the willed motions are those that occur. Similar adjustments are made to correlate physical stimuli with what the patient feels in response to those stimuli.

The authors of the 1990 article describing this work (including, incidentally, Bernard Widrow, the developer of the Adaline model) anticipated the passage of a decade before this innovation could be implemented practically in behalf of patients.

5

SELF-ORGANIZING MAPS

In 1981 Tuevo Kohonen of the University of Helsinki demonstrated that systems could be built that would organize input data without being supervised or taught in any way. The system that Kohonen described was able to perform the mapping of an external signal space into the system's internal representational space, without human intervention. He called the process a *self-organizing feature map* (also describable as an adaptive vector quantizer or AVQ) and showed how it could be performed by a neural network.

Since the time of Kohonen's innovation, he and others have evolved a number of variations on this process. One such variation is illustrated in Figure 5-1.

At the top left of the figure is a signal space consisting of k decision regions, each of which is populated by many n-dimensional binary vectors, $\mathbf{x}\{0,1\}^n$. Any vector represents a sample taken from the signal space, and the dot within each decision region is the centroid of all vectors within that region.

At the top right of the diagram is a two-layered neural network having n input nodes (corresponding to the n-fold dimensionality of the input vectors) and k output nodes (corresponding to the k decision regions), with every input node connected to every output node. The task to be performed by the network is to learn to categorize input signals according to which of the decision regions they come from.

Each of the interconnects between an input and an output node is weighted; these synaptic weightings are designated w_{ij}. In the bottom diagram, a matrix shows the w_{ij} as matrix elements, in a matrix whose row headings designate input nodes and whose column headings designate output nodes. The matrix elements in the jth column constitute an n-dimensional vector, the fan-in (set of synaptic input weights) leading into the jth output node.

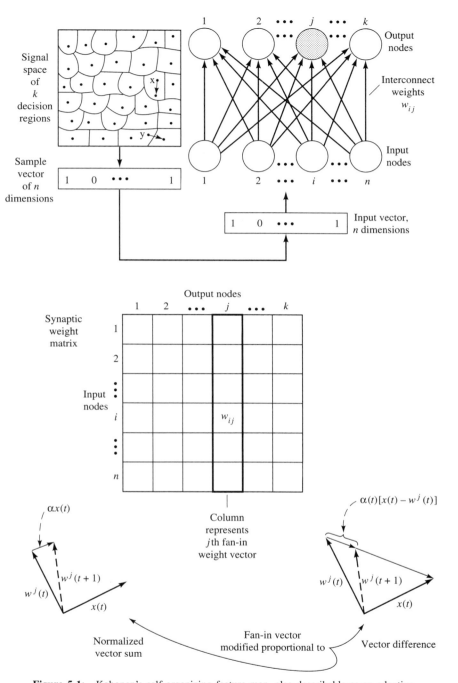

Figure 5-1: Kohonen's self-organizing feature map, also describable as an adaptive vector quantizer (AVQ), carries out an unsupervised feedforward paradigm to group input vectors into classes. After each input vector, lateral competition occurs between network nodes to establish a winning node (the node having components closest to the input vector). This lateral competition brings an element of feedback into the paradigm, so that the AVQ cannot be confined strictly to the feedforward part of the taxonomy chart. [Adapted from Michael Chester, "Neural Networks Move from Theory to Practice," *Electronic Products*, August 1, 1988, p. 19. Garden City, NY: Hearst Business Communications, Inc.]

In the initial state, the synaptic weights have been chosen randomly. That is, the weightings are not related in any way to the signal space. The only thing that relates the neural net to the signal space at all is the fact that it has n input neurons (to match the n dimensions of the signal vector) and k output neurons (to match the k decision regions of the signal space). Except for that broad dimensional correspondence, the network has no a priori knowledge of the signal space.

What happens when an initial vector randomly selected from the signal space is input to the neural net?

First, the similarity of the input vector to each of the k fan-in vectors (vertical columns of the matrix) is determined. This can be done by various methods. For instance, the Euclidean distance between the input vector and each of the fan-in vectors can be calculated at each of the k output nodes. Or the inner (dot) product can be formed between the input vector and each of the k fan-in vectors—a large dot product indicating a high degree of similarity. Whatever the method of comparison, if the jth fan-in vector is declared the one most similar to the input vector, then the jth output node is declared the "winner."

The idea of selecting a winning node and subsequently rewarding that node was a concept that had evolved from Stephen Grossberg's earlier and ongoing work in "competitive learning," and represents an important theme in neural network theory. In Kohonen's network, the reward for winning is that the jth fan-in vector is modified slightly, rotating toward the input vector. This can be done by moving the jth fan-in vector incrementally along the vector difference between itself and the input vector, as shown by the diagram toward the lower right corner of Figure 5-1.

If $\mathbf{x}(t)$ is the input vector during cycle t, then the modified fan-in vector looks like this at the start of cycle $t + 1$:

$$\mathbf{w}^j(t + 1) = \mathbf{w}^j(t) + \alpha(t)[\mathbf{x}(t) - \mathbf{w}^j(t)].$$

Or the synapses fanning into the winning node are changed through a normalized vector sum, rather than a vector difference:

$$\mathbf{w}^j(t + 1) / \|[\mathbf{w}^j(t)\| = [\mathbf{w}^j(t) + \alpha(t)\mathbf{x}(t)] / \|[\mathbf{w}^j(t) + \alpha(t)\mathbf{x}(t)]\|.$$

But as Figure 5-1 shows, this gets us to approximately the same place.

The factor $\alpha(t)$ is a function such as

$$\alpha(t) = .1(1 - t/10^4).$$

This presupposes that 10,000 training inputs are to be carried out and that the incremental changes will get smaller at each successive cycle, reaching 0 at the 10,000th cycle, after which training ends.

The fan-in vectors to all the losing nodes remain unchanged.

The next input vector may be from a very different part of the signal space, and the winning fan-in vector of cycle 1 may not even be a contender in cycle 2. However, there will be another winner, and it will migrate toward the input that it resembled.

In this incremental fashion, each fan-in vector migrates—sometimes with reversals of direction—and the synaptic weightings fluctuate, erratically at first but gradually settling into a fixed pattern.

At the end of the training period, this version of Kohonen's paradigm will result in each fan-in vector approximating the centroid of one of the decision regions. The x and y in the top left diagram represent the chance locations of two fan-in vectors juxtaposed on the signal space at the start of the training process. The arrows show their net migrations during the training, with each of them approaching a nearby (not necessarily the nearest) centroid.

Following the training, a new rule comes into play. Now, in the recall mode, a random vector from the signal space is presented to the network for classification. If the jth vector wins the dot product competition, it is no longer rewarded through a change in synaptic weights. Instead, it turns on a light, indicating that the unknown vector belongs to the jth decision region. In this way, with the synapses stable, the net is prepared to identify any unknown vector from the signal space.

Because he was interested in maintaining topological similarity between the mapped space and the signal space, Kohonen (1982) subsequently rewarded not only the winning neuron but also its eight nearest neighbors (Figure 5-2); all of these were allowed to migrate toward the input vector. The rule was modified for neurons near the edges and corners of the formation because these had fewer neighbors. In another variation, he also extended a partial reward to the 16 next-nearest neighbors to the winner, allowing them to migrate one-quarter the distance of the others.

The result of these topological exercises was not only a pairing of output nodes with decision regions, but a pairing that preserved the topology, so that regions of the neural network that were adjacent to each other mapped regions of the signal space that were adjacent to each other. This kind of mapping is of special significance in representing the way that nervous systems map the parts of an organism's body.

Applications of the Self-Organizing Map

An application conducted by Kohonen involved categorizing phonemes from the Finnish language by means of spectral analysis. Figure 5-3 shows the results. In Figure 5.3a, the node that gave the maximum response to each phoneme is shown. In Figure 5.3b, the phoneme that caused the maximum response for each node is entered into the map. The result confirms a transformation preserving the contiguity of similar phonemes.

Uses of Kohonen's paradigm have continued in numerous contexts requiring the topological mapping of raw data. One example relates to the classification of insect songs (Neumann, Wheeler, Burnside, Bernstein, and Hall, 1990). The project involved the classification of courtship songs produced through wing vibrations by male fruit flies (*Drosophila melanogaster*), according to the genetic strain of the singer.

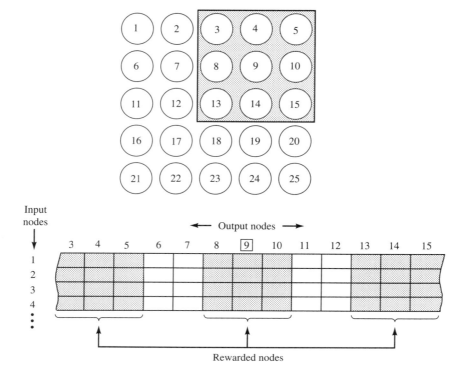

Figure 5-2: In this version of a self-organizing feature map, the winning node and its eight geometrically nearest neighbors are all rewarded through fan-in adjustment. This strategy preserves the topology of the external data field within the network.

An AVQ network of 72 nodes, each having nine input synapses, was used as a front-end classifier. The songs consisted of pulses (of two or three cycles each, at about 225 Hz) separated by interpulse intervals of 35 to 45 milliseconds. Each input to the network represented the features of a single pulse. These inputs were nine-dimensional vectors characterizing each pulse in terms of the time intervals between zero crossings within the pulse.

A song, consisting of a large number of pulses, would result in various nodes being selected, so that a song would finally be represented by a histogram of how often each of the 72 nodes prevailed. Implicit in this process was a considerable compression in the data; each pulse, initially designated by its nine-dimensional vector, was reduced to a scalar label from 1 to 72.

The resulting histograms were then presented to a second neural network based on backpropagation (see the next chapter), which was trained to recognize the song-to-genotype correlations and to categorize unknown songs with a high degree of confidence.

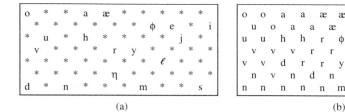

Figure 5-3: Kohonen's mapping of Finnish language phonemes describable by frequency spectra: (a) the node showing maximum response to each phoneme; (b) the phoneme causing maximum response at each node. [From "Self-Organization and Associative Memory," by T. Kohonen, 2nd edition, Springer-Verlag, 1988.]

Other Studies of Topological Mapping

Kohonen's research was by no means the only neural-oriented work being done in those years on topological mapping. Both prior to and concurrent with his work, studies carried out by several other analysts were establishing related principles. In his 1982 paper, Kohonen refers back to studies in topographic projections between two laminar structures by others in the neural network field (Willshaw and von der Malsburg, 1976, 1979; von der Malsburg and Willshaw, 1977; Amari, 1980).

Also taking place during this time period was research by David J. Burr (at the University of Illinois and later at Bell Laboratories) in which he was developing algorithms for mapping pairs of stereo images, one of them being a distortion of the other. This evolved into a sequence of papers on stretching elastic bands or surfaces to match existing contours (see Burr, 1979, 1981, 1983). Even though Burr's analyses at that time did not have a neural reference, his model and Kohonen's turn out to be mathematically equivalent.

In 1987, following similar lines of inquiry, Richard Durbin and David Willshaw from Cambridge University and the University of Edinburgh in the United Kingdom addressed the traveling salesperson problem in terms of topological projection (Durbin and Willshaw, 1987). They simulated the existence of an elastic net (a rubber band) containing randomly located "tour points." This band was superimposed on the map of cities, with an initial center and perimeter close to the center of the apparent distribution of cities. The band is stretched outward to allow it to pass through cities (which act as attractors), gradually assuming an irregular amoeboid shape, while the tension in the net keeps path lengths short. The pairing of tour points and cities that results is equivalent to Kohonen's mapping of synaptic weights to the input vectors of a signal space.

Further evolution of the elastic net concept in relation to TSP was carried out by Burr (1988). In Burr's model, annealing is introduced. The expanding net does not stop at each attractor city that it intersects but continues to stretch outward toward other cities. Another part of the net may capture (intersect) the passed-over city. Later, the net recedes back to intersect any uncaptured cities that remain. This model results in tours within a few percentage points of optimum.

In many areas of research (as in athletics), later efforts have achieved better results than early ones. The shortest routes found by Hopfield and Tank, in their original 30-city tour, were about 19% above the shortest known tour. Durbin and Willshaw, using the same 30-city map that the previous authors used, found the shortest known tour after 1,000 iterations and came within 1% of the shortest known tour for 50- and 100-city cases. Burr found the shortest known tour for 30 cities after 10 iterations, and came within 2% of the shortest for 50 cities after 30 iterations.

A Note on "Selecting a Winner"

The comparison of vectors (to determine which fan-in vector most resembles the input vector) poses an interesting challenge to the integrity of the neural network. At first glance, an external processing element is implied, which can look at all the comparisons and select the best of these.

The trouble is that this would invalidate the neural network's claim to having a fully parallel fault-tolerant structure, having no single central element on which its function depends.

However, competitive learning techniques allow the winning neuron to identify itself—in self-organizing and other types of neural networks. Consider five competing output neurons in a network, whose activation levels are 20, 16, 12, 8, and 4. Suppose that, using an "on-center, off-surround" logic, each feeds back its own output signal to itself, and 1/4 times the negative of that signal to each of the others—so that (in addition to its own positive feedback) each receives the average of the negative feedbacks of the other four. Whenever a neuron's activation becomes negative, it is set to 0 and drops out of the competition. This process, leading to new activation levels, proceeds as in Figure 5-4, rounding off to the nearest unit in each calculation. By the end of eight cycles, only one node has survived the competition. That node updates its synapses, and the network is ready for the next input, with further competitive aftermaths and the updating of another set of synapses.

This particular competitive rule (using the average of the negative feedbacks for the "off-center" signal) represents just one possibility. There are numerous ways in which competitive processes can be performed in order to select a winning node.

One alternative approach would be for each neuron to transmit its output signal as an absolute inhibitor to all of its competitors. It would also set a threshold equal to its own output signal on each of the lines through which it receives inhibitory competitive inputs. Then, the only inhibiting signal to reach a neuron is one larger than its own output.

The receipt of any such signal tells a neuron that it is not the winner of the competition. If, after the expiration of a time delay sufficient to allow all inhibiting

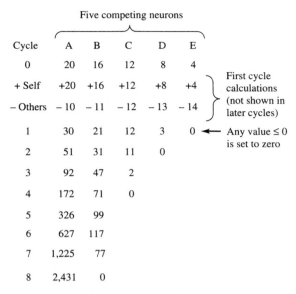

Figure 5-4: Lateral competition among neurons is often referred to as "on-center, off-surround." That is, each neuron acts to enhance its own activity and to suppress the activity of its neighbors. This phenomenon is present in the retinas of higher animals, bringing about the animal's ability to see contrasts in both light and dark areas—because the strength of the perceived image is based on a local reference with respect to the reactions of nearby cells, rather than on a global reference relating to the light intensity. This logic, imitated in neural networks, can be handled in various ways, one of which is illustrated here. Neurons *A–E* are five nodes in a fully connected output layer. Each feeds back its own signal to itself minus the average of the other four, until only one is active (nonzero output). Values of 1/2 are rounded downward.

In an alternative approach, described in the text, each neuron transmits its output as an absolute inhibitor to all its competitors; each also sets a threshold on its incoming inhibitor lines equal to its own output. Thus, it receives an inhibit only from a neuron that has a larger output than its own. In contrast to the several cycles required in this figure, that would resolve the competition in a single cycle.

signals to reach their destinations, a neuron receives no inhibiting signals, it declares itself the winner. This technique would resolve the competition within a single cycle.

6

BACKPROPAGATION

Backpropagation, or "backprop," has been the most popular, most widely implemented of all neural network paradigms. It is based on a multilayered, feedforward topology, with supervised learning.

This paradigm was initially developed and announced by Paul Werbos in the early 1970s in his Harvard University doctoral thesis, and was evolved in a series of his subsequent papers. Werbos was working, not from an engineering implementation point of view, but out of an interest in exploring the functioning of the human brain. He says that "if I were going to give credit to someone for having the first intuitions about this approach, I would pick Sigmund Freud." Werbos quotes Freud's theory of psychodynamics, in which the brain is described as a neural network.

Freud, in addressing the problem of how the brain adapted in time, hypothesized a chemical flow backwards from neuron to neuron, opposite to the forward direction of electrical excitation, to establish the causal pathways. Exposure to this concept triggered Werbos into looking at the backward propagation of errors through a feedforward electronic network, as a model of the learning process.

David Parker at Stanford came up with an independent treatment of backpropagation in 1981. And David Rumelhart, Geoffrey E. Hinton, and Ronald J. Williams independently derived, evolved, and disseminated it as a neural network architecture in the mid 1980s.

A key element in the backpropagation paradigm is the existence of a hidden layer of nodes. This frees the network from the linear limitations of the perceptron. The network is fully connected, with every node in layer $n - 1$ connected to every node in layer n.

A backpropagation network typically starts out with random weightings on its synapses. Then it is exposed to a training set of input data. As it gets these inputs, it also is given, in contrast to the random outputs it is initially producing, the correct output that should go along with every input. As the training proceeds, the network's weights are incrementally adjusted until it is responding more or less accurately. (How accurately depends on how much training it receives and, therefore, on the experimenter's requirement.) At that point, it is ready to categorize unknown inputs in whatever application it was trained for.

Backpropagation belongs to the class of algorithms that perform gradient descent. That is, it is a descendant of the Widrow-Hoff or delta rule.

Among the advantages of backprop are its ability to store numbers of patterns far in excess of its built-in vector dimensionality. On the other hand, it requires very large training sets in the learning phase, and it converges to local minima, which may or may not be global minima. Furthermore, it requires an external computer to adjust its weights.

The structure of a backprop network is illustrated in Figure 6-1. In this case, a three-layered network is assumed, having an input layer, an output layer, and one hidden layer. However, a backprop network can contain greater numbers of hidden layers.

At the bottom of the diagram, the vectors, $\mathbf{x}$, that are to be classified or responded to are entered into the input nodes. Meanwhile, in the supervisory external computer, target vectors, $\mathbf{z}$, are associated with the input vectors. That is, target vector $\mathbf{z}$ is the category that (from the experimenter's point of view) is the desired response to pattern $\mathbf{x}$.

The interconnection weights between nodes at a lower (ith) layer and those at the next upward (jth) layer are randomly set at the start of the training process. As a result of this randomness, the actual output vector $\mathbf{y}$ (issued by the output nodes) will generally be distant from the target vector.

A correction signal, proportional to the difference between the target vector and the output vector, is then fed from the external computer to the network. And (changing in form as they are applied downward through successive hidden layers) the correction signals adjust the synaptic weightings of the network in a direction designed to shift the output vector incrementally toward the target vector. It is this set of correction signals, disseminated backward through the network, that gives the paradigm its name.

Error Surface

Consider a network state vector whose components include all the synaptic weights at all the nodes of a backpropagation network. If there are m synapses in the network, then the synaptic state of the network at any time can be represented as a specific case of this m-dimensional state vector, a point in m-space.

The overall squared error of the network (for a particular m-dimensional synaptic state vector and a particular n-dimensional input vector) is a scalar, equal

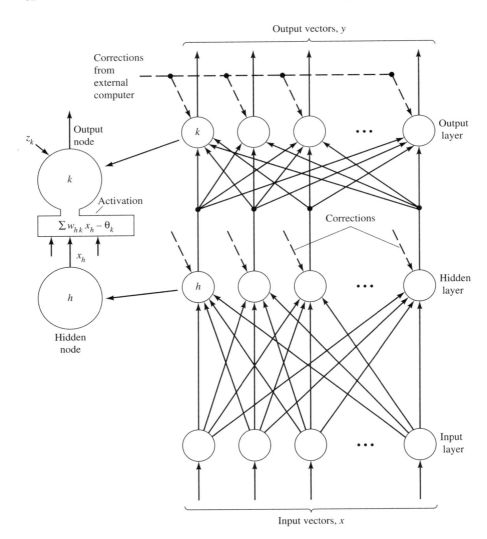

Figure 6-1: Backpropagation network. Backprop is a feedforward paradigm, in which each layer is totally connected to the next higher layer. Correction terms proportional to the differences between target vectors, **z**, and output vectors, **y**, are backpropagated through the network to adjust weights. An external computer applies the correction algorithm.

to half the sum of the squares of the errors,

$$E_p = (1/2)\sum_k (z_k - y_k)^2,$$ (6.1)

over all output nodes. The p subscript refers to the specific input vector pattern that is used.

However, this error can be generalized by averaging it over all input vectors in the sample space. This generates a global error function, $\text{GE} = \sum_p \text{E}_p$.

Viewing the synaptic state vector as an m-dimensional abscissa, the global error function, GE, can be treated as the corresponding one-dimensional ordinate.

The error surface (which reflects an enormous amount of information involving all possible synaptic weights and all possible input vectors) is generally very complex and irregular, containing peaks, craters, ridges, valleys, and slopes. The goal of the backpropagation paradigm is to locate, via gradient descent, a crater or minimum (ideally, a global minimum) in the fixed error surface. The surface itself does not change as a function of time. It is predefined over all possible states of the network, with a topography that is determined by the topology of nodal interconnections and by the vector input space that is to be sampled and over which it was averaged.

In other words, the backprop paradigm is an explorer looking for a crater in a fixed but very complex multidimensional landscape. This crater is the minimum error, and its location is the set of m synaptic weights that, when averaged over the population of input patterns, leads to this minimum.

Generalized Delta Rule

There are a number of derivations of the rules for correcting synaptic weights in a backpropagation network. What is shown here is based on a derivation by Rumelhart, Hinton, and Williams (1986). In the following equations, it is assumed that the nodes of the backpropagation network utilize a logistic signal transfer function. It is also assumed that the analysis focuses first on the output nodes—followed by extension of the process to hidden nodes.

Start by considering the derivative of the error function, E, with respect to the change in synaptic weight leading into an output node. The object of looking at the derivative is to determine the rule for changing weights in such a way as to maximize the descent of the error function along the gradient.

Strictly speaking, the derivative is that of E_{ps}, the error function following presentation of pattern p when the network weight vector is in state s. To avoid carrying along extra subscripts, however, a plain E is used in the followed calculations.

Through chain differentiation:

$$dE/dw_{hk} = dE/dy_k * dy_k/du_k * du_k/dw_{hk},$$ (6.2)

where dE/dw_{hk} is the derivative of the error function with respect to the hth
synaptic weight leading into the kth output node, w_{hk},

this derivative factoring into:

dE/dy_k, the derivative of the error function with respect to y_k, the output signal of the kth output node;

dy_k/du_k, the derivative of the output signal from the kth output node with
respect to the node's internal activation, u_k;

and du_k/dw_{hk}, the derivative of the output node's activation with respect to its
hth synaptic weight.

The next step is to evaluate each of the three derivatives on the right-hand
side (r.h.s.) of (6.2). Start with the derivative of E with respect to y_k, which, from
equation (6.1) is:

$$dE/dy_k = y_k - z_k. \tag{6.3}$$

The second factor on the r.h.s. of equation (6.2) is the derivative of the output
node's signal with respect to its activation. The presence of this derivative requires
that the signal function of each neuron (the transformation that it applies to its
summed inputs or activation) must be continuous and differentiable with respect to
the activation. The logistic function described in Chapter 1 meets these needs. For
the logistic function

$$y_k = [1 + e^{-u_k}]^{-1}, \tag{6.4}$$

where y_k is the output from a node based on its inputs from the nodes at the immediately lower level, and u_k is the summation of those inputs, as expressed in
equation (1.1) of Chapter 1.

Differentiating y with respect to u_k, in equation (6.4) leads to:

$$dy_k/du_k = e^{-u_k}/(1 + e^{-u_k})^2.$$

Using the identity $e^{-u_k}/(1 + e^{-u_k}) = 1-[1/(1 + e^{-u_k})]$,

$$dy_k/du_k = [1/(1 + e^{-u_k})][1 - 1/(1 + e^{-u_k})].$$

That is, $dy_k/du_k = y_k(1 - y_k)$. Since, by definition of the logistic function, y_k is a
positive number between 0 and 1, dy_k/du_k is always positive.

For the last derivative on the r.h.s. of (6.2), the starting point is the definition
of the activation, u_k, as:

$$u_k = \sum_h w_{hk}x_h - \theta. \tag{6.5}$$

Then, the derivative of u_k with respect to the synaptic weight is:

$$du_k/dw_{hk} = x_h. \tag{6.6}$$

But x_h, the input to the output node, is also the output from the hidden node—and, since all nodes are assumed here to have logistic signal functions, x_h is positive between 0 and 1. Therefore this derivative is also positive.

If we substitute the three derivatives into equation (6.2), the derivative of the network error with respect to synaptic weight is:

$$dE/dw_{hk} = (y_k - z_k)[y_k(1 - y_k)]x_h. \tag{6.7}$$

The form of equation (6.7) bears a close resemblance to the delta rule, equation (3.4), developed in the context of the LMS paradigm:

$$\Delta w_i = \eta[d(t) - y(t)]x_i(t). \tag{3.4}$$

In fact, the rule for changing weights in the backprop network is equivalent to the delta rule. Substituting $[z_k - y_k]$ for $[d(t) - y(t)]$, and x_h in the above discussion for $x_i(t)$, (3.4) becomes:

$$\Delta w_i = \eta[z_k - y_k]x_h. \tag{3.4a}$$

From this, and from the fact that both η in (3.4a) and $y_k(1 - y_k)$ in (6.7) are positive, the combination of the two equations shows that:

$$dE/dw_{hk} \sim -|\Delta w_{hk}|. \tag{6.8}$$

The always negative direction of change of the error was assured in the first place by the rule that adjusted the actual output toward the target value.

Recalling that the global error function, GE, is the sum of the pattern-specific error functions, E or E_p, (6.8) leads to

$$dGE/dw_{hk} \sim -|\Delta w_{hk}|. \tag{6.8a}$$

This line of argument demonstrates that the paradigm performs gradient descent, as the global error function of the network decreases in direct proportion to the absolute change in the synapse.

It also suggests a generalized delta rule for backpropagation:

$$\Delta w_{hk} = \eta(z_k - y_k)[y_k(1 - y_k)]x_h. \tag{6.9}$$

Although this derivation is based on the logistic transfer or "squashing" function, the approach can be modified to fit other transfer functions as long as they are continuous and differentiable.

For example, in place of the logistic function, one can use the hyperbolic tangent, also a sigmoid:

$$f(u) = (e^u - e^{-u})/(e^u + e^{-u}).$$

This function is monotonically increasing, with asymptotes to ± 1, rather than 0 and 1, as the argument goes to $\pm\infty$—which is useful when bipolar outputs are wanted. Like the logistic function, the hyperbolic tangent has a simple derivative:

$$f'(u) = [1 + f(u)][1 - f(u)].$$

Synaptic Changes in Hidden Layers

Equation (6.9), expressing the correction to a synapse of the kth output node, can be broken down into the product of an error function, d_k, and the signal x_h from hidden node h to output node k:

$$\Delta w_{hk} = \eta d_k x_h \qquad (6.10)$$

Implicit here is the definition of the error function at the kth node as

$$d_k = \eta y_k(1 - y_k)(z_k - y_k). \qquad (6.11)$$

The only subscript here is k—so that the error function of (6.11) applies to all synapses of the kth output node.

The error term applied to a hidden node must also be considered. The problem with a hidden node is that it is not directly related to the target expectation. The evolution of a rule for applying synaptic changes, not only to output nodes but downward through successive layers, is what has made backpropagation feasible.

The logic that has emerged is this: a hidden node just below the output layer should be corrected in proportion to how heavily it contributed to an output node that is itself heavily in need of correction. Statistically speaking, a hidden node that has a strong connection to a very errant output node is probably a large contributor to that error. So, taking this into account, and once more weighting the error by the slope function, the full error factor for hidden node h becomes

$$d_h = H(1-H)\sum_k d_k w_{hk}, \qquad (6.12)$$

where w_{hk} is the synaptic weight between hidden node h and output node k, H is the output from the hidden node, and d_k is the error at output node k; the product of these two terms is summed over all k, reflecting the relationship of this hidden node to all output nodes that it feeds.

This error is generated in response to a particular input pattern, p, so a more exact version of (6.12) is:

$$d_{hp} = H(1-H)\sum_k d_{kp} w_{hk}. \qquad (6.12a)$$

With correction terms thus established for the nodes of the highest hidden layer, equation (6.12a) is also applied to nodes at the next hidden layer (layer g),

$$d_{gp} = G(1-G)\sum_h d_{hp} w_{gh}, \qquad (6.13)$$

and so forth. The process repeats through all layers, for every layer i feeding into a next higher layer j whose error term has already been established.

Backpropagation Summary

To summarize backpropagation: the weights leading into an output node are adjusted in proportion to the difference between the output node's actual output and its desired or target output; weights leading into hidden nodes are adjusted in proportion to their contributions to errant higher nodes; at the end of the learning phase, the weights are frozen; then, unknown inputs are fed into the stabilized network and are categorized.

It is important to recognize that the post-training input does not cause the network to traverse the error surface, nor does the resulting output have anything to do with gradient descent, which was operative only during the learning phase. All patterns presented to the network after it has been frozen see the same fixed point on the error surface, corresponding to a single abscissa, a network weight vector that combines the effects of all the vectors that were processed during training.

The issue arises, during the training phase, of whether to change the synapses after each vector to which the network is exposed. The alternative is to calculate the cumulative effect of all the vectors in the training set, then make a single change that represents the cumulative information.

Cumulative or batch update approximates true gradient descent, with each input pattern seeing the same network state vector, taking the network directly down the slope to what is (ideally) the global minimum. In the alternative approach of incremental update, each training pattern sees a different state vector, and the process is diluted. However, if the learning rate constant is sufficiently small, the process will still approximate gradient descent.

Advantages of incremental update are seen in its simulation of "a dynamical system which can be studied and perhaps used as a basis for models of actual physical or biological systems" (Pineda, 1989).

Choices of updating tactics and other details of gradient descent are implemented in the external computer, where an algorithm governs the weight changes. In its frozen recall mode, however, the backpropagation network no longer depends on an external computer. In this stage, it can claim the full independence and distributed intelligence characteristic of a neural network.

The backpropagation paradigm is beset by some limitations, alluded to earlier in this chapter. These limitations and their possible remedies are discussed in greater length in a later section of the chapter, following some application examples.

A Hyperplane Model

A geometric model can be used to represent the activations of neurons in a multilayer feedforward network, for a particular network state.

The activations, u, can be interpreted as hyperplanes in synaptic weight space. This is evident from equation (1.1) [or its equivalent, equation (6.5)], the

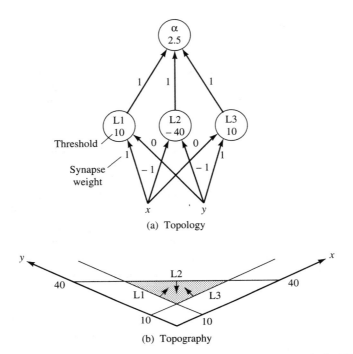

(a) Topology

(b) Topography

Figure 6-2: This feedforward network consists of four neurons—three in the hidden layer and one as the output node. The authors of this example followed a common practice of not treating the input nodes as neurons or as constituting a layer of the network. (The presence of two input nodes in this case establishes a two-dimensional synaptic weight space.) In part b of the figure, it is seen that an input vector in the triangular region $x > 10$, $y > 10$, and $(x + y) < 40$ will turn the output node on. The boundaries here are lines because the boundaries in an n-dimensional space are of dimensionality $n-1$. The decision boundaries in general are hyperplanes. [From Stephen José Hanson and David J. Burr, "What Connectionist Models Learn: Learning and Representation in Connectionist Networks," *Behavioral and Brain Sciences*, Princeton, NJ, Vol. 13, No. 3, 1990.]

equation of a hyperplane. For the sake of visualization, it is helpful to consider a primitive network whose input layer has only two neurons. Then the hyperplanes become two-dimensional planes, with the index i assuming values 1 and 2. Each of these planes represents the fan-in from the two input nodes to one of the nodes in the next layer up.

The equation of such a plane, corresponding to the activation state of the jth neuron, is

$$u_j = w_{1j}x_1 + w_{2j}x_2 - \theta_j. \tag{6.14}$$

A boundary line between activations within this plane that exceed the threshold and those that do not can be established by setting u_j in (6.14) equal to zero:

$$w_{1j}x_1 + w_{2j}x_2 - \theta_j = 0. \tag{6.15}$$

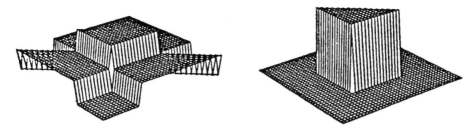

Figure 6-3: These contours show the activation and thresholded output from neuron α of the previous figure. [From Stephen José Hanson and David J. Burr, "What Connectionist Models Learn: Learning and Representation in Connectionist Networks," *Behavioral and Brain Sciences*, Princeton, NJ, Vol. 13, No. 3, 1990.]

Researchers Stephen José Hanson and David J. Burr at Bell Communications Research mapped the topographies for this primitive linear case (Hanson and Burr, 1987). In Figure 6-2, after Hanson and Burr, a backprop network is shown, having three hidden neurons and one output neuron. The threshold for each neuron is indicated, as are connection weights. A further simplification establishes a thresholding logic, so that a node turns on if its inputs match or exceed its threshold.

Two input nodes, accepting inputs x_1 and x_2, are implicit in the figures. In feedforward networks, input nodes do nothing except provide fanouts to higher layers, so they are often omitted from diagrams, and not always considered as constituting a layer. Hanson and Burr, for instance, describe this as a "two-layer" network (hidden and output layers), rather than a three-layer network.

Based on the synapse weightings, it is clear that hidden neuron L1, with a threshold of 10, turns on if input $x_1 \geq 10$. Similarly, L3 turns on if $x_2 \geq 10$. But the weights going into L2 from both input nodes are negative (inhibitory), so that neuron will turn on only if $x_1 + x_2$ stays sufficiently small. Since L3 is activated whenever its input is greater than or equal to -40, it will turn on only when $(x_1 + x_2) \leq 40$.

Output neuron A, with a 2.5 threshold, will turn on only if L1, L2, and L3 are all on. This condition is equivalent to the state of the network being inside the triangular region of Figure 6-2b. That is, $x_1 \geq 10$, $x_1 \geq 10$, and $(x_1 + x_2) \leq 40$.

Figure 6-3a plots the summed inputs to neuron A, and Figure 6-3b presents the thresholded output of A. When the step function thresholding is smoothed by a logistic, the abrupt plateaus of Figure 6-3 are replaced by the rounded contours of Figure 6-4.

A Neural Speech Synthesizer

One of the more vivid demonstrations of backpropagation was performed by Terrence Sejnowski and Charles Rosenberg of Johns Hopkins University (Sejnowski and Rosenberg, 1986), who taught a network to perform speech synthe-

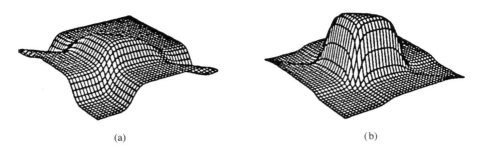

(a)   (b)

Figure 6-4:   The same model as Figure 6-3, but using a sigmoid transfer function.
[From Stephen José Hanson and David J. Burr, "What Connectionist Models Learn:
Learning and Representation in Connectionist Networks," *Behavioral and Brain
Sciences*, Princeton, NJ, Vol. 13, No. 3, 1990.]

sis from written text. What distinguished the behavior of their NETtalk from existing speech synthesizers was the fact that (as one would expect of a neural network)
it was not given explicit rules for the translation of written text into phonemes.

NETtalk's name reflects the name of a well-known speech synthesis program, DECtalk, from Digital Equipment Corporation. In processing text, DECtalk
looks at the ASCII codes of keyboard-entered text through a window 7 characters
wide, with text symbols restricted to the 26 letters of the alphabet, comma, period,
and the space between words, for a total of 29 possibilities. The program focuses
on the center character in this window and applies context rules having to do with
the triplet of flanking letters on either side in order to establish the parameters of
the phoneme. Then it delivers the parameters to the back-end circuitry that generates the voice sounds. There are three options for the voice—man, woman, or
child. All this is based on sophisticated phonetic rules, supplied by specialists in
the voice field.

The training of NETtalk was carried out not only using backpropagation, but
also through another paradigm—the Boltzmann machine, a probabilistic model
developed earlier by Sejnowski and his colleagues (see Chapter 10). Results were
similar with both paradigms.

In teaching NETtalk to speak, Sejnowski and Rosenberg set all weights to
random initial values. The network that they were using had 7 input groups of 29
units each (corresponding to the 7-character window of DECtalk and the 29 character identities), for a total of 203 input nodes. A single hidden layer contained 80
nodes, and the output layer contained 26 nodes, representing 23 speech features,
plus three nodes relating to stress and to syllable boundaries. This made a total of
309 nodes, and because each layer was fully connected to the next layer up, there
was a total of 18,629 connections.

Because of its random weights, NETtalk started out by translating the printed
inputs into gibberish. However, the correct phonemes were provided as training

inputs to the output nodes, borrowing on the well-established logic present in DECtalk. Gradually, as errors were propagated back through the network, NETtalk's output became more coherent.

The experimenters also ran their outputs through the backend of DECtalk, selecting the child voice option. What they heard initially was like the babbling of a child that has not yet learned how to talk, producing sound "uncannily similar to early speech sounds in children," according to Sejnowski and Rosenberg. Then, in successive stages, they heard the sounds of a child learning to speak—and finally speaking clearly.

It is illustrative of the tacit nature of neural networks that, even though it was taught by a rule-based system, NETtalk contains no rules. Instead, its phonetic knowledge is encoded in a set of synaptic weights. Subsequent efforts to correlate the configuration of weights with the knowledge gained were unsuccessful. Furthermore, if the whole experiment is repeated from scratch, with a new initial set of random weights, and the network is then retrained, the final arrangement will be totally different from before—not just a simple transformation, but a completely independent configuration. Nevertheless, with this entirely different network, it may again provide about the same level of performance.

Other Applications

Among the myriad of uses to which backpropagation has been put, the recognition of spoken or written text has been one of the more prominent. Burr has applied backprop to the recognition of both spoken and handwritten numerals (Burr, 1986). As referenced in Chapter 2, Richard Lippmann has used the paradigm for spoken vowel recognition. There are numerous other language recognition examples in the literature.

Along similar lines, backpropagation has been applied to the recognition and classification of animal sounds—such as its use in conjunction with AVQ in recognizing insect songs, described in the last chapter.

In the referenced insect song application, the 72 output nodes of the self-organizing map (described in Chapter 5) feed into 72 input nodes of the backpropagation network. The 72-element vector that is transferred between networks represents the normalized activation histogram of an insect song over 72 pulses. The experimenters, knowing the genotype of the insect that produced the song, feed a target vector to the output nodes. This target vector is defined as the tag for that genotype. The network is then trained over a few genotypes, each with its assigned vector tag. At the end of the training process, the backpropagation network, with weights fixed, is able to assign insects to genotypes strictly on the basis of their songs.

It is worth noting at this point that a different network paradigm, the "functional link network" developed by Yoh-Han Pao, combines both unsupervised cluster-producing capabilities and supervised learning. The first stage of the functional link network does the clustering and then feeds its outputs into the supervised stage, which uses the delta rule. Because of the preprocessing that is done in the first stage, however, the second stage is able to perform its function at a sophisticated level without the presence of a hidden layer (Pao 1988, 1989; Pao and Beer, 1988; Klassen, Pao, and Chen 1988). Feeding the insect song to this network would provide an interesting performance comparison to the AVQ-backprop sequence.

Other pattern recognition applications of backpropagation have included such examples as the removal of noise from EKG signals; sonar target discrimination; and radar target recognition. HNC has used the paradigm for pattern classification in diagnosing brake system performance.

Limitations and Remedies

Backpropagation has been the workhorse of the technology in its early years and has been used in the bulk of practical applications for neural networks. When a very large body of data is available for training, and when extensive memory and time are available for that training process, it represents a slow and moderately reliable way to get to a solution. In some cases, it may take thousands or even hundreds of thousands of sweeps through the training set to educate the network. Hence, the paradigm's success in the field is marred by its sheer computational demands.

The existence of local minima in the error surface is compounded by the existence of multiple global minima—since many different weight permutations can lead to the same input/output transformation.

The history of backpropagation is thronged with various patchwork fixes to adjust the rates at which weights are changed and to deal with the multiplicities of global and local wells. These have succeeded to varying degrees, but at the cost of introducing complexity, as well as often requiring the experimenter to customize the remedy to the application.

Rumelhart, Hinton, and Williams observed that the weight changes that occur in the course of the paradigm should theoretically be infinitesmal, in order to represent true gradient descent. The weights in a real network need to be incremented in finite steps. The constant of proportionality, η, in equations 6.9 through 6.11, sets a scale for the size of these steps. But problems arise as the learning rule is applied in different regions of the error surface. Where the surface is relatively flat, the gradient descent proceeds very slowly. Where the slope of the surface is steep, the changes occur rapidly and may result in oscillation about a minimum.

Attempts to optimize the learning rate through a judicious choice of η are delicate. If η is made too small, the process is interminable. If η is made too large, the state of the network (in terms of its weight values) can go into oscillation.

Rumelhart et al proposed one remedy in their 1986 paper. They introduced a *momentum* term—an inertial leftover from cycle $(t - 1)$ of weight changes just prior to the current cycle, t. This is designed to smooth the transitions. Equation

(6.9) is generalized like this:

$$\Delta w_{ij} = \eta d_j x_i + \alpha \Delta w_{ij}(t-1). \qquad (6.16)$$

The second term provides the inertia, with constant α determining the degree of this effect.

In the insect song example described previously, the experimenters used the logistic with cumulative updating, along with an adaptation based on the "delta-bar-delta" rule originated by R. A. Jacobs (1988). This rule replaces the learning coefficient, η, with a learning coefficient matrix, μ_{ij}. An exponentially weighted moving average of Δw_{ij} over n passes through the training set multiplies the current value of Δw_{ij}. If the product is positive, learning is assumed to be stable (current weight change going in the same direction as the moving average) and μ_{ij} is updated using the rule

$$\mu_{ij} = \mu_{ij} + k,$$

where k is a coefficient about an order of magnitude less than μ_{ij}. But, if the product is negative, indicating instability (w_{ij} changing in a direction opposite to the moving average), then μ_{ij} is updated according to

$$\mu_{ij} = (1 - \theta)\mu_{ij},$$

where θ is a positive number between 0 and 1; for this application, a value of 0.2 was found to produce consistent convergence.

The result was, according to the experimenters, "to produce more stable convergence by quickly decreasing the learning coefficient when crossing a 'valley,' but not letting it increase too quickly when on a smoothly sloping section of the error surface."

Recurrent Backpropagation

In their 1986 paper on backpropagation, Rumelhart, Hinton, and Williams suggested the possibility that the network could combine feedback and feedforward mechanisms. This combination has been explored subsequently in further detail by various authors, including Almeida (1987), Pineda (1989), and Williams and Zipser (1989a).

In the Williams and Zipser model, the backpropagation network consists of a single layer of n nodes. The inputs fanned in to each neuron in this layer are the m components of input vector $\mathbf{x}$ (one of which can be a bias set to 1) and the n components of output vector $\mathbf{y}$ from the previous cycle (Figure 6-5).

There is a single time-step delay through the network, with the outputs $y(t)$ feeding back to the neurons at the same time as external inputs $x(t)$. In the starting cycle, t_0, since $\mathbf{y}$ is not yet available as an output, it must be assigned initial components. In all subsequent cycles, $y(t)$ is produced from the previous cycle's inputs, $x(t-1)$ and $y(t-1)$.

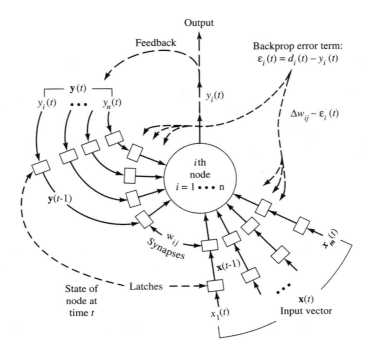

Figure 6-5: The diagram shows any one of the n neurons in the single layer of a recurrent backpropagation network. The ith neuron receives the m components of the input vector, $\mathbf{x}$, and outputs the ith component of the output vector $\mathbf{y}$. All n components of the output vector appear at the inputs of all neurons, at the start of the next cycle, along with the next input vector. Thus, there is a one-time-step delay through the network. Each neuron, since it receives all components of both $\mathbf{x}$ and $\mathbf{y}$ at each cycle, sees the same inputs as all other neurons. But, as in standard backprop, each component arrives through a distinct synapse, and each neuron's set of $m + n$ synaptic weights is unique. In a teacher-forced version of the paradigm, some or all components of the backprop target vector, $\mathbf{e}$, are fed back to the inputs in place of components of $\mathbf{y}$. Both input synapse modification and feedback combine to give the network the composite property of supervised feedback. Its applications focus on relating input and output temporal sequences.

Thus, the inputs that the network is given include $\mathbf{y}(t_0)$ initially, and the vector sequence $\mathbf{x}(t)$ over the course of the paradigm, as t steps from t_0 through some final value t_f. The network's response is the vector sequence $\mathbf{y}(t + 1)$.

In summary, the paradigm maps a temporal input sequence to a temporal output sequence. In a subsequent paper, the authors define its generic tasks to include "sequence classification, where the input is the sequence to be classified and the desired output is the correct classification, which is to be produced at the end of the sequence," and "sequence production, in which the input is a constant pattern and the corresponding desired output is a time-varying sequence" (Williams and Zipser, 1990).

Specific tasks that have been taught to the network include performance of an exclusive OR (XOR) operation between inputs separated by a delay of from two to four cycles; recognition of the order in which two specified events occurred, independent of the number of intervening events; the production of sine wave oscillations, and parsing parentheses in long text strings to balance left and right parentheses (Williams and Zipser, 1989b).

For the backprop aspect of its operation, the network undergoes supervisory training, with the input synapses being shifted according to the generalized delta rule, to move components y_k in the direction of the desired output vector, e_k. It is assumed that the target values are not necessarily known for all outputs, and therefore the synapses that are adjusted by this procedure are generally a subset of all the synapses. Furthermore, since the known target outputs may not relate to a fixed set of nodes, the membership in this subset may itself be variable during the course of the paradigm.

Among the variants of the paradigm that Williams and Zipser describe is a "teacher-forced" mode, in which the target outputs, e_k, rather than the actual outputs, y_k, are fed back to some of the inputs.

Recurrent backpropagation is interesting not only in opening up a hybrid area combining feedback and supervised feedforward, but also in its operation on temporal sequences. It is not the only neural technique for processing temporal sequences. Other sequence-oriented paradigms have been devised, including the "outstar avalanche" (Grossberg, 1969, 1970, 1971), the "spatiotemporal pattern recognizer" (Hecht-Nielsen, 1987), and the "temporal associative memory" (Kosko, 1988a).

7

LEARNING LAWS AND CONTINUED TAXONOMY

The taxonomy of Chapter 1 appears again in Figure 7-1—this time with some meat on its bones. We have now dealt with paradigms representing each of the quadrants of the taxonomy chart. Backpropagation, Kohonen's self-organizing feature map, and the Hopfield net are the classical paradigms of supervised feedforward, unsupervised feedforward, and feedback architectures, respectively. Furthermore, the perceptron and the LMS paradigm, forerunners of backprop, join it in quadrant I. In subsequent chapters, other paradigms will be assigned to sectors of this taxonomy.

The taxonomy, however, remains a loose one, with paradigms tending to spill over the boundaries. This appears in the fact that both the perceptron and backpropagation have variations including feedback. Furthermore, the self-organizing map (or AVQ), in its lateral competition between nodes, exercises a limited form of feedback.

Given this fuzzy taxonomy, how do we know which paradigm to select for a given application? What is the practical significance of the quadrants?

In most applications, quadrant I is the simplest to use. Particularly in problems where feedback is not present and where external information is available for use in supervising the learning process, backpropagation is feasible. It has the advantage of being able to store a very large number of exemplars, compared to the feedback cases—along with the disadvantage of needing very large training set exposure.

As the situation becomes more complex—perhaps because of the absence of supervisory information with which to teach the network, or a goal of modeling dynamic systems—the experimenter needs to move to other quadrants.

If, for example, a problem is to establish boundaries between various classes

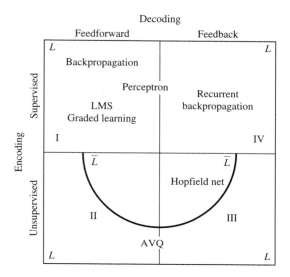

Figure 7-1: The taxonomy with categorized examples. Some, however, resist categorization, as shown by their overlap of the boundaries. (Modified from Kosko.)

of information, then it is impossible to operate in quadrant I, because quadrant I presumes that you know the class boundaries a priori, in order to provide the correction signals. Then, the natural place to operate would be in quadrant II, which is the habitat of clustering paradigms. In applying the quadrant II paradigms, you know how many classes you wish to establish, and you let the paradigm determine the boundaries.

A greater degree of generality is found in quadrant III, where the number of classes as well as the boundaries between them may be unknown at the outset. These feedback nets are also particularly interesting in their behavior because they are dynamic systems. The penalties for operating in this comparatively subtle terrain include a more severely limited storage capability—where, as we have seen, the maximum number of attractors or potential wells is highly sensitive to the dimensionality of the data.

Learning Laws

In 1949 Donald Hebb put forth a theory of learning in which he hypothesized that if the output of a neuron X in a nervous system repeatedly stimulates a second neuron, Y, to fire, then the pathway from X to Y becomes increasingly efficient in conveying that stimulus. There is much more to Hebb's theory than this; however, this is what he is best known for.

Figure 7-2: Hebbian learning. Synapse w_{ij} learns in proportion to the product of the concurrent output signals from neurons i and j, connected via that synapse.

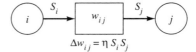

$$\Delta w_{ij} = \eta\, S_i S_j$$

The Hebbian learning rule, for a synapse w_{ij} between the ith and jth neurons, is:

$$\Delta w_{ij} = \eta S_i S_j$$

where S_i is the output signal transmitted from the ith neuron to the jth, and S_j is the concurrent output from the jth neuron. The rule states that when these two quantities, S_i and S_j, are concurrently large, the synapse between the two neurons will be strengthened (Figure 7-2). Or, in more specific terms, if the jth neuron is stimulating the ith neuron and (whether as a result of that stimulus or of other stimuli) the ith neuron is activated, then learning takes place at the synapse. The constant η is a constant of proportionality indicating the strength of the effect; and the learning increment is Δw_{ij}.

In contrast to the Hebbian law, the Widrow-Hoff or delta rule, which we met in Chapter 3, and again in Chapter 6 at the output nodes of a backprop network, assumes the existence of a teacher. It appeared in Chapter 3 as:

$$\Delta w_{ij} = \eta(z_k - y_k)$$

where z_k is the target output and y_k is the actual output from the kth neuron.

When the delta rule is adapted, as was described in Chapter 6 in a backprop-agation context, a more specialized learning law results, taking into account not only the difference between an idealized target output and an actual output, but also special rules for modifying synapses between hidden and output nodes.

Unsupervised Learning Laws

Bart Kosko of the University of Southern California writes: "Unsupervised learning laws are first-order differential equations that describe how synapses evolve in time with locally available information. . . . Locality allows asynchronous synapses to operate in real time" (Kosko, 1990b).

The dependence only on local information is important in a few ways. First, from the standpoint of biological evolution, it is more believable that intelligence grew from local interconnections between neighboring cells than from some intrinsically complicated phenomenon operating remotely.

Assuming that learning is expressed through the changing of synaptic weights, there is very little information locally available to a synapse. It is exposed to its own state and to the states of the two neurons that it links—and that is all. For the biological neuron, there are external events (*parasynaptic effects*) going on in its immediate vicinity, such as biochemical changes, the actions of glial cells, and background physical effects such as mechanical vibrations, temperature changes, and electromagnetic flux. Kosko combines all of these as noise, as will be shown near the end of Chapter 9.

For biological as well as electronic systems, this simplification has the appealing quality of separating the operation of the nervous system from extraneous perturbations. Furthermore, to the experimenter who wishes to model biological neurons, it has to be good news that this modeling can be accomplished using a model based exclusively on nodes and their interconnections—and that the overwhelming morass of parasynaptic effects need not be part of the picture.

Second, whether in biological nervous systems or in electronic hardware, the dependence only on local information implicitly increases redundancy and fault tolerance. There is no central unit to oversee or correct the operation of the network—therefore no vital element whose loss is critical.

With these principles in mind, let's come back now to a synapse that sees only its own state and that of the two adjacent neurons. The synapse in the following discussions has a weight w_{ij}, and it lies on the line bringing the output signal, S_i, from the ith neuron to the input of the jth neuron—whose output signal is S_j.

The rate at which the synapse varies can be expressed, in a very general form, as

$$\dot{w}_{ij} = f(w_{ij}, S_i, S_j, \dot{S}_i, \dot{S}_j),$$

where f is (so far) an arbitrary function.

Suppose, in the simplest case, that the synapse is changing only as a function of its own state. The resulting law (which is also a sublaw appearing implicitly in several more complete learning laws) is this:

$$\dot{w}_{ij} = -w_{ij}.$$

That is, $dw/dt = -w$, and therefore $w = w_0 e^{-\alpha t}$, where α is a constant of integration and w_0 is an initial state of the neuron at time $t = 0$. This equation likens the neuron to a discharging capacitor, or the release of a stretched massless spring. It represents an exponential decrease of memory in the absence of adjacent neuronal activity—in other words, a forgetting.

In order to learn, a synapse needs to outdo this exponential decay term with supportive signal outputs from the two neurons that it connects. The signal Hebb law uses the products of the two signals:

$$\dot{w}_{ij} = -w_{ij} + S_i S_j. \tag{7.1}$$

The Hebbian property here stems from the activity of the two concurrent signals.

A variant is the competitive learning law, which takes the following form:

$$\dot{w}_{ij} = -w_{ij} S_j + S_i S_j.$$

Factoring out S_j, this becomes:

$$\dot{w}_{ij} = w_{ij} + S_j (S_i - w_{ij}), \tag{7.2}$$

Here, S_j modulates the learning rate.

It isn't necessarily obvious, at first, why equation (7.2) represents a competitive process. The underlying assumption is that the upper-layer neurons compete with each other. In this lateral competition, each neuron in a layer sends negative (inhibiting) outputs to all of the others in its layer; the greater the activation level of the neuron, the more strongly negative the inhibitory signals it transmits. Through an iterative process, this leads to a single winner. (See Chapter 5.)

In practice, the output signal, S_j, is usually either a step function or a very steep sigmoid. So it can be assumed that S_j is approximately 1 (at the winning node) or 0 (at one of the losers). Fitting this into (7.2), losers don't change, but the winning node changes its input synapses.

Other variations on the fundamental Hebbian learning law have been developed, such as the "classical differential Hebbian" learning law:

$$\dot{w}_{ij} = -w_{ij} + \dot{S}_i \dot{S}_j, \tag{7.3}$$

which makes learning a function of the rates of signal change in the neurons, not of the absolute signal values. The differential Hebbian law (dropping "classical") takes both signals *and* signal velocities into account:

$$\dot{w}_{ij} = -w_{ij} + S_i S_j + \dot{S}_i \dot{S}_j. \tag{7.4}$$

In 1989 Kosko proposed another variant, the differential competitive law:

$$\dot{w}_{ij} = \dot{S}_j (S_i - w_{ij}). \tag{7.5}$$

This substitutes a "learn only if change" logic for the "learn only if win" logic of (7.2). The signal velocity in (7.5) is described by Kosko as a "local reinforcement mechanism." Its sign tells whether the jth node is winning or losing, and its magnitude says by how much.

8

ADAPTIVE RESONANCE

The contributions of Stephen Grossberg of Boston University to neural network theory have been voluminous and pervasive in their influence. Since 1964 he has been publishing papers and books in this field, which have gradually coalesced into Grossberg's theory of adaptive resonance.

A good starting point in tracing adaptive resonance is a 1980 article by Grossberg in the *Psychological Review*, entitled "How does a brain build a cognitive code?" This paper looks into the encoding of sensory input data by biological neurons.

However, Grossberg does not investigate this by starting with the anatomy and physiology of nerve cells. Rather, he proceeds from the logical examination of what it is that a living nervous system must be able to do.

One question he poses is this: "How can a coding error be corrected if no individual cell knows that one has occurred?" This question is examined in the context of the erroneous associative cues to which we are exposed in a rich, fluctuating environment.

He illustrates the limits of classical (Hebbian) conditioning with the metaphor of two lovers sharing a turkey dinner. If passive feedforward association of stimuli were sufficient to establish conditioning, why wouldn't these people get into the confusion of wanting to consume their lovers and mate with turkeys? While allowing that some quirky behavior patterns can be induced, Grossberg observes that we are generally pretty good at maintaining coherence in response to stimuli.

The model that is then posed in the *Psychological Review* article involves two fields of neurons, which we will symbolize here as F^x and F^y. The field F^x is an idealized representation of a group of neurons close to the sensory input, whereas F^y represents a higher level. As an example of F^x, Grossberg gives the lateral geniculate nucleus (LGN), which he refers to as the waystation closest (in some species) to the visual receptors, and, as an example of F^y, the visual cortex, where internal representations and memories of visual stimuli are processed and stored.

Figure 8-1 illustrates the encoding issue. In Figure 8-1a, suppose that the system has learned, or perhaps is genetically predisposed to know, that the encoding of input pattern x_1 produces the internal representation y_1. (The details of the encoding process, which occurs within the arrow between F^x and F^y, need not be known in the context of Grossberg's argument.)

Then, suppose that, at a subsequent time, as shown in Figure 8-1b, an erroneous encoding occurs, in which input x_2 evokes y_1. Grossberg asks how this false encoding can be recognized and suppressed. Certainly not within F^y, because, so far as F^y knows, the pattern present in F^x is x_1.

The logical conclusion is that feedback must occur, in which F^y sends back to F^x the input pattern that it expects to be present there (Figure 8-1c). So, F^y sends back pattern x_1. The juxtaposition of generally uncorrelated x_1 and x_2 combine to form a more or less flat or noiselike pattern—an indication that an encoding error has occurred. If there hadn't been an erroneous encoding, a match or resonance between layers would have occurred, as in Figure 8-1d.

The mismatch condition of Figure 8-1c must lead to a suppression of pattern x_2, so that the activity leading to the false encoding will not continue to fortify that encoding. But that's not enough. The erroneous pattern across F^y also needs to be suppressed. This correction cannot be based in F^x, Grossberg reasons, because F^x has no information as to what pattern is present in F^y. In fact, whatever field initiates the corrections to the y field must be able to inhibit all cells in the y field, because any combination of those cells may be involved. Grossberg hypothesizes a nonspecific "arousal" center that is triggered along with F^x upon the introduction of a signal into the system. Figure 8-2 shows the branching of a stimulus into both the specific route through F^x and the nonspecific route through arousal center A.

The existence of nonspecific arousal paths was well established in biological research prior to Grossberg's work. As an example of nonspecific arousal, Grossberg notes the fact that you elicit a reaction if, in the middle of a conversation with a friend, you suddenly slam your hand on the table.

It is the very nonspecificity of the arousal center that makes it the logical source for broad inhibition to field F^y.

The next question that Grossberg addresses is this: What in the cycle of events following the mismatch brings the arousal center into play to suppress the pattern across F^y? The mere absence of a pattern in F^x cannot do it—otherwise waves of arousal would be continually triggered in the absence of significant input stimuli.

The mechanism that Grossberg hypothesizes is taken through its consecutive stages in Figure 8-2. Field F^x, so long as it has a pattern active across it, inhibits the arousal center (Figure 8-2a). It is only when the x field is suppressed subsequent to

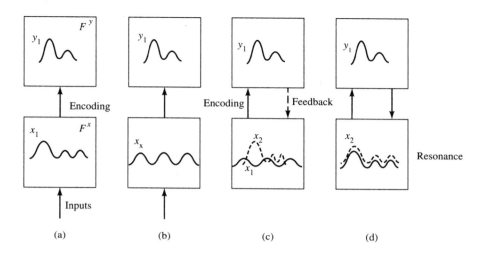

Figure 8-1: Correction of false encoding (after Grossberg). This series of diagrams shows how a higher level neural field of a human or animal brain would correct a false encoding of input data. The correct encoding is shown in a. In part b, a different input arriving from the lower level F^x erroneously stimulates the same response. Grossberg demonstrates that the false encoding must be corrected by feedback from the higher level, F^y, of the pattern that it expects to be present at F^x. The returned pattern washes out the lower level pattern at c, if the encoding was false—or confirms it (d) if the encoding was correct. See the text for fuller detail.

Figure 8-2b that it relinquishes its inhibition of A (Figure 8-2c). At that point, the nonspecific arousal is released to suppress the pattern in the y field.

If the inhibition is to be successful in suppressing the erroneous response pattern, y_1, while leaving cells of the y field free to respond rapidly to any new stimulus, then the degree to which any cell is inhibited should be proportional to how active it has been in representing the erroneous pattern. So a graduated inhibition appears across F^y, in which every cell is inhibited in direct proportion to its level of activity when the wrong pattern was encoded.

Then, if pattern x_2 is again input to the system, another chance at correct encoding occurs, with the cells that were most implicated in the discredited pattern being the ones most punished—that is, excluded from the next attempt to form the correct response to x_2.

The inhibition that was generated at the arousal center must last long enough to block any tendency of y_1 to reappear in response to x_2. The correct response should then be available from the less punished cells—those that were relatively or fully inactive in the formation of the distorted response.

The upgoing pattern x_2 and the responses to x_2 in level F^Y go through a series

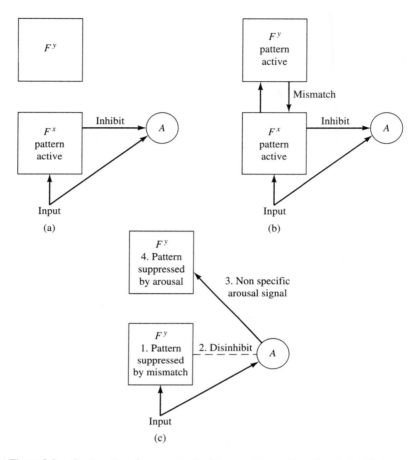

Figure 8-2:   Continuation of response to the false encoding problem. How is the falsely generated pattern at F^y dispelled after the suppression of the pattern at F^x? Grossberg hypothesizes an arousal center, A, which is triggered by the collapse of the pattern at F^x and which, in turn, suppresses the pattern at F^y. (After Grossberg.)

of rapid reverberations with false responses being quenched by the mechanism described previously until a matched response is obtained.

At this point, the analysis comes up against the next potential snag. If y_2, the correct response to x_2, is available in F^Y, then why didn't it appear in the first place? Or, equivalently, if y_2 didn't appear, then does that mean that cells able to generate it are not present in F^Y? And, if the ability to create y_2 is intrinsically absent in F^Y, or absent after the suppression of the cells that were active in generating incorrect response y_1, then how can the ability to create y_2 develop or redevelop?

Thus, it would seem that the suppression of the erroneous higher level pattern following x_2 would tend to leave the higher level idle upon the repetition of x_2.

(An early repetition is assured if x_2 comes from a stimulus that the environment is continuously supplying at that time.) Grossberg concludes, in fact, that the organism would be limited in this way if feedforward mechanisms were solely involved.

However, the possible presence of lateral competition among the neurons in F^Y provides an alternative hypothesis. When the neurons forming pattern y_1 are suppressed, the remaining neurons in F^Y are left free to compete. Their competitive interaction would tend to enhance small existing differences in their activity levels, building these into strongly contrasting differences. The result would be the creation of a pattern y_2 as a response to x_2.

That is, the competitive process can generate configurations in which slightly active elements suppress their competitors and enhance themselves to become highly active. (This quality was demonstrated in Chapter 5 in relation to Kohonen's AVQ paradigm.) Minor, random initial variations in a symbolic terrain become major features. This, Grossberg observes, is a feasible model for how responses to newly-learned stimuli could form.

Implied is the likelihood that x_2 is triggered by an experience that is new to the organism, its very novelty contributing to its erroneous evoking of known pattern y_1. The suppression of y_1 and the formation of a new upper-level pattern, y_2, enable the organism to encode its response to a new stimulus.

In summary, the described mechanisms establish the means by which a living or conceptual system could "build a cognitive code." When encoding has occurred and mismatches have been corrected, the pattern formed at the lower level matches the expectation at the higher level and the communication between levels becomes supportive—a state of resonance. It is this adaptive resonance that provides the underlying theme as well as the name for Grossberg's theory.

These ideas were subsequently embodied in paradigms. The paradigms show ways in which to implement the principles of pattern matching and competition in artificial neural networks.

The ART Paradigms

Paradigms based on adaptive resonance theory (ART) have been described by Gail Carpenter and Stephen Grossberg. ART1 is the version that takes binary inputs, whereas ART2 takes continuous-valued inputs.

An ART1 geometry is shown in Figure 8-3. The exemplar patterns are stored in the synapses. There are both "bottom-up" synapses, b_i^j, and top-down synapses, t_i^j. These correspond to the intercommunications between fields F^x and F^y in the theoretical model. Because ART1 (referred to simply as ART in the following discussion) undergoes learning, these synapses change with time.

In Figure 8-3, the jth bottom-up exemplar, a vector $\mathbf{b}^j$ (with components b_i^j), represents the synaptic input weights of the jth top-layer neuron. On the other hand, the jth top-down exemplar, $\mathbf{t}^j$ (with components t_i^j), is a vector representing the input weights from the jth top-layer neuron to each of the bottom-layer neurons.

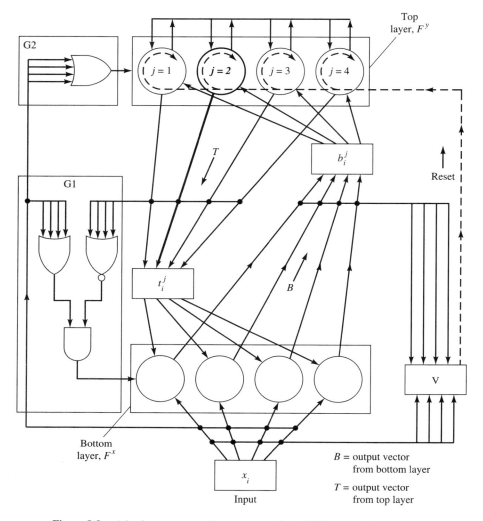

Figure 8-3: Adaptive resonance. The geometry of the ART1 feedback network. See the text for full details.

Thus, each bottom-up exemplar is stored in the synapses of a particular top-layer neuron. But each top-down exemplar, associated with a particular top-layer neuron, is distributed among the synapses of the various bottom-layer neurons. Inner products of incoming vectors with these exemplars determine degrees of similarity. A particular bottom-up exemplar, $\mathbf{b}^j$, is multiplied by a vector $\mathbf{x}$ (input during cycle τ), to produce a scalar output u^j, a measure of similarity between $\mathbf{x}$ and $\mathbf{b}^j$:

$$u^j = \sum_i x_i b_i^j \qquad (8.1)$$

This is illustrated in Figure 8-4.

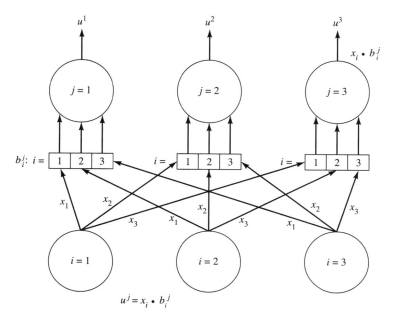

Figure 8-4:   The role of the bottom-up exemplars, b_i^j, in ART1.

Using this notation, we can now look into the behavior of the network. Although the behavior of ART is described by differential equations, finite equations approximate it. These equations describe the initial and changing values of the synapses and the interactions of the input vectors with the synaptic weights.

To begin with, the top-down synapses, t_i^j are all initialized to 1. The bottom-up synapses, b_i^j, are all initialized to some common value $< [L/(1 - L + N])$, where L is a small constant greater than 1 (L often being set to 2) and N is the number of input nodes—that is, the dimensionality of the input vectors.

Each one of the nodes in the bottom layer receives three inputs—a logic signal from the circuitry (G_1) to the lower left in Figure (8-3); the input signal (x_i); and the signal from the upper layer, mediated by the top-down synapses, t_i^j. At least two of these inputs must be positive for the node to be activated (a two-thirds rule).

When an input vector, $\mathbf{x}$, is introduced into the ART network, the presence of at least a single 1 bit in $\mathbf{x}$ activates the OR gate in G1. The NOR gate in G1 is true because there are, as yet, no signals coming down from the upper layer. Therefore, the AND gate in G1 outputs a 1 to each of the lower nodes. Because the inputs to these nodes (through the top-down synapses, t_i^j) are still zero, and because G1 provides each node with one of the two inputs needed for its activation, the ith node will be triggered if and only if input $x_i = 1$. That means that $\mathbf{x}$ will pass through the bottom layer unchanged, and $\mathbf{B}$, the output vector from the bottom layer, will be identical to $\mathbf{x}$.

The dot product of $\mathbf{x}$ with the bottom-up synapses then establishes the acti-

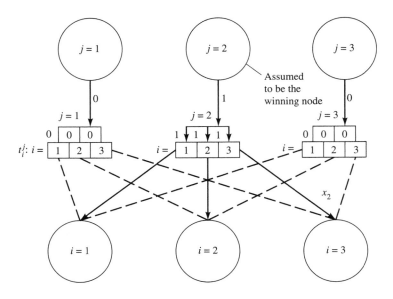

Figure 8-5: The role of the top-down exemplars, t_i^j, in ART1.

vations at the upper nodes, as already indicated by (8.1). And, without transformation, these nodes provide output signals, u^j, equal to those activations.

Next, lateral inhibition is performed, in which each of the upper nodes feeds inhibiting signals to its neighbors and activating signals to itself, proportional to its own activation. This is the competitive process by which only one of these nodes remains active.

In the first cycle, with all the synapses initialized to the same values, a random selection determines the winner; after that, the winner will be the upper node whose fan-in forms the largest dot product with the input vector—that is, the one most like the input vector. Then, if the Jth node wins (letting capital J indicate the winner, in contrast to lower-case j, indicating any arbitrary node), then only the Jth neuron sends an output to the lower layer.

Furthermore, the downgoing output signal from the Jth node of the upper layer is not the activation, u^J. That activation level played its only part when it made node J the winner. But the output from the winning node to the lower layer is a simple 1, which multiplies the components t_i^J of the Jth top-down synaptic vector. (see Figure 8-5.)

The unit signal from the Jth node does something else. By triggering the NOR gate in G1, it resets G1 to zero. Now, based on the 2/3 rule, a lower level neuron becomes active only if its sees a 1 component from the input vector (still the input of cycle τ) AND if it sees a 1 component from t_i^J, the top-down synapse. The only top-down synapses that can participate in this are those for which $j = J$.

But the Jth node is only a conditional winner at this point. A vigilance test has to be performed to establish whether the vector is sufficiently close to the exemplar stored as $\mathbf{t}^J$, the corresponding top-down synaptic vector.

Under initial conditions, with all the t_i^j of the synaptic array initialized to the same starting value, there is no special reason to expect a good match. But good matches will be prevalent later, as the network trains itself.

The vigilance test requires that the following inequality be fulfilled:

$$\sum_i x_i t_i^j \Big/ \sum_i x_i > \rho, \tag{8.2}$$

where ρ is the vigilance parameter, determined ahead of time by the experimenter.

Because the top-down exemplar, $\mathbf{t}^j$, and the input vector, $\mathbf{x}$, are both binary, the left-hand side (l.h.s.) of inequality (8.2) is a measure of the bit agreement between them. The numerator, being the dot product of the two binary vectors, is a scalar equal to the number of 1s that the vectors have in common—in other words, their logical AND. The denominator is just the sum of the 1s in the input vector. The ratio has a value between 0 and 1; and in order for the exemplar to be selected, it must exceed the preset vigilance parameter, also a number between 0 and 1.

The vigilance test takes place as follows: With no unit signal from G1, the ith lower level node will be active only if t_i^j and x_i are both 1s; in other words, the node performs a logical AND of t_i^j and x_i. The output bits are summed and passed to the vigilance logic, V, as the dot product $\sum_i x_i t_i^j$. The vigilance logic also has $\sum_i x_i$ available to it, directly from the input vector, so it has all the information it needs to perform the test of equation (8.2), resetting the winning node's output to 0 if the test fails. Note that all this is still happening in the first cycle of network operation—cycle τ.

If the l.h.s. of (8.2) does not exceed ρ, then the match established by the bottom-up logic is nullified, and the output of the winning Jth node is temporarily set to zero and excluded from the paradigm. Then the bottom-up process is repeated, with the same input vector being input again, to select a new conditional winner, also subject to the vigilance test.

With the confirmation of a winner that passes the vigilance test, accompanied by the offset of the input vector, the G2 circuit (whose OR gate switches to *false*) issues a softer reset to all upper nodes—that is, a reset to zero that does not exclude them from the continuing paradigm. Now the network is ready to receive the next input vector.

In presetting the value ρ, the experimenter is determining how "grainy" the categorization will be. A high value of ρ means that matches will be relatively hard to make, with the result that many exemplars and many categories will be established. A lower value of ρ means a faster, coarser learning process with fewer exemplars and categories.

At this point, a natural question arises: Why should the bottom-up and top-down synapses constitute different and possibly conflicting exemplars? The answer is that these two classes of ART exemplars are formed in different ways and play different roles in the paradigm. How they differ becomes apparent in the context of how they are modified.

As with many paradigms, the synapses are modified only when they are associated with a winning node. If the vigilance test is affirmative, then the input vector has been accepted in class J by both bottom-up and top-down exemplars. In that case, both exemplars are moved closer to the input vector that they just classified—as we have seen, for instance, in Kohonen's self-organizing feature map in Chapter 5. However, the two kinds of ART synapses follow different learning rules.

For the winning top-down synapse, the learning rule is very straightforward. The top-down exemplar vector in cycle τ, symbolized as $\mathbf{t}^J(\tau)$ and the input vector, $\mathbf{x}$, are compared in a logical AND operation whose output generates the new synapses, $t_i^J(\tau + 1)$:

$$t_i^J(\tau + 1) = x_i \cap t_i^J(\tau). \tag{8.3}$$

In the case of the bottom-up synapses, the new values of the winning b_i^j are based on a weighted version of (8.3):

$$b_i^J(\tau + 1) = [x_i \cap t_i^J(\tau)] \ / [(L-1) + \sum_i x_i t_i^J(\tau)]. \tag{8.4}$$

In equation (8.4), the new b_i^j values are functions of the new values of t_i^j, but modified (as a function of the constant L) according to how many bits of the $t_i^j(\tau)$ are 1s, which is what the summed expression in the denominator expresses. In fact, the new bottom-up exemplar, $\mathbf{b}^J(\tau + 1)$, is penalized, so far as new inputs are concerned, in proportion to how many 1s are present in the new top-down exemplar.

At first glance, this is a strange result. A large number of 1s is just what you would expect from a winning exemplar. Why does it now appear as a penalty?

This penalty is designed to eliminate a bias in favor of exemplars that are supersets of other exemplars. The extreme example is found in a vector that is all 1s. It would win every competition in both bottom-up and top-down processes, resulting in a degenerate network. In general, various degrees of degeneracy would result from wins going to relatively dense vectors, automatically able to generate high scores in both the competition and the vigilance test, without having any real resemblance to the input vector, but merely having a predominance of 1s.

By countering this automatic bias, equation (8.4) introduces a principle of parsimony into the network. As the b_i^j adjust themselves according to (8.4), a strong bottom-up exemplar tends to be one that can produce a high score, yet one adapted toward a top-down exemplar that is not oversaturated with 1s. In general, this will tend to select exemplars that are intrinsically close to the input vector, rather than those that merely overwhelm the comparison through having a multitude of 1s.

If the vigilance test looks at every conditional winner in turn and keeps rejecting them, it will finally see a vector that is still in its initial state—a $\mathbf{t}^J$ whose terms, t_i^j, are all still set to unity. Such a vector automatically passes the vigilance test—and thus becomes the exemplar for a new case—that is, it forms the start of a category for an input vector that does not fit into any of the established classes.

However, a vector $\mathbf{b}^J$ associated with this top-down exemplar will be penalized according to the excess of 1s that it inherits. Less dense bottom-up exemplars are more likely to win in later cycles. Also, through the erosion of going through intersections with not-very-dense input vectors, new top-down winners will tend to thin themselves.

Thus, the two halves of the recognition cycle supplement and counterbalance each other. They do this with a mathematical elegance reminiscent of Yossarian's point of view in Joseph Heller's *Catch-22*, when he considered a logic that had "an elliptical precision about its perfect pairs of parts that was graceful and shocking, like good modern art."

As the network accepts an exemplar pair, with agreement between the initial competition and the later vigilance test, it is in its state of adaptive resonance with regard to the current input. Furthermore, this network resolves a stability/adaptability dilemma. The exemplars that it forms are relatively stable; yet, it has room to adapt to new information that does not fit into any of its exemplars.

When the network is related back to the underlying theory of adaptive resonance, it is clear that the processes of encoding between two fields F^x and F^y and correcting false encodings have been implemented. The selection of a winning node through the initial competition, corrections through the vigilance test, and the subsequent temporary disabling of provisional but unacceptable winners model the theory.

ART2, not detailed here, represents a direct extension of these principles to the case of continuous inputs. In order to handle a continuous range of values, the lower level field, F^x, has multiple sublevels and multiple gain controls, to establish the multiple threshold levels corresponding to the continuous data. Further developments include ART3, which models chemical gating, and a fuzzy version of ART.

A Note on Parsimony

As part of the ART paradigm, Carpenter and Grossberg took an elegant approach to prevent a very dense vector from winning a dot product competition, whether or not it bore much resemblance to the exemplar. It is important to observe that this pitfall can be much reduced, whatever the paradigm, if input vectors and stored exemplars are sparse. If, for example, we are considering vectors having 100 binary components, of which 6 or 7 (at most) are 1s, then the problem goes away. In this sparse environment, the vector whose dot product with the stored exemplar is the largest is very probably the vector that most closely resembles that exemplar.

The benefits of sparse or dilute coding, explored by Grossberg (1976, 1986) and others, echo the earlier discussion of Hopfield nets, where the optimum density of 1s was set at $\log_2 n$ for an n-dimensional vector. For a 256-element vector, that means that, ideally, there should be eight 1s.

9

BIDIRECTIONAL ASSOCIATIVE MEMORY

Bidirectional associative memory, or BAM, is a more sophisticated descendant of autoassociative memories, such as the Hopfield net. A major evolution of BAMs through several models has been taking place in recent years, primarily through the work of the BAM's originator, Bart Kosko of the University of Southern California.

In an autoassociative memory, an input vector that is "A-like" will recall stored vector **A**, an input vector that is "B-like" will recall stored vector **B**, and so forth. And, of course, **A** recalls itself and **B** recalls itself. The autoassociative nature of such a memory is further indicated by the fact that the exemplar vectors are multiplied by their own transposes in order to generate the terms of the synaptic matrix.

In contrast to this, a BAM associates vector pairs $\mathbf{A}^x$, $\mathbf{B}^x$, such that $\mathbf{A}^x$, when input to the network, recalls $\mathbf{B}^x$, and vice versa. And this bidirectionality is built into the terms that make up the BAM synaptic matrix, as joint functions of $\mathbf{A}^x$ and $\mathbf{B}^x$. The bidirectionality also shows up in the architecture of the network. Unlike the single, totally interconnected layer of the Hopfield net, the BAM has two layers, each of which is totally connected to the other (Figure 9-1), with inputs going both ways. This symmetric structure corresponds to the two sets of vectors that are to take turns in recalling each other.

Figure 9-2 illustrates the generation of a BAM, using an example from an article by Kosko (1988a). In this example, the 15-dimensional vectors **A** are to be paired with the 10-dimensional vectors **B**, so that $\mathbf{A}^1$ is paired with $\mathbf{B}^1$, $\mathbf{A}^2$ with $\mathbf{B}^2$, and so on. As with the Hopfield net, a bipolar transformation is made, substituting -1s for 0s, to replace $\mathbf{A}^i$ with $\mathbf{X}^i$ and $\mathbf{B}^i$ with $\mathbf{Y}^i$. Then, the synaptic matrix, **W**, is generated by the formula:

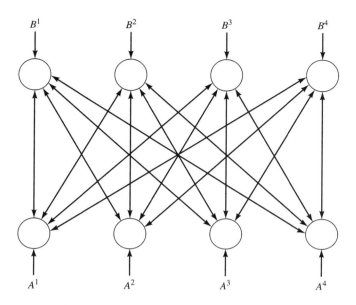

Figure 9-1: Architecture of a BAM (bidirectional associative memory). The BAM and its descendants are feedback networks developed by Bart Kosko. In contrast to the autoassociative Hopfield network, these are heteroassociative networks. The neurons are in two layers, and each neuron in one layer communicates reciprocally with all neurons in the other layer.

$$\mathbf{W} = \sum_k (\mathbf{x}^k)^T \mathbf{y}^k$$

Bidirectional associations between vectors whose dimensionalities are free to differ generate matrices that are not necessarily square and symmetric—as they must be in the case of the Hopfield. Another contrast relates to the fact (see Chapter 4) that the main diagonal of a Hopfield matrix is commonly zeroed, to eliminate the unwanted condition of neurons feeding back to themselves. Here, no such self-feedback is implied by the main diagonal, and there is no zeroing. A BAM matrix on-diagonal term W_{ii} is the strength of coupling between neuron i in the X field and neuron i in the Y field.

Now, in Figure 9-2, when $\mathbf{W}$ is multiplied by $\mathbf{A}^1$, and subsequently thresholded, $\mathbf{B}^1$ should be recalled. When the multiplication is carried out, with the row vector $\mathbf{A}^1$ forming an inner product with each column of $\mathbf{W}$, this vector is generated:

$$\mathbf{A}^1\mathbf{W} = (12, 10, 4, 4, -4, -4, -12, -12, 12, 12).$$

Using a threshold that sets all negative elements to 0 and all nonnegatives to 1, the output vector becomes:

$$(\mathbf{A}^1\mathbf{W})' = (1, 1, 1, 1, 0, 0, 0, 0, 1, 1),$$

$A^1 = (1\ 0\ 1\ 0\ 1\ 0\ 1\ 0\ 1\ 0\ 1\ 0\ 1\ 0\ 1)$ $B^1 = (1\ 1\ 1\ 1\ 0\ 0\ 0\ 0\ 1\ 1)$

$A^2 = (1\ 1\ 0\ 0\ 1\ 1\ 0\ 0\ 1\ 1\ 0\ 0\ 1\ 1\ 0)$ $B^2 = (1\ 1\ 1\ 0\ 0\ 0\ 1\ 1\ 1\ 0)$

$A^3 = (1\ 1\ 1\ 0\ 0\ 0\ 1\ 1\ 1\ 0\ 0\ 0\ 1\ 1\ 1)$ $B^3 = (1\ 1\ 0\ 0\ 1\ 1\ 0\ 0\ 1\ 1)$

$A^4 = (1\ 1\ 1\ 1\ 0\ 0\ 0\ 0\ 1\ 1\ 1\ 1\ 0\ 0\ 0)$ $B^4 = (1\ 0\ 1\ 0\ 1\ 0\ 1\ 0\ 1\ 0)$

$x^1 = (1\ -1\ \ 1\ -1\ \ 1\ -1\ \ 1\ -1\ \ 1\ -1\ \ 1\ -1\ \ 1\ -1\ \ 1)$ $y^1 = (1\ \ 1\ \ 1\ \ 1\ -1\ -1\ -1\ -1\ \ 1\ \ 1)$

$x^2 = (1\ \ 1\ -1\ -1\ \ 1\ \ 1\ -1\ -1\ \ 1\ \ 1\ -1\ -1\ \ 1\ \ 1\ -1)$ $y^2 = (1\ \ 1\ \ 1\ -1\ -1\ -1\ \ 1\ \ 1\ \ 1\ -1)$

$x^3 = (1\ \ 1\ \ 1\ -1\ -1\ -1\ \ 1\ \ 1\ \ 1\ -1\ -1\ -1\ \ 1\ \ 1\ \ 1)$ $y^3 = (1\ \ 1\ -1\ -1\ \ 1\ \ 1\ -1\ -1\ \ 1\ \ 1)$

$x^4 = (1\ \ 1\ \ 1\ \ 1\ -1\ -1\ -1\ -1\ \ 1\ \ 1\ \ 1\ \ 1\ -1\ -1\ -1)$ $y^4 = (1\ -1\ \ 1\ -1\ \ 1\ -1\ \ 1\ -1\ \ 1\ -1)$

$$W = \begin{bmatrix}
4 & 2 & 2 & -2 & 0 & -2 & 0 & -2 & 4 & 0 \\
2 & 0 & 0 & -4 & 2 & 0 & 2 & 0 & 2 & -2 \\
2 & 0 & 0 & 0 & 2 & 0 & -2 & -4 & 2 & 2 \\
-2 & -4 & 0 & 0 & 2 & 0 & 2 & 0 & -2 & -2 \\
0 & 2 & 2 & 2 & -4 & -2 & 0 & 2 & 0 & 0 \\
-2 & 0 & 0 & 0 & -2 & 0 & 2 & 4 & -2 & -2 \\
0 & 2 & -2 & 2 & 0 & 2 & -4 & -2 & 0 & 4 \\
-2 & 0 & -4 & 0 & 2 & 4 & -2 & 0 & -2 & 2 \\
4 & 2 & 2 & -2 & 0 & -2 & 0 & -2 & 4 & 0 \\
0 & -2 & 2 & -2 & 0 & -2 & 4 & 2 & 0 & -4 \\
0 & -2 & 2 & 2 & 0 & -2 & 0 & -2 & 0 & 0 \\
-2 & -4 & 0 & 0 & 2 & 0 & 2 & 0 & -2 & -2 \\
2 & 4 & 0 & 0 & -2 & 0 & -2 & 0 & 2 & 2 \\
0 & 0 & -2 & -2 & 0 & 2 & 0 & 2 & 0 & 0 \\
0 & 0 & -2 & 2 & 0 & 2 & -4 & -2 & 0 & 4
\end{bmatrix}$$

$W = \sum_i x^{i^T} y^i$

$A^i W \rightarrow B^i$

$B^i W^T \rightarrow A^{\,i}$

Figure 9-2: The generation of a BAM synaptic matrix. The mathematics are similar to those used to generate a Hopfield matrix. Rather than vectors multiplying themselves to form outer products, however, associated vector pairs are multiplied together. The figure shows that vectors A^i and B^i are converted to bipolar forms x^i and y^i. Then, the outer products of $(x^i)^T$ and y^i are summed to form the synaptic matrix, W. When vector A^i multiplies the matrix, its associated vector, B^i, is recalled, and vice versa. (After Kosko.)

which equals B^1. And, in similar fashion, each of the A^i recalls the corresponding B^i. Running the paradigm backward, when any B^i multiplies W^T, thresholding produces A^i.

When an unknown vector, not equal to any of the eight vectors that generated W, is applied to W, it usually requires a number of recall cycles before converging to a stable vector pair. This is analogous to the reverberation of a Hopfield network as it recalls a stored vector.

For example, if the vector

$$\mathbf{B}^x = (1, 1, 0, 0, 1, 1, 0, 0, 0, 0)$$

is presented to the synaptic matrix of Figure 9-2, it produces output

$$\mathbf{A}^x = (1, 1, 1, 1, 0, 0, 1, 1, 1, 0, 0, 1, 1, 1).$$

Neither $\mathbf{B}^x$ nor $\mathbf{A}^x$ is one of the stored exemplars. $\mathbf{B}^x$ resembles $\mathbf{B}^3$, but with errors in the last two bit positions; $\mathbf{A}^x$ resembles $\mathbf{A}^3$, but with errors in bits 4 and 12.

The BAM paradigm calls for the input of $\mathbf{A}^x$ back through the transposed synaptic matrix. This cycle correctly summons $\mathbf{B}^3$—and $\mathbf{B}^3$, in turn, summons $\mathbf{A}^3$. When $\mathbf{A}^3$ is processed through the matrix, it recalls $\mathbf{B}^3$. The matrix is now stable, have reverberated through only two cycles to reach a stability point.

As with the Hopfield net, the convergence of a BAM corresponds to a local energy minimum. The energy function for a solution that recalls a vector pair ($\mathbf{A}$, $\mathbf{B}$) is $-\mathbf{AWB}^T = -\mathbf{BW}^T\mathbf{A}^T$. For instance, in the example of Figure 9-2, $-\mathbf{A}^1\mathbf{WB}^T = -54$ and $-\mathbf{B}^1\mathbf{W}^T\mathbf{A}^T$ yields the same scalar result.

The energy of an arbitrary input/output pair, prior to stabilization, does not generally fall at a minimum. Nevertheless, as in the Hopfield net, there are exceptions—cases in which induced minima will form—attractors that associate vector pairs never intentionally stored. Kosko estimates that the number of exemplar pairs that can be stored without significant interference can be as large as the dimensionality of the smaller of the two exemplar classes; thus, for the example of Figure 9–1, ten exemplar pairs could be stored.

However, there are techniques for increasing this capacity. Karen Haines and Robert Hecht-Nielsen (Haines and Hecht-Nielsen, 1988) show that the use of variable thresholds for the different nodes, along with sparse code, can raise the capacity of a BAM to as high as 2^n vectors.

Kosko has broadened the stabilizing property of the BAM by proving the generalization that "every real matrix is bidirectionally stable." The reader is referred to Kosko's 1988 paper for the proof; or one can carry out an exercise by writing an arbitrary matrix, multiplying it by an arbitrary binary vector, and continuing from there through sequences like those of BAM recall.

For instance, construct the arbitrary matrix

$$
\begin{matrix}
2 & -3 & 0 \\
1 & 4 & -3 \\
-4 & 2 & 3 \\
1 & 0 & 2
\end{matrix}
$$

Multiplying the columns by an arbitrary binary input vector, col [0 1 1 0], produces row [−5 3 0], which thresholds to [0 1 1]. When the transposed matrix is then multiplied by [0 1 1], the product is col [−3 1 5 2], which thresholds to [0 1 1 1].

Next, when [0 1 1 1] multiplies the transposed matrix, it recalls [0 1 1], and stability has been reached. The solution is then the vector pair [0 1 1], [0 1 1 0]. There may be other pairs defining potential wells in this matrix, which would be summoned by other input vectors.

But the matrix was not constructed from stored vector pairs. Instead, the exercise "discovers" a vector pair implicitly stored in the matrix.

The simplicity of the BAM generally lends itself to pencil-and-pad exercises of this type. Or the operation of the BAM—or any other paradigm—can be demonstrated using neural scratchpad software (such as the "Brain Simulator" from

Neural Network Laboratory, a division of Abbot, Foster & Hauserman Company, San Francisco), on which the user can define a paradigm, specifying network architecture, synaptic weights, thresholds, and inputs. Once defined in such a program, the paradigm can be put into action to display the outputs of the neurons.

TAM

The BAM concept can be extended to what Kosko calls a "temporal associative memory" or TAM. In the TAM, he lets the ith vector operate on a synaptic matrix, $\mathbf{W}$, to evoke the $(i + 1)$st vector. If the $(i + 1)$st vector is applied to $\mathbf{W}$, it, in turn, evokes the $(i + 2)$nd, and so forth. But if any vector operates on the transposed synaptic matrix, $\mathbf{W}^T$, the temporal sequence operates in reverse, with the $(i + 1)$st vector recalling the ith, and so on.

To illustrate this case, Kosko uses four vectors, $\mathbf{A}^1$, $\mathbf{A}^2$, $\mathbf{A}^3$, and $\mathbf{A}^4$, with:

$$\mathbf{A}^1 = (1, 0, 0, 1, 0, 0, 1, 0, 0, 1)$$
$$\mathbf{A}^2 = (1, 1, 0, 0, 1, 1, 0, 0, 1, 1)$$
$$\mathbf{A}^3 = (1, 0, 1, 0, 1, 1, 1, 0, 1, 0)$$
$$\mathbf{A}^4 = (1, 0, 0, 1, 0, 0, 1, 0, 0, 1)$$

The synaptic matrix, $\mathbf{W}$, is generated as $\sum_i \mathbf{X}^i \mathbf{X}^{i+1}$, where the $\mathbf{X}$s are the bipolar transforms of the $\mathbf{A}$s. By letting the last vector, $\mathbf{A}^4$, recall the first, $\mathbf{A}^1$, the temporal sequence proceeds in a loop. Then the expression for $\mathbf{W}$ becomes:

$$\mathbf{W} = (\mathbf{X}^n)^T \mathbf{X}^1 + \sum_{i=1}^{n-1} (\mathbf{X}^i)^T \mathbf{X}^{i+1}$$

$\mathbf{W}$ takes us around the loop $\mathbf{A}^1$, $\mathbf{A}^2$, $\mathbf{A}^3$, $\mathbf{A}^4$, $\mathbf{A}^1$, . . . , while $\mathbf{W}^T$ takes us around the other way, $\mathbf{A}^4$, $\mathbf{A}^3$, $\mathbf{A}^2$, $\mathbf{A}^1$, $\mathbf{A}^4$, ...

MAM

Although the fundamental BAM is a two-layered structure without hidden layers, Kosko notes that it can be generalized to multiple layers. But adding layers to a BAM does not necessarily have to be done internally in the form of hidden layers. This point is illustrated by a multidirectional associative memory (MAM) described by Masafumi Hagiwara of Keio University in Yokohama.

The simplest case of the MAM uses three layers. Each pair of the layers is involved in a reciprocal exchange, as in a BAM. The two-sided game of catch that is played by the BAM becomes a three-sided game in the three-layered MAM, abbreviated here as a "3-MAM."

The synaptic matrix between any two layers of the 3-MAM is generated just as if they were the two layers of a BAM. Thus, if vectors $\mathbf{A}^i$, $\mathbf{B}^i$, and $\mathbf{C}^i$ are the inputs to neural layers A, B, and C, respectively, and if the bipolar transforms of (A^i, B^i, C^i) are (X^i, Y^i, Z^i), then three synaptic matrices are generated:

$$I = \sum_i (X^i)^T Y^i \text{ (synapses between neuron layers } A \text{ and } B)$$

$$II = \sum_i (Y^i)^T Z^i \text{ (synapses between neuron layers } B \text{ and } C)$$

$$III = \sum_i (X^i)^T Y^i \text{ (synapses between neuron layers } C \text{ and } A)$$

These matrices represent the storage of vector triplets, in associations such as (A^1, B^1, C^1) and (A^2, B^2, C^2). The input of any one of the vectors into its corresponding layer evokes the two associated vectors to recall the full stored triplet.

Actually, the flow of information in the 3-MAM is a little more complicated than a three-sided game of catch. There are two balls in circulation—a ball that circulates "clockwise" and a reflected ball that circulates "counterclockwise." If a vector is input to layer A, a dual output is evoked from layer B: the direct output from B is transmitted to layer C, and the reflected output from B is transmitted back to layer A. The operation must be synchronous, so that a neuron receives its clockwise and counterclockwise inputs simultaneously.

Each neuron, as it receives its two inputs (through two different sets of synapses) sums the two sets of weighted inputs to determine its activation. Then, in BAMlike manner, the neuron issues a 1 if its activation is nonnegative and otherwise issues a 0.

Hagiwara points out the advantages of the MAM, not only in the richness of its multiple associations, but also in its noise immunity. If the input to one layer is critically noise-contaminated, the introduction of a relatively noise-free vector to any other layer will serve to suppress the noise and bring the system to equilibrium.

There is an implied design tradeoff in the introduction of the third and higher layers that constitute the MAM. The designer needs to determine whether, in any given case, the additional performance outweighs the penalties in complexity and memory storage requirements.

ABAM

With the adaptive bidirectional associative memory, or ABAM, Kosko takes his model into an environment of continuous inputs and establishes a paradigm that includes adaptation. The following two equations serve as a useful starting point to describe the network dynamics:

$$\dot{x}_i = -x_i + \sum_j S_j(y_j)W_{ij} + I_i, \tag{9.1}$$

$$\dot{y}_j = -y_j + \sum_i S_i(x_i)W_{ij} + J_j, \tag{9.2}$$

In equations (9.1) and (9.2), I_i and J_j are constant or slowly varying external input vectors, W_{ij} is the synaptic weight between the ith and jth nodes, the S values are the I/O signals generated at the nodes, and x and y are the associated paired activations resulting from the operation of the paradigm—at first varying, later stabilizing. The terms $-x_i$ and $-y_j$ indicate the exponential decay of the activation (as discussed in Chapter 4 and in Chapter 7).

These equations clearly represent a generalization of the Hopfield model, equation (4.5), with bidirectionality as an extension.

When the terms x_i and y_j become equal to zero, equations (9.1) and (9.2) have reached a stable condition. Then, with the external inputs set to zero, the equations reduce to the discrete BAM case:

$$x_i = \sum_j S_j W_{ij},$$

$$y_j = \sum_i S_i W_{ij}.$$

If the synapses of the network described in equations (9.1) and (9.2) are allowed to adapt, a third equation is needed. For the signal-Hebb law, the synaptic learning equation that accompanies (9.1) and (9.2) looks like this:

$$\dot{W}_{ij} = -W_{ij} + S_i(x_i)S_j(y_j). \tag{9.3}$$

The additive structures of (9.1) and (9.2) can be transformed into a shunting form through the transformations $b_i(x_i) = x_i - I_i$; $b_j(y_j) = x_j - J_j$. When amplification factors $a_i(x_i)$ and $a_j(y_j)$ are included, the following equations result:

$$\dot{x}_i = -a_i(x_i)[b_i(x_i) - \sum_j S_j(y_j)W_{ij}], \tag{9.4}$$

$$\dot{y}_j = -a_j(y_j)[b_j(y_j) - \sum_i S_i(x_i)W_{ij}], \tag{9.5}$$

where $a_i(x_i)$ and $a_j(y_j)$ are greater than or equal to 0.

And, staying the same,

$$\dot{W}_{ij} = -W_{ij} + S_i(x_i)S_j(y_j). \tag{9.6}$$

Equations (9.4), (9.5), and (9.6) constitute the adaptive BAM or ABAM model.

If the two fields of (9.4) and (9.5) are allowed to collapse into one, this model reduces back to the earlier Cohen-Grossberg autoassociative model (Cohen and Grossberg, 1983):

$$\dot{x}_i = a_i(x_i)[b_i(x_i) - \sum_j W_{ij}y_j(x_j)],$$

with $a_i(x_i) > 0$. The difference in sign between this equation and the collapsed ABAM merely reflects a different convention in defining terms, not a conceptual difference.

The Cohen-Grossberg model was a precursor (by several months in publication date) to the continuous Hopfield model. This reflects the parallel investigations that Hopfield on the west coast of the United States and Grossberg and his colleagues on the east coast were conducting. The two models are equivalent.

The Noise-Saturation Dilemma

The shunting form chosen by Grossberg and found also in the shunting version of the ABAM is significant in terms of the "noise-saturation dilemma," which Grossberg addressed in several of his early works (Grossberg, 1977, 1978, 1980). He stated the problem as follows: "All cellular systems face the following dilemma. If their inputs are too small, they can get lost in noise. If the inputs are too large, they can turn on all excitable sites, thereby saturating the system and rendering it insensitive to input differences across the cells."

Grossberg considered a population of cells subject to a stimulus I, with the ith cell receiving an input I_i. Then, letting B represent the number of excitable sites in the ith cell, and $x_i(t)$ the number of those that are excited at time t, the number of unexcited sites in the cell is $B - x_i(t)$. This leads to:

$$\dot{x}_i = -Ax_i + (B - x_i)\,I_i,\qquad(9.7)$$

where $i = 1, 2, 3, \ldots, n$.

In (9.7), the first term on the right, $-Ax_i$, represents exponential decay of the excited population, with decay rate A. The second term, $(B - x_i)\,I_i$, represents the excitation process acting on previously dormant sites. Suppose that the stimulus, I_i, experienced by the ith cell is the product of the cell's sensitivity, θ_i, and a general background intensity of the stimulus, I:

$$I_i = \theta_i I\qquad(9.8)$$

Substituting this expression into (9.7), letting the derivatives, $\dot{x}_i$, go to zero at equilibrium, and collecting terms leads to:

$$x_i = (B\theta_i I)/(A + \theta_i I).$$

Therefore, as I becomes very large, x_i approaches the total site population B, a saturated state.

Faced with this dilemma, Grossberg posed the following alternative to (9.7):

$$\dot{x}_i = -Ax_i + (B - x_i)I_i - x_i \sum_k I_k.\qquad(9.9)$$

The subtracted final term, in which $k \neq i$, represents the competitive influence of other cells inhibiting the ith cell—the on-center, off-surround concept that characterizes lateral competition.

But, $x_i I_i + x_i \sum_k I_k$ add, for $k \neq i$, to $x_i I$.

Now, when this substitution is made, when (9.8) is substituted into (9.9), and when the system comes to equilibrium, the expression for x_i becomes:

$$x_i = (B\theta_i I)/(A + I).$$

The resulting limit for x_i as I becomes very large is now

$$x_i = \theta_i B,$$

and, with the excited population proportional to sensitivity or gain factor, θ_i, the noise-saturation dilemma is averted.

The fact that a resolution was reached on the basis of (9.9), with its multiplicative term, established the basis for a shunting rather than additive relationship for neural systems.

ABAM: Implementation

If the ABAM equations are to be simulated on a computer in finite form, they can be approximated by substituting Δx_i, Δy_j, and ΔW_{ij} for the derivatives. Whether in its continuous form or in finite form, with weights initially set to random values, the system will rapidly converge to a stable state after receiving inputs. Kosko (1988b) shows convergence to be a negative exponential function of time, or of the number of oscillations of the network.

The stable x, y pair and associated weights resulting from initial input $S_i(x_i)$ and its counterpart $S_j(y_j)$ will, at convergence, have dug an attractor basin in the associative memory. Whereas the discrete BAM depends on being constructed from exemplar vectors, this one goes through adaptive learning, developing an attractor state in response to the input vector pair.

The stable vector pair and synaptic states resulting from two initial input vectors are not analytically predictable. That is, the coordinates defining the attractor are not explicit functions of the input pair that created it. Rather, the network's response is the de facto definition of the attractor.

In order to develop multiple attractors, the network is exposed to inputs from several different vector pairs. However, it is not generally desirable to take the development of any single attractor state to a point of saturation because it will tend to obliterate earlier attractors and dominate attempts to train the network to later inputs.

There is a strategy for avoiding this. After the network is briefly exposed to an input, the subsequent reverberations can be quickly interrupted, long before a steady state is reached. Then training starts in response to a different input pair, and this too is interrupted. Subsequently, the first pair is again input to the network, sculpting the first basin a little deeper. In this way, the multiple attractors are formed in an intermittent fashion.

The multiple processes continue in this turn-taking fashion, until the network has thus been sculpted with multiple basins. Subsequent to this training period, the synapses are fixed, and the network is open to the recall process.

Recall is initiated by a single input vector. As in the case of the discrete BAM, this vector will evoke a vector in the other layer, and the processes take place by which any BAM gravitates toward an attractor state.

However, separation of the training and recall processes into two distinct phases is not strictly necessary. With the weights left free to change, a newly input vector pair that is close to an existing attractor state may recall that state, instead of defining a new attractor.

CABAM

Kosko went on from the ABAM to develop further extensions. One of these, which he called the competitive ABAM or CABAM, includes an explicit competitive term, by which the winning neuron inhibits others in its own layer. This is equivalent to the lateral inhibition in Grossberg's theory, or to the logic in Kohonen's self-organizing map that lets only the winning fan-in modify itself in the direction of the input vector.

The ABAM activation equations, with competition terms included, look like this:

$$\dot{x}_i = -a_i(x_i)[b_i(x_i) - \sum_j S_j(y_j)W_{ij} - \sum_k S_k(x_k)Q_{ki}],$$

$$\dot{y}_j = -a_j(y_j)[b_i(y_j) - \sum_i S_i(x_i)W_{ij} - \sum_h S_h(y_h)R_{hj}].$$

The second summation in each equation represents interactions among neurons within a layer. Thus, the expression for $\dot{x}_i$ includes the effects of signals from neurons in the x-layer, via synapses Q_{ki}—an interconnection matrix limited to the interior of the x-layer. Similarly, $\dot{y}_j$ shows the effects of signals from within the y-layer via R_{hj}. For the effects to be competitive, the weights within these competitive terms are typically 0 along the diagonal of the synaptic matrix (no feedback from a neuron to itself) and negative off the diagonal (each neuron inhibiting others). This lateral inhibition is usually modeled as being distance-dependent, with inhibition weights inversely proportional to distance.

The more positive the signal is from any neuron, the more it inhibits its competitors, whereas a neuron with low activation will do little to inhibit its competitors. If the radius of competition within a field is assumed to be sufficiently large, and the competitive weights sufficiently strong, then, at equilibrium, the resulting output vectors will each contain all 0s except for a single 1. The result is a set of clearly distinguishable, orthogonal solutions.

In contrast to the noncompetitive ABAM, the CABAM provides sharply resolved attractor states, and the ambiguity of slipping into a spurious well is averted. Where N is the lesser of the CABAM's two array dimensions, there are N possible stable states—an immediate result of the orthogonality described above.

In this region of no more than N solutions, the CABAM operates as a crisper classifier than the ABAM. But, for ventures into the more ambiguous realms of $>N$ attractors, the uncompetitive ABAM remains viable. Its use is more appropriate to global optimization problems, the simulation of learning processes, and the exploration of induced exemplars.

RABAM

A crucial underlying issue relating to all neural networks is that of robustness and the ability to withstand various levels of random noise. Mathematical paradigms that operate flawlessly on paper are of limited use if, when put into electronic systems, they cannot withstand disturbances from the outside world.

When considered as simulations of living nervous systems, neural networks have additional reasons for needing to be resistant to a multitude of external perturbations. Many biologists have criticized neural models as being simplistic because they do not take into account the wide variety of biochemical effects that occur in the vicinity of synapses.

Kosko addresses these issues with the "random adaptive bidirectional associative memory," or RABAM. In his diffusion RABAM he perturbs the neurons and synapses with Brownian motion terms:

$$dx_i = -a_i(x_i)[b_i(x_i) - \sum_j S_j(y_j)W_{ij}]dt + dB_i, \tag{9.10}$$

$$dy_j = -a_j(y_j)[b_j(y_j) - \sum_i S_i(x_i)W_{ij}]dt + dB_j, \tag{9.11}$$

$$dW_{ij} = -W_{ij} + S_i(x_i)S_j(y_j) + dB_{ij}. \tag{9.12}$$

In (9.10) and (9.11), the terms dB_i and dB_j represent independent random processes within the neurons, whereas in (9.12) dB_{ij} represents independent random processes within the synapses. These equations constitute the diffusion RABAM.

The learning law expressed in (9.12) is the signal Hebb law. However, as Kosko points out, this can be replaced with the competitive diffusion law,

$$dW_{ij} = S_j(y_j)[S_i - W_{ij}]dt + dB_{ij} \tag{9.13}$$

if S_j is sufficiently steep. Or, with tighter constraints, the differential Hebb or differential competitive laws can be used instead.

Kosko also states the RABAM theorem in a less rigorous noise notation, by adding a noise term to each of the ABAM equations.

$$\dot{x}_i = -a_i(x_i)[b_i(x_i) - \sum_j S_j(y_j)W_{ij}] + n_i, \tag{9.14}$$

$$\dot{y}_j = -a_j(y_j)[b_j(y_j) - \sum_i S_i(x_i)W_{ij}] + n_j, \tag{9.15}$$

$$\dot{W}_{ij} = -W_{ij} + S_i(x_i)S_j(y_j) + n_{ij}, \tag{9.16}$$

$$E(n_i) = E(n_j) = E(n_{ij}) = 0, \qquad (9.17)$$

$$V(n_i) = \sigma_i^2 < \infty, \quad \sigma_j^2 < \infty, \quad \sigma_{ij}^2 < \infty. \qquad (9.18)$$

If the noise terms have means of zero (9.17) and finite variances (9.18), the network will stabilize.[1] The theorem is proved (Kosko, 1990b, 1992a) for these different versions of the RABAM, through demonstration that the Lyapunov condition is met.

Stabilization in the presence of noise is not obvious a priori for systems in general. If, for instance, an inertial guidance system was subject to large noise levels, its state could be perturbed on a major scale. Sensors returning erroneous inputs would generate false correction terms, throwing the system off course and generating spurious correction signals whenever the vehicle happened to move back toward the proper course. In general, it would continue to generate correction signals to placate an imaginary error function. Under these circumstances, the error would compound, and the system behavior would diverge radically.

In contrast to that scenario, the RABAM theorem states that a feedback neural network will not diverge but will stabilize, with the mean-squared network velocities converging to the variance of the noise.

Figure 9-3 illustrates the dynamics of the system. The intrinsic mean-squared velocity vector of the network, added to the noise variance vector, yields the effective mean-squared velocity that an observer would see.

For a system unable to stabilize in the noise environment, the intrinsic mean-squared velocity would tend to increase, representing the compounding effects of the noise on system performance, as in the inertial guidance example.

What the RABAM theorem shows is that the intrinsic mean-squared velocities of the ABAM (or any other feedback ANN) diminish exponentially—taking the network to its smallest possible level of randomness in the presence of the noise: the variance of the noise itself. In other words, the system will vibrate about its equilibrium condition with a statistical distribution characteristic only of the noise, not compounded by a resulting runaway system error.

The RABAM theorem indicates that this stability extends to all feedback neural network paradigms. Furthermore, it assures us of the structural stability of the paradigms themselves.

Kosko suggests a demonstration, which the reader may want to try. It is not a proof but has intuitive appeal. Add some random noise to each memory element, w_{ij}, of a discrete additive BAM and to each neuron's activation, following each iteration of the paradigm—and watch it stabilize.

A color demonstration of the RABAM model is provided in a software package, Neural Network Library, from HyperLogic Corp., a company based in

---

[1] Since variance is expressed as the second moment of a probability density function, it isn't hard to define a distribution whose variance is infinite. For instance, if the noise density function in a system were $1/\pi(1 + x^2)$, known as "Cauchy noise," the variance would be the integral of $[x^2/\pi(1 + x^2)]dx$, which diverges as x becomes indefinitely large. But, for finite limits of integration of Cauchy noise, no matter how large, the RABAM paradigm converges.

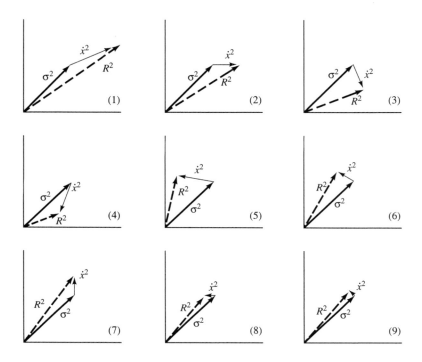

Figure 9-3: Convergence of the RABAM (random adaptive bidirectional associative memory). The diagrams show the convergence of the effective mean-squared velocity of RABAM output, R^2, approaching the variance of input noise, σ^2, as the squared velocity of the network, $\dot{x}^2$, drops exponentially toward zero.

Escondido, California. (The library's main purpose is to enable the C programmer to develop neural network applications, using various paradigms.) The RABAM demo includes an input window, showing the fluctuations of noise about a vector that is being presented to the network. A concurrent output window shows the initially large fluctuations of neural states about an idealized output vector, and shows these gradually approaching an equilibrium condition no noisier than the perturbations on the input vector. Other windows show other statistics of the fluctuation, as well as the user-selected parameters of the network.

Kosko has shown that the RABAM model represents the most generalized expression of unsupervised feedback paradigms, subsuming all other occupants of the lower right quadrant of the taxonomy (Kosko, 1990b). The matrix operations of the ABAM and CABAM (extended to incorporate random effects in the RABAM) are a generalized representation of operations leading to stability or resonance between the input and output vectors of a quadrant III neural network.

VARIATIONS ON NEURAL THEMES

There are many interesting variants on neural network paradigms, involving such aspects as probabilistic models and mixed architectures of various kinds that take selected elements from two or more existing paradigms.

This chapter surveys a variety of neural network models. The inclusion of these paradigms in a mixed and miscellaneous chapter does not indicate that they are less advanced than those occupying dedicated chapters. Their placement here stems from the fact that they are less widely used at this time or are singular variants rather than representatives of broad architectural classes. In fact, some of these miscellaneous paradigms have strengths that may eventually enable them to usurp their better known predecessors.

The Boltzmann Machine, a Probabilistic Model

In molecular physics, the Boltzmann distribution provides the probability density function for the kinetic energies of particles in a gas of absolute temperature, T. The probability that any given particle has an energy between E and $E + dE$ is proportional to $e^{-E/kT}dE$, where k, the Boltzmann constant, is a universal physical constant.

This statistical function was carried over into neural networks by David Ackley, Geoffrey Hinton, and Terrence Sejnowski in 1985. Specifically, they hypothesized a fully connected Hopfield-type network of neurons in binary states 0 (off) and 1 (on), with the kth neuron having a probability p_k of being in the *on* state, where,

$$p_k = 1/(1 + e^{-\Delta E_k / T}). \tag{10.1}$$

95

In this equation, ΔE_k is the energy gap between the *on* and *off* states of the neuron, and T is analogous to a system temperature. The network's global energy, summed over all nodes, is $\sum_{i<j} w_{ij} x_i x_j$, where w_{ij} is the weight leading into node i from node j, and x_i and x_j are the binary nodal signals.

The motivation that led to the development of this model, whose details will be presented, was based on limitations of the Hopfield network in converging to a local rather than a global minimum. For some applications, that is not an issue; when the goal is to converge to the stored vector closest to the input vector, the potential well that is wanted is the nearest, not the deepest one. In optimization problems, however, the global minimum is what is sought.

First it is necessary to be able to escape from local minima. Consider Figure 10-1. A ball rolling on a surface, if its energy is sufficiently low, can get trapped in a local minimum that is not only higher than the global minimum but perhaps higher than other minima of interest. The way to free the ball and make it roll uphill is to "kick" it, so that it is ejected from the trap like a pinball hit by a spring mechanism. In neural terms, noise needs to be added to the situation—something to make the ball oscillate randomly in the local trap until it makes an excursion over a nearby maximum, and thus downward along the next downslope.

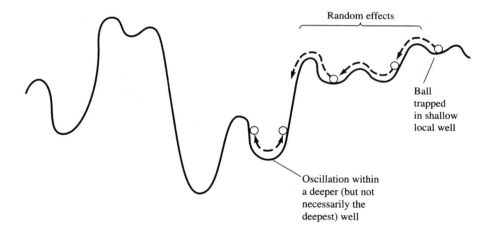

Figure 10-1: The Boltzmann machine (a neural network operating on a statistical principle) derives its name from the Boltzmann distribution of molecular velocities, whose mathematical form it borrows. This diagram presents the analogy of a ball coming to rest in a potential well, which may not be the deepest such well in the terrain. However, applied energy can jolt the ball out of the local well, in which case it may find the global minimum of the terrain. Similarly, the stable state reached in a feedback network may represent a local minimum. Adjusting a parameter that corresponds to temperature (in the molecular parallel) moves the network state out of the local well. Later, the network is "cooled" again to allow it to converge—ideally into a deeper potential well. The entire cycle is called "simulated annealing," because of its resemblance to the temperature cycles that metals undergo as they are strengthened.

In the molecular model, random input comes from temperature. In the work of Ackley et al., the T term, an adjustable "temperature" parameter, fills that role.

The energy gap, ΔE_k, for the kth node, is shown to equal the node's activation function—that is, the weighted sum of all inputs from other nodes:

$$\Delta E_k = \sum_i w_{ki} x_i. \qquad (10.2)$$

Equations (10.1) and (10.2) establish that each node will oscillate between the *on* and *off* states, depending on the inputs it is receiving.

The system as a whole will also oscillate, with this oscillation occurring about a dynamic global equilibrium. The relative probabilities of occurrence of any two global system states, A and B, having energies E_A and E_B, are:

$$P_A/P_B = e^{-(E_A - E_B)/T}. \qquad (10.3)$$

This equation fulfills the necessary requirement that when the two energies are equal, the relative probability is 1. As energy level E_A becomes much larger than E_B, the probability, P_A, of level A becomes much smaller than the probability, P_B, of level B. Ackley et al. point out a nice property of equation (10.3): the difference of the logs of the probabilities for two global states becomes (with $T = 1$) the difference in their energies.

It is also clear that a high temperature adds to the randomness of the situation, and that the system, quickly escaping from shallower global wells, will find its dynamic equilibrium in the vicinities of deeper wells. Even in a deeper well, however, it will tend to be unstable because of the continuing strongly random effects. Conversely, with the temperature parameter low, the system is more likely to gravitate toward the nearest local solution and stay there.

Having control over the temperature parameter, experimenters can tune the network. Those who want to emulate an associative memory—for instance, for pattern recognition applications—could choose a low temperature parameter; the minimum that is sought in that case is not necessarily the deepest but is the one closest to the input vector. Those whose applications call for an optimum or near optimum global solution to a problem could choose a high temperature, which would tend to shake the system free from merely local minima.

There is a mixed strategy that leads to a fast search for deep global minima and then a slower search in order to stabilize in one of the deeper of those. This is done by starting the system at a high temperature to facilitate its fast search and then lowering the temperature to allow stabilization. Because of its resemblance to the physical process of annealing a metal by taking it through that sort of temperature progression, this cycle is referred to as *simulated annealing*.

In order to train the network, all visible nodes are clamped to represent the input and output exemplars. After the system has settled into approximate equilibrium (*approximate* in that there will always remain some degree of random motion), an input vector is introduced into the system for categorization. Some subset of the visible nodes is clamped, with the signals on the clamped nodes being the components of the input or test vector. The global state of the visible nodes after restabilization is the system's response to the input.

Ackley, Hinton, and Sejnowski also provide a learning paradigm for the Boltzmann machine. Consider two connected neurons, i and j, and define two probabilities to be measured when the network is at equilibrium. First, p_{ij} is the probability that both of these neurons are simultaneously in the *on* state during the training phase, when the visible units are clamped. Secondly, p'_{ij} is the probability that both of these nodes are simultaneously on in the run phase. Then, as Ackley et al. demonstrate analytically, the learning law for the synapses is:

$$\Delta w_{ij} = \epsilon \, (p_{ij} - p'_{ij})$$

where ϵ is a scaling factor.

If there is a difference (in going from training phase to recall phase) in the probability of the two neurons being concurrently in the *on*-state, the synapse will change in such a way as to reduce that difference. The learning law has the favorable property seen in many neural networks of being dependent only upon local information at the two nodes and the synapse between them. Yet, operating between all pairs of connected nodes, the law determines the global state of the network.

The Hamming Network

The logical structure underlying the Hamming network was described in relatively early works—by Steinbuch in 1961 and Taylor in 1964. Its more recent presence in the neural network scene stems from independent proposals in 1987: Baum et al.; Domany and Orland; Lippmann et al. The authors who advanced the concept in that year generally viewed the Hamming net as a practical alternative to the Hopfield net. Like the Hopfield net, it performs an autocorrelation function—but it includes a competitive layer that forces rapid convergence in categorizing input vectors.

Illustrated in Figure 10-2, the Hamming or unary net is a resident of the lower left quadrant of the taxonomy. That is, it is a feedforward network, which classifies inputs without instruction. Like the Hopfield network and the BAM, it acts as a content-addressable memory.

Although not all interconnections are shown in the figure, the input and output layers of the Hamming net are fully connected to the intermediate layer. The synapses between the input nodes and the intermediate nodes are constructed, in the creation of the network, from the input exemplars. But this differs from the Hopfield net and the BAM in how the construction is carried out.

Rather than taking the outer products of exemplars with themselves (or their bidirectional associates), and summing these outer products to form a matrix of synapses, the Hamming paradigm stores the fan-in to each middle layer neuron as an exemplar vector. In other words, each of these fan-ins looks as if it was gener-

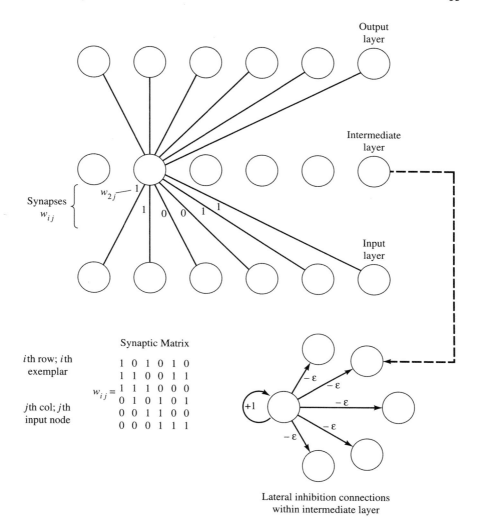

Figure 10-2: The Hamming net, like the AVQ, uses unsupervised feedforward. However, its use of lateral inhibition gives it a toe-hold in the feedback category. Its stored vectors are built into it at its creation, so it is a nonlearning network. The intermediate layer is fully connected to I/O layers. (Interconnections are shown here only for the winning intermediate node.) The Hamming net's stored vectors fan in to the intermediate layer nodes.

ated by a Kohonen self-organizing map. Instead of this being the endpoint of the paradigm, however, it is only the beginning. The exemplar vectors are simply defined, at the outset, as the fan-ins to the middle layer. Here, we are in a nonlearning situation.

Consider an input vector, as it is presented to this preset arrangement. It will tend to find its largest dot product with the fan-in vector that it most resembles.

At this point, the competitive factor comes into play. The design goal of the network is to have only *one* intermediate node *on*, and all others *off*. This suggests lateral inhibition within the intermediate layer, and that is what is done. The nodes in this layer are fully interconnected, with each one feeding itself an input equal to its own activation, while feeding each of the others an input $-\epsilon$ times its own activation, where ϵ is a constant less than $1/M$. (M is the number of intermediate nodes, and, since each of these nodes stores one exemplar, it is also equal to the capacity of the network in stored exemplars.)

The sequence in which the paradigm is performed is as follows: an input vector is introduced to the input nodes, is left there long enough to initialize the outputs of the middle layer, and is then removed. The network will then go through several iterations, as the competitive process takes place within the middle layer.

When the dust settles, with the network stable, only one intermediate node remains on—the node whose task it is to recognize that particular exemplar or something very close to that exemplar. A single node having that specialized recognition function is known as a *grandmother cell*, based on the illustrative idea of a single neuron in a person's brain firing when that person sees and recognizes his or her grandmother.

The same principle was used by Grossberg in storing a pattern in the synapses of a node, in an arrangement he called an "instar."

Suppose that a small Hamming network containing 64 grandmother cells accepts 10-bit input vectors. The network would be able to process 1024 distinct binary vectors, most of them noisy, sorting them into 64 classes.

Various authors describe different ways in which to tap the output of a winning grandmother cell. The cell could, when connected as in Figure 10-2, output a vector identical to its own synaptic fan-in. This output would then selectively turn on the output neurons corresponding to the cell's own 1 bits.

Baum et al. (1987) make this arrangement still more complex by having the winning cell address the output layer through a weight matrix that is the transpose of the input matrix. This seems like overkill when all that is needed is to identify the winning grandmother and thus the identity of the stored vector. In fact, the authors come to essentially that conclusion, saying, "Even more simply, the unary output of the grandmother level can itself be taken as an address and fed into standard RAM."

Lippmann (1987) compares Hamming net performance with that of a Hopfield net. He illustrates the comparison by assuming that 100-bit vectors are to be categorized into ten classes. The Hamming net would need 1100 I/O connections, 100 inputs to each of 10 grandmother cells plus a 10-by-10 array; the Hopfield would need nearly 10,000, a 100-by-100 array minus main diagonal elements.

Lippmann also notes that the Hamming net is an optimum minimum error classifier of random, independent inputs, and that it always produces a stored vector as its response. Its deterministic structure, of course, precludes spontaneous attractors.

This network is called a Hamming network because it outputs the exemplar whose Hamming distance from the input vector is the smallest. Or it is called a unary network because only a single intermediate node stays activated.

Brain-State-in-a-Box (BSB)

The brain-state-in-a-box (BSB) paradigm, developed by James Anderson, Jack Silverstein, Stephen Ritz, and Randall Jones at UCLA in 1977, is an ancestral relative of the Hopfield net. It gets its name from the fact that output vectors are constrained to lie within a multidimensional mathematical box—a hypercube.

The exemplar vectors that generate the synaptic matrix are bipolar, having components equal to 1 and -1. Given that these vectors are n-dimensional, the vertices of the limiting hypercube are n-tuplets.

The synaptic matrix, W, is generated by the summation:

$$W = \sum_i \lambda_i (x^i)^T x^i$$

where the x^i are the generating bipolar vectors and the λ_i coefficients are eigen-values weighting each vector's outer product. The resulting matrix, except for the λ_i, is like the matrix in the Hopfield network. Like the Hopfield net, this matrix is to be used as an autoassociator. However, the BSB can be made into a heteroassociator, in which case the matrix is like a BAM matrix:

$$W' = \sum_i \lambda_i (x^i)^T y^i$$

When an unknown vector, X, is presented to the autoassociative matrix, W, the output at the end of cycle $t + 1$ is:

$$X(t + 1) = aW[X(t)] + bX(t), \tag{10.4}$$

where a and b are predetermined constants. As equation (10.4) indicates, the output is a linear combination of the input vector and its product with the matrix. In n-space, there are $2n$ vertices toward which various solutions will converge.

Figure 10-3 presents an example of an autoassociative BSB, based on five five-dimensional exemplars. In this example, there are 32 vertices, such as (1, 1, 1, 1, 1), $(-1, -1, -1, -1, -1)$, and so on. The five exemplars, defined over $\{-1, 1\}$, establish five of these vertices. For computational simplification, a common value of $\lambda_i = .2$ has been set in this example for all five of the outer products—although, in general, the λ_i will differ from one another, in the range from 0 to 1.

The constants a and b of (10.4), as well as the coefficients, must be chosen so that no component of the output vector falls outside the interval $[-1, 1]$ in the

$$
\begin{array}{lrrrrr}
x^1 = & 1 & -1 & 1 & 1 & -1 \\
x^2 = & 1 & 1 & 1 & -1 & -1 \\
x^3 = & 1 & 1 & -1 & 1 & 1 \\
x^4 = & -1 & 1 & -1 & 1 & 1 \\
x^5 = & -1 & -1 & 1 & 1 & -1
\end{array}
$$

(a) Generating bipolar vectors, $\mathbf{x^i}$

$$
\begin{array}{rrrrr}
5 & 1 & 1 & -1 & -1 \\
1 & 5 & -3 & -1 & 3 \\
1 & -3 & 5 & -1 & -5 \\
-1 & -1 & -1 & 5 & 1 \\
-1 & 3 & 5 & 1 & 5
\end{array}
$$

(b) Synaptic matrix, $\mathbf{w}$

$$
\begin{array}{rrrrr}
1 & .2 & .2 & -.2 & -.2 \\
.2 & 1 & -.6 & -.2 & .6 \\
.2 & -.6 & 1 & -.2 & -1 \\
-.2 & -.2 & -.2 & 1 & .2 \\
-.2 & .6 & 1 & .2 & 1
\end{array}
$$

(c) Synaptic matrix, weighted by eigenvalues, λ_i

$$
\begin{bmatrix} -.2 \\ .4 \\ -.1 \\ .2 \\ -.3 \end{bmatrix}
$$

(d) Input vector, $\mathbf{x}$

$$
\begin{array}{rrrrr}
-.20 & -.04 & -.04 & .04 & .04 \\
.08 & .40 & -.24 & -.08 & .24 \\
-.02 & .06 & -.10 & .02 & .10 \\
-.04 & -.04 & -.04 & .20 & .04 \\
.06 & -.18 & -.30 & -.06 & -.30
\end{array}
$$

(e) Product of weighted synaptic matrix and input vector

$-.12 \quad .20 \quad -.72 \quad .12 \quad .12$ ⟵ (f) Output vector from product

$-.20 \quad +.40 \quad -.10 \quad +.20 \quad -.30$ ⟵ (g) Addition of input vector

$-.32 \quad .60 \quad -.82 \quad .32 \quad -.18$ ⟵ (h) Output vector from cycle 1

⋮

$-.67 \quad 1 \quad -1 \quad 1 \quad 1$ ⟵ (i) Output vector at the end of cycle 3

Figure 10-3: Numerical example for the neural network called brain-state-in-a-box (BSB). It is an autoassociative feedback network, resembling the Hopfield net.

first cycle. (In the example shown in the figure, $a = b = 1$ fulfills the requirement.) When, in any subsequent cycle, the paradigm forces any component outside the $[-1, 1]$ range, this result is overridden, and a hard limit of 1 or -1 is assigned to the errant component.

The result of the paradigm is that the output moves, after a few cycles, to the periphery of the hypercube, usually to one of its vertices. Ideally, it will approach the vertex of the exemplar that most resembles the input vector.

In the example shown in the figure, the input vector, $(-.2, .4, -.1, .2, -.3)$ most resembles exemplar $\mathbf{X^4}$ $(-1, 1, -1, 1, 1)$—agreeing in four of five algebraic signs. The convergence of the output to $\mathbf{X^4}$ is rapid; at the end of three cycles, the output is $(-.67, 1, -1, 1, 1)$, with only the first term lagging, but well on its way to its destination at -1.

As the authors of the original BSB article (Anderson et al., 1977) demonstrated, the paradigm operates in the presence of random noise, with the probability of successful classification of an input vector being inversely proportional to the variance of the noise. The addition of the noise can be a simple addition of a random variable, symmetrical about zero, to each component of the input.

If a reward is given the eigenvalue corresponding to the vertex the paradigm converges to, a BSB network can undergo learning. Anderson et al. recommended that the winning eigenvalue, λ_i, be incremented according to the relationship

$$\lambda_{new} = 1 + g(\lambda - 1) + \eta,$$

where η is a learning constant and g is a decay factor. For sample calculations that the authors presented, the parameters used were $\eta = .3$ and $g = .9$ or $.95$.

Vertices that are not selected are punished, with only the decay factor playing a part:

$$\lambda_{new} = 1 + g(\lambda - 1).$$

The Neocognitron

Along with his colleagues at the NHK Broadcasting Science Research Laboratories in Tokyo, Kunihiko Fukushima has developed feedforward neural paradigms based on a complex, hierarchical geometry. Fukushima's first paradigm, announced in 1975, was the *cognitron*. Since that time he has elaborated on the cognitron with the more advanced *neocognitron*. The discussion here will focus on the neocognitron (Fukushima, Miyake, and Ito, 1983), which incorporates the earlier model.

The neocognitron is a cascaded logical structure that operates in the manner of a succession of specialized sieves in order to extract and categorize information. Its development stems from attempts to model the ways in which the human cerebral cortex processes visual images from the retina, to perform pattern recognition.

Simulated on a computer, the input layer of the neocognitron represents a two-dimensional array of optical receptor cells. Neurons in a second layer categorize features from the input layer, such as vertical or horizontal lines, diagonal lines of various orientations, and step structures.

A third layer processes the features detected by the first layer, determining their locations in the visual field. Higher layers are trained to induce (from the shapes and locations of the features detected) the presence of particular geometric patterns.

Figure 10-4 shows how a neocognitron that has been trained to recognize numerals would respond to the input of the numeral 5. The input numeral occupies the input layer, U_0. The entirety of this layer is mapped by each of 12 sets of synapses (a_1), each set oriented toward a particular kind of feature. Thus, the top a_1 set in the diagram extracts horizontal line segments from the pattern, the seventh a_1 set extracts vertical line segments, and so on.

The results of these mappings are that the mapped features appear in the 12 planes of the U_{s1} layer. Furthermore, the location of a mapped feature corresponds

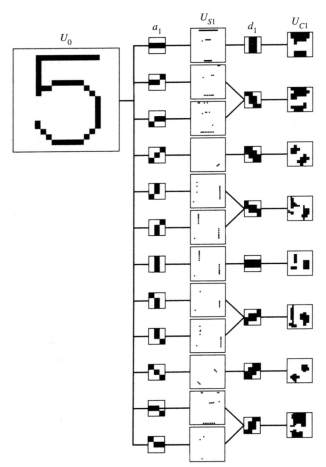

Example of response of cells of layers U_0, U_{S1}, and U_{C1}, and
synaptic connections between them

Figure 10-4: Cells of the neocognitron perform successive feature extraction to iden-
tify a numeral. [Kunihiko Fukushima, Sei Miyake, and Takayuki Ito, "Neocognitron: A
Neural Network Model for a Mechanism of Visual Pattern Recognition," *IEEE
Transactions on Systems, Man, and Cybernetics*, 13(5), pp. 826–834, September–
October, The Institute of Electrical and Electronic Engineers, Inc., 1983.]

to its location in the original pattern. Thus, the mapped horizontal lines appear at
the top, middle, and bottom of the U_{s1} plane—corresponding to the horizontal segments in the numeral 5.

As successive layers process this information, inasmuch as the detected input
shows horizontal segments at top, middle, and bottom, and vertical segments at top
left and bottom right (as well as other geometric specifics involving the locations

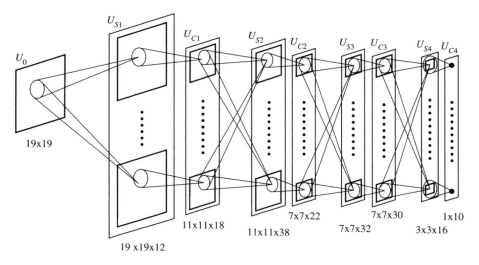

Schematic diagram illustrating synaptic connections between layers in necognitron

Figure 10-5: Successive layers of the neocognitron. [Kunihiko Fukushima, Sei Miyake, and Takayuki Ito, "Neocognitron: A Neural Network Model for a Mechanism of Visual Pattern Recognition," *IEEE Transactions on Systems, Man, and Cybernetics*, 13(5), pp. 826–834, September–October, The Institute of Electrical and Electronic Engineers, Inc., 1983.]

of certain diagonal and step structures), the input pattern can be categorized. There is enough information available to detect a 5 from among the possible digits 0–9.

However, a pattern recognizer should be font-independent. Ideally, it should be able to do what we do: recognize a variety of digits, printed or scrawled, in various distorted shapes and orientations.

In 1982, Fukushima, in a paper coauthored with S. Miyake, announced the ability of the evolving neocognitron to exhibit tolerance to deformations. (It already was tolerant to shifts in position of the input figure.) The neocognitron's tolerance is partially represented in Figure 10-4, as the synaptic sets d_1 map the U_{s1} planes into the U_{c1} planes. (*S* stands for *simple* because of the direct mapping that occurs at this level, and *C* stands for *complex* because of the more sophisticated generalization that occurs there.)

Where horizontal features are located in U_{s1}, the d_1 synapses provide vertical spread; where vertical features are located, they allow horizontal spread; and, in general, an orthogonal broadening of the active regions in the U_{s1} planes is performed.

For example, the top set of synapses in the diagram would map any horizontal line near the top of U_{s1} into a broad horizontal band at the top of U_{c1}. The point is that a horizontal bar at the top is a characteristic of numerals 5 and 7, but various

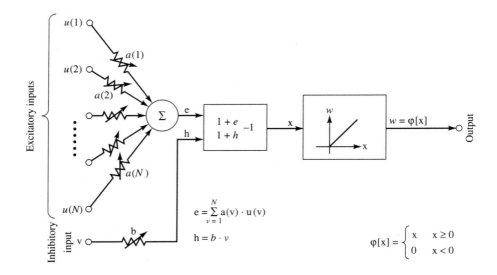

Figure 10-6: The neurons of the neocognitron accept both excitatory and inhibitory inputs. The excitation of the neuron is $x = [(i + e)/(1 + h)]^{-1}$, where e is the summed excitatory input and h is the inhibitory input. [Kunihiko Fukushima, Sei Miyake, and Takayuki Ito, "Neocognitron: A Neural Network Model for a Mechanism of Visual Pattern Recognition," *IEEE Transactions on Systems, Man, and Cybernetics*, 13(5), pp. 826–834, September–October, The Institute of Electrical and Electronic Engineers, Inc., 1983.]

print fonts and various people writing in hand will draw that bar in different ways and at different relative heights in the figure. The U_{c1} plane that handles high horizontal bars responds to all of these in the same way, activating the same general region of neurons.

The general structure of the neocognitron is shown in Figure 10-5, presenting the number of neurons within each layer. For instance, the second layer from the left contains twelve sublevels or planes, each with 19×19 neurons.

With successively higher layers, the network is no longer looking at single features such as horizontal or vertical line segments, but at increasingly complex combinations of features. Finally, at the right of Figure 10-5, the structure has funneled the data down to 10 neurons corresponding to the 10 digits to be recognized. At this level only one neuron is active, indicating the recognized digit.

An early model of the neocognitron operated in the unsupervised (quadrant 2) mode. In a later development it operates in a supervised (quadrant 1) mode. In either case, excitatory inputs to a neuron from neurons in the preceding layer are combined according to the usual summed products of weights and inputs (Figure 10-6).

The typical neuron also has an inhibitory input connection from the next layer down. The excitation of a neuron is:

$$x = [(1 + e)/(1 + h)] - 1,$$

where e is the summed excitatory input and h is the inhibitory input.

Excitatory interconnections lead from clusters in the nth layer to nearby neurons in the $(n+1)$st layer, while inhibitory interconnections lead from those cell clusters to the favored neurons' neighbors in the $(n+1)$st layer. This has the usual effect of sharpening the responses of neurons, making the winning nodes stand out among their suppressed competitors. Also, the synapses of winning neurons are reinforced, as the network experiences repeated exposure to a class of patterns.

In the unsupervised mode, the neocognitron models biological learning, developing its own (not fully predictable) way of classifying the various input patterns.

The supervised mode is needed in teaching the network to recognize numerals or alphabets or other symbol sets where the categories are preassigned. In that case, training signals are used to reinforce the input synapses of selected cells, concurrent with the presentation of the input signal that is to be categorized.

In the neocognitron, this selective training starts at the lower layers and is gradually shifted upward, as the training moves to higher levels of complexity.

The version of the neocognitron represented in Figure 10-5 requires 14,529 neurons, and the number of synapses is far greater than this. It has been an important construct in the analysis of biological learning. Although it has been particularly important in representing visual learning, it is not restricted to that area; the input patterns at the lowest layer and the output constructs at the top layer can, of course, be applied to any area of data organization.

Restricted Coulomb Energy

Based on a three-layer architecture, restricted coulomb energy (RCE) is a proprietary paradigm belonging to Nestor Inc., and was created by Leon Cooper, Charles Elbaum, and Douglas Reilly, all from Nestor. It got its name from the way it models attractor basins, analogous to the Coulomb law of attraction between particles of opposite electrical charge—with some restrictions on how this attraction operates. (Although it is also said to be named after the initials of its inventors: Reilly, Cooper, and Elbaum.) RCE is a supervised feedforward paradigm, oriented toward pattern recognition.

Figure 10-7 shows the geometry of the network. Input nodes are fully connected to the internal nodes, and the internal nodes are selectively connected to the output nodes. An output node operates as an OR gate. If any of its inputs are active, it produces an output—otherwise it does not.

In Figure 10-8, a vector space models the intermediate node logic. Here a simple two-dimensional case is shown, involving two input nodes. But the model generalizes immediately to n dimensions. The circles in the diagram are the attrac-

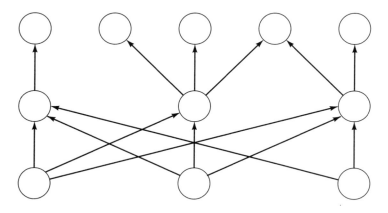

Figure 10-7: Three-layer topology of an RCE (restricted coulomb energy) network from Nestor, Inc. Input nodes are fully connected to the internal nodes, and the internal nodes are selectively connected to the output nodes. An output node operates as an OR gate. If any of its inputs are active, it produces an output—otherwise it does not. The RCE is a supervised feedforward network, but one that differs significantly in concept from backpropagation. (Modified from materials supplied by Nestor Inc.)

tor basins, whose centers are located by the synaptic weight vectors, $\mathbf{W}^i$, of the internal nodes. (Vectors have an origin at an arbitrary point in this plane and their ends are marked as points.) The radii of the basins, λ^i, are internal node thresholds.

If an input vector, $\mathbf{F}$, falls within an attractor basin, then the internal node associated with that attractor basin is activated. In Figure 10-8, the terminus of input vector $\mathbf{F}$ lies within basin 1. Therefore, the intermediate node corresponding to 1 would turn on.

This is equivalent to requiring that the absolute value of the vector difference, $\mathbf{F} - \mathbf{W}^1$, be less than λ^1:

$$\|\mathbf{F} - \mathbf{W}^1\| < \lambda^1.$$

Notice that an input vector could fall within any one of the three attractor basins of the diagram, or could fall in the space between basins, activating none of the internal nodes. It could also fall within the region of overlap between basins 1 and 2, activating both of the corresponding nodes.

Consider the operation of RCE, in a very simple case involving only two input nodes and two patterns that are to be recognized: A and B.

At the start of the training process, there are only input nodes. No internal nor output nodes exist until the paradigm generates them. Of course, the physical elements and interconnections exist that can be assigned to nodes, but they are not functioning parts of the network until they are assigned. Therefore, the network is free of an overhead of surplus nodes, whose presence would slow the operation of the paradigm. The network is always exactly as big and complex as it needs to be—and no more.

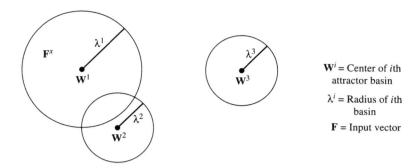

Figure 10-8: A vector space models the logic of an internal node in the RCE network. Vectors $\mathbf{W}^i$ and $\mathbf{F}$ have a common origin (not shown) within this space. The synaptic weight vector $\mathbf{W}^i$, determines the location of an attractor basin (shown as a circle) in the vector space. The radius, λ^i, of the ith basin corresponds to the node's threshold. If an input vector, $\mathbf{F}$, falls within an attractor basin, then the internal node associated with that attractor basin is activated. The point $\mathbf{F}$ in this figure represents an input vector in basin 1, and it therefore turns on internal node 1. (Modified from materials supplied by Nestor Inc.)

Now a two-dimensional input vector is presented to the two input nodes of this virgin network. Input vector F does not fall in an attractor basin because no basins are yet present.

At this point, a supervisory input takes place. The network is told the class of the input vector. Assume, in this case, that it is an instance of pattern class A. An internal node is assigned whose weight vector coincides with input vector $\mathbf{F}$. An output node is assigned to the identification of pattern A. And the four existing nodes of the network are interconnected, as shown in Figure 10-9.

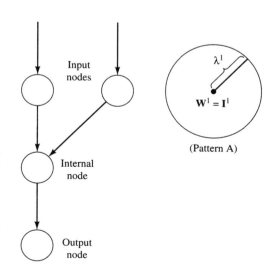

Figure 10-9: The beginning of an RCE network. Nodes are activated as they are needed. (a) initial nodes; (b) first attractor basin. Its location, W^1, has been set to match the first input vector, I^1, and its radius, λ^1, has been set to a default value. The network has been told that input vector I^1 belongs to "pattern A." (Modified from materials supplied by Nestor Inc.)

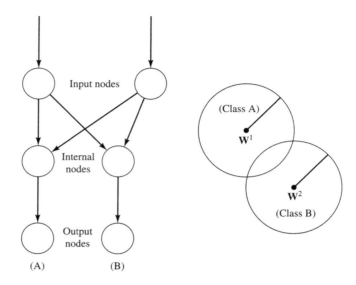

Figure 10-10:   The RCE network grows, with attractor basins for patterns of classes *A* and *B*. (Modified from materials supplied by Nestor Inc.)

Also shown in this figure is the network's one attractor basin. It has a weight vector $\mathbf{W}^1$ that is identical to $\mathbf{I}^1$, the only input vector that the network has seen. The radius of this first basin is set to a network default value, λ^1.

If a second vector presented to the network has a terminus within the attractor basin defined by $\mathbf{W}^1$, λ^1, then it is automatically classified as an *A*-type pattern, triggering an output at the lone output node—and the network does not grow. Suppose, however, that the next vector presented falls outside the first basin. And suppose that the supervisory input tells the network that this is a class *B* pattern.

The initial result of this event is illustrated in Figure 10-10. A second internal node is added, providing a *B*-type attractor basin, and an output node that identifies *B* patterns is also added. The connections are as shown in the figure.

The radius of the second basin can be no larger than the network default, and must also be no larger than the distance to the nearest other weight vector. In other words, even though basins may overlap, no basin can include the center of another basin. At this early stage, this requirement happens to be identical to taking the default radius—but that will quickly change.

What happens if a third input vector falls in the overlap region of the two basins? First, it triggers, both internal nodes, resulting in signals from both output nodes. At this point, a supervised input occurs again, telling the network that this is (for instance) an *A*.

At the left of Figure 10-11, the *x* marks the location of the third input vector, in the region common to the two basins. But the designation of the new vector as class *A* means that the *B*-basin must contract just enough to exclude the new vec-

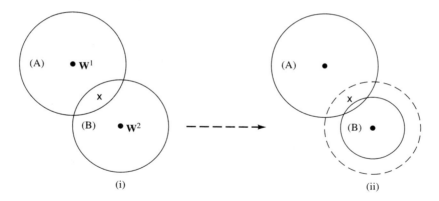

Figure 10-11: Contraction of an RCE basin. This happened when a new vector arrived at x in panel i. Supervisory input declared the new vector to be of type A. Therefore (in panel ii), the basin assigned to pattern type B shrank, leaving the new vector exclusively in A. (Modified from materials supplied by Nestor Inc.)

tor. At the right of the figure, the new configuration is shown. The dashed contour marks the initial boundary of the second basin. But that is now history, and the solid contours show the two basins as they will now function.

As consecutive training vectors are presented to the network, they will blanket the entire decision space with attractor basins. As training progresses, these basins will eventually approximate the contours of the underlying phenomena A

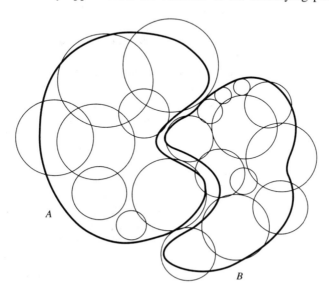

Figure 10-12: Following the logic of the earlier figures, training vectors generate multiple basins approximating contours of underlying phenomena A and B. (Modified from materials supplied by Nestor Inc.)

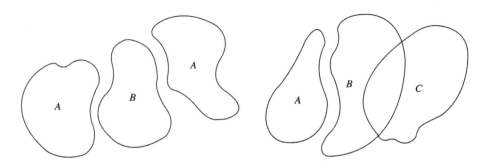

Figure 10-13: Attributes of RCE: it is able to classify disjoint regions; after having learned initial categories (in this case, *A* and *B*), it can then adapt, at a later stage, to learning a new and unanticipated category (*C*). It will adjust its *A* and *B* boundaries as needed to adapt to the presence of *C* in the sample space. (Modified from materials supplied by Nestor Inc.)

and *B*, whose patterns are to be distinguished (Figure 10-12). Subsequent to training, an unknown vector presented to the network will be automatically classified according to the type of basin within which it falls

One of the strengths of RCE is that it has no difficulty at all in separating nonlinearly separable decision regions. More than that, it readily handles disjoint regions (Figure 10-13).

Another of its strengths is that it can learn new categories, introduced at a later stage. A network that has learned to distinguish classes *A* and *B* can be taught to distinguish pattern *C* from either of these—even though the experimenters may not have known of the existence of *C* at the outset of their work. If, for example, as in Figure 10-13, *C* has a decision boundary with *B*, but not with *A*, the training could continue with the presentation of only *B*- and *C*-related vectors.

Nestor has taken its paradigm through further evolution by combining two or more RCE networks into a multiple network, arbitrated by a controller. This complex of networks, named the Nestor Learning System (NLS), is illustrated in Figure 10-14. In this figure, it is assumed that three different attributes of the patterns under study are used to create the input vectors. Suppose that parameters related in some specific way to frequencies, slopes, and peaks in waveform patterns are extracted as possible classifiers. If each of these parameters has certain advantages in performing classifications, it is reasonable to suppose that their combination will be more effective than any one taken alone.

In the figure, it is assumed that a vector extracted from an unknown pattern produces no answer (falls between basins) in RCE1, produces a definite "*A*" response from RCE2, and gives an ambiguous "*A* or *B*" response from RCE3. The controller, receiving these inputs, believes RCE2 and classifies the pattern as *A*. The next pattern sampled, however, may be more readily distinguished by one of the other networks, so the controller is able to select from the most definitive of its multiple inputs.

There are various logics by which the controller can make its decision. The table in Figure 10-14 lists three possibilities for a three-network complex. The

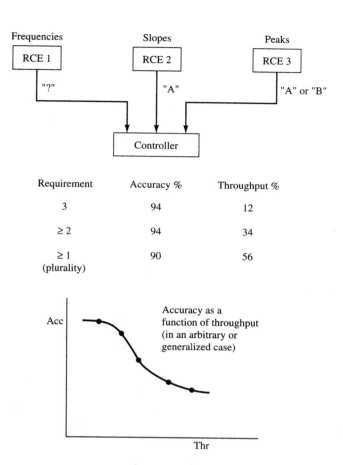

Requirement	Accuracy %	Throughput %
3	94	12
≥ 2	94	34
≥ 1 (plurality)	90	56

Figure 10-14: The Nestor Learning System (NLS) draws on multiple RCEs to make a decision. The separate RCEs may be processing different parameters in the data field—such as frequencies, slopes, and peaks. The system has various ways in which it can combine the results of the different networks. In the three-RCE case, as shown in the table, it can require unanimous agreement among the three, majority, or plurality. The more stringent the demand (e.g., unanimity), the greater the accuracy but the lower the throughput. (Modified from materials supplied by Nestor Inc.)

most conservative requirement is that all three networks must agree before a pattern is classified. This leads to a high accuracy but a relatively low throughput. An intermediate case calls for classification if two or more of the networks agree; in a sample study performed by Nestor, this led to no degradation in accuracy, while increasing throughput—as shown in the table entries. Finally, the most tolerant logic accepts classification from one or more of the networks, so long as that classification represents a plurality—for instance, one network saying that the pattern is "*B*" and the others silent or ambiguous—or two of the networks agreeing.

Of course, the values in this table are tied to the particular study and cannot be generalized. However, the monotonic decrease of accuracy and monotonic increase in throughput is a general property in going from conservative to tolerant logic.

The general idea of attraction/repulsion via a Coulomb model is the basis for other paradigms. One example of a generic paradigm of this type is the a classifier-based model by Peggy Israel and Cris Kotsougeras (1989). This relies on an associative memory and a Coulomb network to retrieve objects that match both a noisy retrieval cue and a classification constraint.

Dystal, a Biological Model

A learning law proposed by Alkon, Blackwell, Barbour, Rigler, and Vogl (1990) gives rise to a neural network called Dystal—an acronym derived from "*dynamically stable associative learning*". Dystal is a paradigm that specifically sets out to model biological nervous systems. Studies of the marine snail *Hermissenda crassicornis* and the rabbit have provided key elements of the model. In addition to modeling biological systems, the paradigm seems likely to be efficient when implemented in electronics.

In the Dystal model, there are two different kinds of synapses or pathways—those carrying unconditioned stimuli (UCS), corresponding to the innate drives of the animal, and those carrying conditioned stimuli (CS), corresponding to the stimuli to which the animal learns to respond. The synapses that carry the UCS are called *flowthrough connections*, and those carrying the CS are called *collateral connections*.

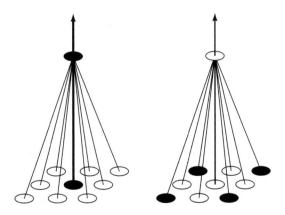

Figure 10-15:   Dystal: In part a, the neuron at the top accepts multiple collateral inputs (light lines) but only one flowthrough input (heavy line). In part b, the neuron at the top accepts only collateral inputs. In both diagrams, neurons having flowthrough connections are represented by solid circles. The connection between two such neurons defines a flowthrough path, which carries unconditioned stimuli (UCS). The collateral paths carry conditioned stimuli (CS). (Modified from Alkon et al., 1990.)

As studies ever since Pavlov have demonstrated, an animal can be taught to associate artificial signals (CS) with rewards and penalties. In Dystal, this association is represented by simultaneous activity along flowthrough and collateral connections. When there is such simultaneous activity, the weight on the collateral path (which is where the learning takes place) is increased. The flowthrough paths maintain constant large weightings.

Along with the two kinds of synapse defined in Dystal, there are also two kinds of neuron, defined on the basis of what kinds of input paths they take. These are illustrated in Figure 10-15. A flowthrough neuron is one having a flowthrough input. Furthermore, although it may have multiple collateral inputs, it has just one flowthrough input.

On the other hand, a collateral neuron can be fed by multiple flowthrough and collateral neurons along collateral paths.

Because the learning process that takes place on a collateral synapse is based entirely on the concurrent activity along paths from flowthrough neurons into the same node, the usual learning modes found in ANNs do not occur. Furthermore, whether or not the postsynaptic neuron fires does not play any part in the changes in synaptic weights. Dystal learns neither through feedback, nor supervision. Collateral synaptic weights, which start at low values, are changed at a node according to these rules:

1) The weight is increased if the collateral path and paths from all flowthrough neurons to that node carried signals in both of the last two cycles.

2) The weight stays the same if the collateral path carried a signal in both of the last two consecutive cycles, but any path from a flowthrough neuron leading into that node did not.

3) The weight is decreased unless the collateral path carried a signal during *both* of the last two consecutive cycles.

4) Assuming that the minimum allowable weight is 0 and the maximum 1, any decrease in the present weight level, w, is proportional to w, and any increase is proportional to $1 - w$.

There are several advantages to this schema. First, the paradigm is sensitive to temporal relationships. Second, because the network depends on neither feedback nor supervision for its learning process, it is flexible with regard to how it is connected, accepting feedforward, lateral, or feedback connections. Third, the computational burden is reduced in contrast to supervised or feedback networks.

With regard to this last point, the authors of the article [Alkon et al., 1990] point out that "Essentially all of the currently popular neural network designs implicitly or explicitly use the output of a neural element in the adjustment of weights on its input." They summarize the contrast with the observation that Dystal has a computational complexity proportional to N, the number of weights to be determined, whereas paradigms dependent on the firing of the postsynaptic neuron are complex proportional to N^2 or N^3.

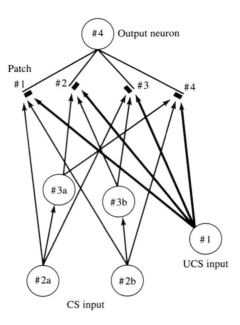

Figure 10-16: In the generalized version of Dystal, synaptic weights are associated with patches (#1–#4) rather than individual connections. Inhibitory inputs (lines tipped with circles) feed into "interneurons" #3a and #3b, which send negative signals to the patches. The patches make Dystal sensitive to relatively subtle variations in complex input patterns. (From Alkon et al., 1990.)

As the Dystal network learns, it remains in a condition of dynamic equilibrium. That is, the weights on collateral synapses do not reach fixed values, but continue to respond to changing stimuli. While these changes are occurring, the system is not moving toward some defined equilibrium or endpoint not yet attained. In this respect, Dystal differs from networks having distinct training and recall stages.

A more generalized version of Dystal can learn anticorrelations as well as correlations. Figure 10-16 shows the part played by indirect connections (via "interneurons") and the use of "patches."

The collateral neuron can send a direct stimulus to the output neuron, or it can send an inhibiting signal via the interneuron. Furthermore, the output neuron has patches, each of which receives UCS and CS inputs from various source neurons. Rather than synaptic weights existing on individual connections, they exist on the patches and are therefore sensitive to entire patterns of signals. The Dystal rules regarding the concurrent existence of UCS and CS signals still apply. But the high or low synaptic weights evolve on the patches and therefore represent the composite situation along multiple lines. The result is that a much larger number of differentiable patterns can be stored.

Drive Reinforcement Model

A paradigm similar in certain ways to Dystal is the earlier drive reinforcement model of A. Harry Klopf. In both paradigms, weight changes at a synapse correlate with recent local activities. These paradigms can be seen as temporal extensions of Hebbian learning.

Drives in the drive reinforcement model are defined as signal levels, and *reinforcers* are defined as changes in signal levels. The model makes three basic assumptions (Klopf, 1988):

1) Instead of correlating levels of pre- and postsynaptic activity, the model correlates *changes* in presynaptic levels with *changes* in postsynaptic levels.
2) Instead of correlating approximately simultaneous changes in these two levels, it correlates earlier presynaptic changes with later postsynaptic changes.
3) The change in synpatic weight is proportional to the present synaptic weight.

A further condition of the drive reinforcement model is that the levels of activity to which the neurons react are frequencies rather than amplitudes. Because they are frequencies, they cannot be negative.

Furthermore, only positive changes in presynaptic signals (moving toward higher frequencies) affect neuronal learning. This is based on the intuitive concept (also demonstrated more rigorously by Klopf) that learning is promoted by an increase in presynaptic signal levels, not by a fading of that activity as it falls toward zero. However, the synapse that is being conditioned can be either excitatory or inhibitory in its effects.

These learning effects are represented in equation (10.5):

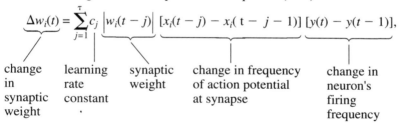

$$\Delta w_i(t) = \sum_{j=1}^{\tau} c_j \left| w_i(t-j) \right| \, [x_i(t-j) - x_i(t-j-1)] \, [y(t) - y(t-1)],$$

| change in synaptic weight | learning rate constant · | synaptic weight | change in frequency of action potential at synapse | change in neuron's firing frequency |

where:

$w_i(t)$ = weight of synapse i at discrete time t;
Δw_i = change in the weight of synapse i;
τ = longest interstimulus interval over which conditioning is effective;
c_j = learning rate constant;
j = interstimulus interval;
x_i = frequency of action potential at synapse i;
y = measure of frequency of firing for neuron.

Because the change in synaptic weight is proportional to the current synaptic weight, the weight cannot become zero—that would freeze any further change in the weight, and learning at that synapse would cease to be possible. Therefore, the model hypothesizes a small positive number, close to zero, as the lower bound on the absolute value of the weight.

A side effect of the inability of a synaptic weight to pass through zero means that excitatory (positively weighted) synapses remain excitatory, and that inhibitory (negatively weighted) synapses remain inhibitory. Klopf points out that this condition is consistent with the known physiology of biological synapses.

The output of a neuron follows the usual neural network formulation:

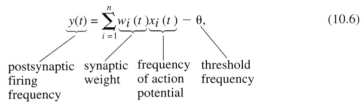

$$y(t) = \sum_{i=1}^{n} w_i(t)\, x_i(t) - \theta, \tag{10.6}$$

postsynaptic   synaptic   frequency   threshold
firing   weight   of action   frequency
frequency   potential

Because $y(t)$ is a frequency, it cannot have a negative value. So, if the right-hand side of equation (10.6) swings negative, with the sum of the weighted inputs falling below threshold, $y(t)$ is set to zero.

It can be seen that the combined effects of equations (10.5) and (10.6) allow for negative changes in synaptic weights—that is, the restriction that only positive change in presynaptic signals contributes to learning does not mean that synaptic weights increase irreversibly.

Equation (10.6) shows that the postsynaptic firing frequency, $y(t)$, will become smaller as the inputs, $x_i(t)$, become smaller. We know, from the conditions placed on equation (10.5), that no corresponding reduction in synaptic weights occurs as a direct response to the diminished inputs. However, the weights do diminish as a result of a decreasing $y(t)$ feeding back into equation (10.5)—and, therefore, they diminish indirectly in response to the diminished inputs.

Like Dystal, drive reinforcement was designed to represent biological systems. In tests of his model, Klopf reports that drive reinforcement simulates learning in numerous details, including such effects as trace conditioning (CS offset preceding UCS onset), delay conditioning (CS onset preceding UCS onset and CS offset occurring at the same time as or after UCS onset), preexposure (nonreinforced presentation of a CS prior to reinforced presentation), and interstimulus interval effect.

Klopf foresees the possibility of making behavioral observations in a mathematical setting that simulates "not only the neural network, but also a simplified organism controlled by the neural network and a simplified environment with which the organism is interacting" (Klopf, 1988).

11

FUZZY THEORY

We have become accustomed, in our environment of computers, to an all-or-nothing logic. We see it in a two-state logic, symbolized through the binary digits (bits) 0 and 1.

In neural networks, also, a two-state logic has generally been employed. Although the inputs to neurons and the synaptic weights that multiply these inputs can be either discrete or continuous over a range of values, each of the output neurons in most ANNs is either ON or OFF.

But another kind of logic is possible, based on a multiplicity of possible logic states of an output neuron—for instance, eleven output signal levels, represented by the decimal values 0, .1, .2, . . . 1.0. The system that deals with these multiplets is called *fuzzy logic*. It was originated by a Polish mathematician, Jan Lukasiewicz, in the 1920s and was paralleled in the work of quantum philosopher Max Black in the 1930s involving "vagueness" structures (Black, 1937). The theory went through major evolution beginning in the 1960s through the work of Lofti Zadeh of the University of California at Berkeley (Zadeh, 1965).

Fuzzy logic has something in common with neural networks: both resemble our instinctive thought patterns. Fuzzy logic contains concepts that correlate with the gray-area terms that people use— "sort of," "mostly," "very," and "not much." The "fuzziness" index, on a scale of 0 to 1, is a measure of membership in a set.

Consider the class of stormy nights. It is not necessarily obvious whether a particular night belongs to this class. If, on the night in question, a strong warm wind is blowing, membership of that night in the class of stormy nights might be designated as .2. If there is a 15-knot wind blowing and it is raining, the night might have a .6 membership in the stormy night class.

On the other hand, a balmy spring night would have a membership of 0 in the class of stormy nights, and a gale with pelting rain and lightning would have a membership of 1. In both of these cases, the fuzzy variable has become "crisp."

A fuzzy vector (consisting of fuzzy units or "fits," not binary units or "bits") is a list such as A = 0   .3   .7   .4   .8. The fits of a crisp vector are all 1s and 0s.

If each fit of a fuzzy vector is adjusted to the nearest crisp value, then the nearest crisp vector can be located. For example, in the case of fuzzy vector **A**, mentioned in the previous paragraph, the nearest crisp vector is:

$$\mathbf{M} = 0 \quad 0 \quad 1 \quad 0 \quad 1.$$

Conversely, the farthest crisp vector from **A** is $N = 1 \quad 1 \quad 0 \quad 1 \quad 0.$

The distance between **A** and the crisp vectors can be defined in various ways—for instance, as the length of the difference vector between **A** and the crisp vector—or, more simply, as the sum of the adjustments that were necessary to make **A** equal to the crisp vector. Using the latter method, the distance from **A** to nearby **M** is 1.2, and its distance from **N** is 3.8.

Kosko defined a fuzzy entropy (measure of uncertainty)—the ratio of:

$$\|(\mathbf{X} - \mathbf{M})/(\mathbf{X} - \mathbf{N})\|,$$

for any fuzzy vector **X**, where **M** is the nearest and **N** the farthest crisp vector from **X**. In the case of vector **A**, the entropy is about .32.

The *pathological vector* is the fuzzy vector whose fits are all .5. It represents the fuzziest (least certain) possible vector in its *n*-dimensional space. Equidistant from all crisp vectors, the fuzzy vector has an entropy of 1.0. In general, fuzzy entropy is defined on a scale from 0 to 1.

Kosko has also defined a directed graph known as a *fuzzy cognitive map*, or FCM (Figure 11-1). This case shows fuzzy cause-and-effect relationship between bad weather and driving speed. The strengths of the causal arrows between nodes can be represented by fits. Of these, only the "always" from "patrol frequency" to "driver caution level" is crisp—equal to 1.

The topology of an FCM has to look familiar. It resembles that of a neural network.

Functions of Fuzzy Vectors

It is important to recognize that fuzzy theory is distinct from probability theory. There are superficial resemblances between the two theories: like fuzzy membership, probability is also defined on a scale from 0 to 1. Furthermore, unity, in each of these systems, has a similar-sounding definition. A probability of 1 represents certainty of occurrence of an event; a fuzziness of 1 represents certainty with respect to an entity belonging to a particular set.

One of the areas of contrast between fits and probabilities is seen in logical OR (union) and logical AND (intersection) operations. The union of probabilities

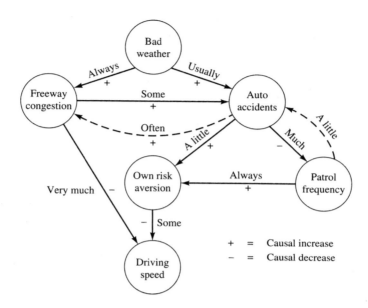

Figure 11-1: Fuzzy cognitive map (FCM). [From Bart Kosko and John S. Limm, "Vision as Casual Activation and Association," *Proceedings of the Society for Photo-Optical Instrumentation Engineers (SPIE)*, September 1985, Bellingham, Washington.]

A and B, the probability that at least one of the two events will happen—is expressed as:

$$A \cup B = A + B - AB.$$

And the intersection of the two, the probability that both will happen, is:

$$A \cap B = AB.$$

In fuzzy logic, the union of A and B is defined as the larger of the two, and their intersection is the smaller of the two. Let's see how this works in practice.

Let the two fuzzy vectors be defined as follows:

$$\mathbf{A} = 0 \quad .3 \quad .7 \quad .4 \quad .8 \text{ (as above)}$$
$$\mathbf{B} = .8 \quad .2 \quad .6 \quad .7 \quad .9$$

Then, on a component-by-component basis, the union of the vectors (fuzzy OR) is found by taking the larger component in each comparison:

$$\mathbf{A} \cup \mathbf{B} = .8 \quad .3 \quad .7 \quad .7 \quad .9$$

The intersection of the vectors (fuzzy AND) is generated from the lesser elements in the component-by-component comparison:

$$\mathbf{A} \cap \mathbf{B} = 0 \quad .2 \quad .6 \quad .4 \quad .8$$

Another important function is the complement of a fuzzy vector. The complement to **A** is formed by subtracting each component of **A** from unity:

$$\bar{A} = 1 \quad .7 \quad .3 \quad .6 \quad .2$$

It is interesting to observe that the intersect of A with its complement is not zero; there is an overlap of A with not-A:

$$A \cap \bar{A} = 0 \quad .3 \quad .3 \quad .4 \quad .2$$

Also, the union of *A* with its complement (not-*A*) is not unity—that is, it does not span the entire sample space:

$$A \cup \bar{A} = 1 \quad .7 \quad .7 \quad .6 \quad .8$$

Like behavior that is "not according to Hoyle," these fuzzy behaviors are "not according to Aristotle."

Fuzziness versus Aristotle

Given two fuzzy vectors, how do we know whether one is a subset of another? In a form of logic based on membership, the nature of "subsetness" is crucial. It so happens that the way subsetness is defined in fuzzy logic poses a challenge (though by no means the first) to all-or-nothing Aristotelian logic. Aristotelian thinking, despite historic challenges from several directions, remains a major influence on our thought processes—evidenced, for example, in the designs of computer logic circuits.

Consider two of the basic tenets of Aristotelian logic, the law of noncontradiction and the law of the excluded middle. The law of noncontradiction says that a statement, *A*, and its negation, not-*A*, are mutually exclusive. To an Aristotelian, an animal is either a cat or a non-cat; therefore, it can't be both a cat and a non-cat. In set theory terms, this is expressed by the requirement that the intersection of **A** and not-**A** must equal zero:

$$A \cap \bar{A} = 0.$$

The law of the excluded middle says that a statement and its contradiction cover all cases. Cats and non-cats include every animal. In other words, the union of **A** and not-**A** must span the entirety of the event space within which **A** and not-**A** are defined:

$$A \cup \bar{A} = 1.$$

Both of these Aristotelian precepts are opposed, as we have seen, by the fact that a fuzzy vector and its complement form a non-zero intersect and a non-unity union. Now let's continue the assault on Aristotle with a look at fuzzy subsetness.

The membership of a sample space, *x*, in one of its own subsets, *A*, can be symbolized as $m_A(x)$. For instance, to what extent is the sample space of all animals contained within the subset of cats? The answer to that question, incidentally, may be the percentage of animals that are cats—or it may involve the degree of "cat-ness" in sampled animals.

Based on an earlier definition by Zadeh, Kosko defines *dominated member-ship* as the case in which every element in fuzzy set A is less than or equal to the corresponding element in fuzzy set B:

$$A \subset B \text{ iff } m_A(x) \leq m_A(x) \text{ for all } x.$$

Thus, A is a dominated subset of B if $A = 0 \quad .3 \quad .7 \quad .4 \quad .8$ and $B = .5 \quad .6 \quad .7 \quad .7 \quad 1.0$.

However, Kosko poses this issue: suppose that two vectors, $\mathbf{R}$ and $\mathbf{S}$, from the same space, are of very high dimensionality—each having, for instance, a million components. Suppose further that vector $\mathbf{R}$ is smaller than $\mathbf{S}$, element for corresponding element, in all but one of these components. Then it would seem that $\mathbf{R}$ should be considered a subset of $\mathbf{S}$ to some very large degree.

Motivated by considerations of this kind, Kosko (1990a) derives a theorem that establishes the membership of one set within another. He starts by defining M, the cardinality or size of a fuzzy vector, as the sum of its elements. Thus, a three-dimensional vector $Z = .3 \quad .9 \quad .2$ would have a cardinality of $M = 1.4$. The theorem then proceeds (ad rigorem) to show that the subsetness of a vector $\mathbf{A}$ with respect to a vector $\mathbf{B}$ is:

$$S(\mathbf{A},\mathbf{B}) = M(\mathbf{A} \cap \mathbf{B})/M(\mathbf{A}). \tag{11.1}$$

The proof of the theorem (Kosko, 1990a) is not shown here. But let's look at some of its effects.

If, as before:

$$\mathbf{A} = 0 \quad .3 \quad .7 \quad .4 \quad .8,$$
$$\mathbf{B} = .8 \quad .2 \quad .6 \quad .7 \quad .9, \text{ and}$$
$$\mathbf{A} \cap \mathbf{B} = 0 \quad .2 \quad .6 \quad .4 \quad .8,$$

then to what extent is each a subset of the other? The sizes or cardinalities are:

$$M(\mathbf{A}) = 2.2,$$
$$M(\mathbf{B}) = 3.2,$$
$$M(\mathbf{A} \cap \mathbf{B}) = 2.0.$$

Then, according to equation (11.1), $\mathbf{A}$ is a subset of $\mathbf{B}$ to the extent $S(\mathbf{A},\mathbf{B}) = 2.0/2.2 = .909$. $\mathbf{B}$ is a subset of $\mathbf{A}$ to the extent $S(\mathbf{B},\mathbf{A}) = 2.0/3.2 = .625$.

This theorem corresponds to a fundamental axiom of probability theory. The probability that events A and B will both occur, $P(A \cap B)$, equals the probability of A's occurrence multiplied by the probability that B will occur, given the preceding occurrence of A:

$$P(A \cap B) = P(A) \, P(A,B),$$

or, rearranging terms:

$$P(A,B) = P(A \cap B)/P(A).$$

The functions in this equation correspond to those in equation (11.1), both within the syntax of the equation and in the mathematical definitions of the individual functions. Kosko's proof, operating from the fundamental concepts of fuzzy theory, leads to the derivation of what has previously been an unproved axiom in probability theory.

What implications do these results have for probability theory? From a fuzzy theory point of view, the sample space of coin tosses has degrees of membership in the subsets of "heads" and "tails," and the occurrence of heads or tails in a coin toss is a representation of the corresponding partial membership. This would place us in a universe where there is uncertainty—but not an uncertainty founded on randomness, rather an uncertainty with regard to degrees of membership.

There are well-known models in physics for the fundamental uncertainty in the concurrent position and momentum of an electron (or other fundamental particle). On the one hand, the electron can be seen as having a probability distribution regarding its location and kinematics. Or the electron can be thought of as smeared out in a diffuse region, so that, to varying degrees, it is in several places at once. Generally, physicists have viewed these two pictures as equivalent models for the behavior of particles.

Kosko's results tend to overthrow this equivalence, making the fuzzy model more fundamental than the probabilistic one.

Probability theory is currently under attack along another front, having to do with chaotic effects. Recurring states or cyclic patterns of states (chaotic attractors) may describe the motions of seemingly random atmospheric weather patterns or of interstellar gases.

The authors of an article on chaos in *Scientific American* (Crutchfield et al., 1986) show an interesting example of a chaotic process in a phenomenon known as Poincaré recurrence. A painting of Henri Poincaré (whose *circa* 1903 mathematical theories have been among the origins of modern chaos theory) is displayed on a computer screen. A stretching operation is performed on the picture elements (pixels) of the screen, making each pixel longer and thinner in the diagonal direction of stretch. This not only distorts the painting, but pulls parts of it off the screen. They are brought back, however, because a second rule is used; the displaced pixels are reinserted at other edges left vacant by the stretching operation.

This deterministic process quickly smears the screen into a random-looking pattern of colors. However—and this is where the "recurrence" comes in—after many cycles, the painting of Poincaré gradually reappears out of the whirl of colors; but it reappears in blurry, ghostlike, multiple, overlapping images. Then, as the process continues, this montage of Poincarés disappears again—-only to reappear after many more cycles as a single image, only partially dimmed from its original form.

How fuzziness relates to chaos—and how probability theory will hold up, attacked from different directions by each of these—is still uncertain.

In the meanwhile, applications of fuzzy theory have been particularly active in Japan, at every level from early research to products on the market. Areas of focus have included such diverse uses as a hand-held Kanji character reader, a fuzzy C compiler, automobile cruise controls, water pressure control in bathroom showers, and translators between spoken Japanese and American phrases.

A great deal of activity was underway in China, too, before the military suppression that took place there in 1989, with estimates of more than 10,000 researchers in the field. Following the events in Tiananmen Square in Beijing, however, this activity was reportedly discontinued.

Much of the Chinese fuzzy work was inspired by Pei-zhuang Wang, the director of Beijing University's Institute of Fuzzy Systems and Knowledge Engineering. Wang also pioneered a Tokyo-based company in the field of fuzzy theory—Apt Instrument Corporation (later known as Aptronics.)

A Fuzzy Neural Underwater Sound Detector

In 1988, W. R. Taber and R. O. Deich, both employed by General Dynamics in San Diego, set out to develop a system that would classify the sources of underwater sounds. The sensors that they were working with were a set of hydrophones, devices designed to detect the amplitudes and frequencies of sound waves through water. The experiments that were carried out dealt with both ship and marine mammal sounds.

As an aside, the distances that underwater sounds are able to travel with minimal attenuation is remarkable. When the sound waves are propagated through undersea "sound channels," they are detectable across geographic distances. For instance, hydrophones in Hawaii are able to detect the sounds of ships or orcas ("killer whales") in the Arctic.

The channels that preserve sound waves over such long distances are formed as a result of fortuitous combinations of pressure and temperature contours, ultimately stemming from current flow patterns and salinity concentrations. They form tunnels within which sound waves are captured and collimated, reflecting off the boundaries of the channel as they propagate. These sound channels are analogous to electromagnetic wave guides.

Taber and Deich decided on a neural network sensitive to time-varying inputs that would latch the best matches to its exemplars, replacing these only when subsequent better matches came along. The arrangement devised was the structure illustrated in Figure 11-2, consisting of multiple neuron rings.

A single ring consists of multiple neurons connected in a circular series arrangement like a string of Christmas tree lights. As shown in the figure, all neurons are identically configured, except for having different sets of synaptic input weights.

The figure shows the detailed anatomy of the jth neuron in one of these rings. The neuron performs the dot product of the mth incoming vector with its stored exemplar, in the usual neural fashion, to determine its activation. However, it also enhances this activation with two other terms: its previous activation, from

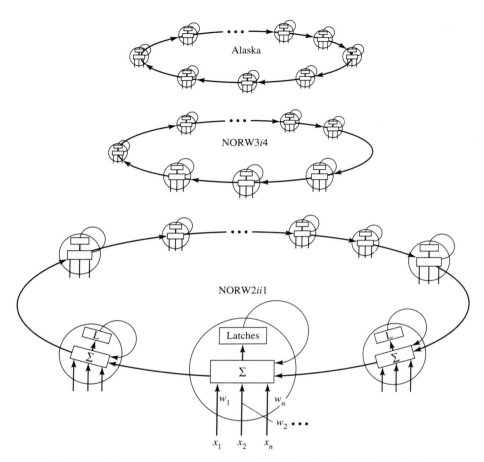

Figure 11-2: Dot product neurons with latches are used in the fuzzy neural ring. One latch stores any activation that exceeds the previously stored activation in that neuron. A second latch stores the time at which this occurs.

cycle $m - 1$, and the present activation of neuron $j - 1$, just upstream in the ring. That is, a neuron is somewhat stimulated by events in the recent past and in its local vicinity.

Now, suppose that the exemplars stored in this ring are based on the sound pattern from a particular variety of Norwegian orca, "NORW2ii1" in the nomenclature assigned by Taber et al. (Taber, Deich, Simpson, and Fagg, 1988). The exemplars were developed from calls of NORW2ii1 orcas, typically about one-half second long. The calls (and the calls of all orcas analyzed for this project) were divided into 20 time slots of 32 milliseconds each. A Fourier transform was applied to the spectrum within each of these sequential slots, dividing the sound into 60 frequency bands. Each of these frequency bands was then characterized by a power coefficient equal to the absolute value of the Fourier coefficients at each frequency.

The 60 power coefficients are the values used to form the synaptic input weights of the neurons. That is, the coefficients taken from time slice 1 become the weights for neuron 1, those from slice 2 become the weights for neuron 2, and so forth.

The arrangement of the neurons in a ring, where there is no real first or last neuron, relates to the fact that (although exemplars can be stored in a temporal sequence from 1 to N) incoming data are liable to start at any part of the cycle. This unpredictability in phase is not as characteristic of discrete signals like orca calls as it is of more periodic processes, such as the revolution of a ship's propeller. The ring structure takes care of the periodic case because the time slice recognized by the jth neuron is identified as the jth time slice, no matter where it occurs in the sequence.

In the orca study, the 20 60-dimensional vectors from the 20 different time slots of NORW2ii1 are stored in the 20 neurons of the ring. Similarly, the signatures of other varieties of orca are stored in other rings.

Now, what happens when an orca call is detected on the hydrophones of ring V, the ring whose stored weightings match NORW2ii1? At the outset, the ring does not know whether it is hearing NORW2ii1 or some other type of orca—or even some other kind of conflicting sounds, such as a ship's propeller.

As in the development of the exemplars, the unknown sound is divided into 20 sequential slots, and the 60 coefficients are extracted from each slot. Then, as testing begins, the 60 incoming coefficients, x_i, from the first selected slot, are input as vectors into each of the 20 neurons. The activation of each neuron is determined by how well the input vector matches its own synaptic vector; at the start of the test, the term corresponding to a neuron's past activation is 0; however, the present activation level of the $(j - 1)$st neuron is transmitted to the jth neuron and contributes to its activation.

Notice that the weighted raw activation itself is passed on by each neuron. This is one hint that we are entering the fuzzy realm. The fuzzy logic, unfulfilled by mere *on* and *off* states of neurons, needs to draw on the graded activation levels themselves.

At the end of this first cycle, each neuron, as well as passing its activation along in the ring, retains that activation in its latch.

Next, the coefficients from the second sampled time slot are input in parallel to all 20 neurons, and a new set of activations is determined—this time, influenced in part by the earlier activation level. At this point, a neuron stores the new activation only if it exceeds the activation in the latch.

The activations are determined by:

$$x_i \text{ (new)} = x_i \text{ (old)} + A[-ax_i \text{ (old)} + bI_1 + cI_2]^+,$$

a variant on the spatiotemporal pattern recognizer (Hecht-Nielsen, 1987).

where: x_i = activation for neuron i,
          A = attack factor,
          I_1 = activation from previous neuron,
          I_2 = dot product of input vector with synapses,
          a = decay constant,
          b = gain from activation from previous neuron,
          c = gain for dot product,
          $[\ ]^+$: the bracketed expression, if < 0, is set = 0.

Each neuron gets inputs not from all others, but only from its immediate predecessor in the ring, and it sends its output only to itself and to its immediate successor in the ring. (However, bidirectional rings are possible, with information traveling in either direction.)

The process continues, with the coefficients of time slot 3 being broadcast simultaneously to all neurons.

Throughout the paradigm, each neuron saves its activation in its latch only if it is larger than the activation that is resident there. Also, at the time that it latches its activation, it also latches the time.

The final result is that all neurons store the highest activations that they experience, recording the times at which these peaks occur. This recorded history correlates with the best matches made to incoming data, although it also includes the influence of local spatiotemporal events in the ring.

Given that NORW2ii1 is itself the unknown call, its input vectors should find relatively close matches to the exemplars, leading to relatively large activations of the neurons. An orca call very different in its properties from NORW2ii1 would generally produce small activations of the neurons. And calls that are somewhat NORW2ii1-like in their signatures would tend to produce intermediate activations.

Notice that, as shown in Figure 11-2, other rings in the vicinity are set to recognize other orca calls: Alaska, NORW3i4, and so on.

The next issue is how to use fuzzy logic to associate a particular unknown signal with the pattern stored in a particular neuron ring. First, activations are listed for the 20 neurons in each of the 10 rings. Activations span a scale from 0 to 1.0, rounded off to the nearest decimal value. For the Alaska orca, for example, the activation sequence was 0, 0, 0, . . . , 1, 1, 1, 1, 1 (where the omitted activations are all 0s), the total activation, α, for this call type thus equaling 5. For the NORW2ii1 orca, the activation sequence was: .1, .3, .5, .7, .8, 1.0, . . . , 1.0, 0, 0 (where the 11 omitted activations are all 1s), and therefore α = 15.4

The sum of all 200 activations (combining the 10 rings) was found, and each value of α was normalized relative to this grand total, to produce *certainty ratios*. Then, each certainty ratio was normalized to the largest one (NORW2ii1) to produce fuzzy membership. The results came out as shown in Table 11-1.

The incoming signal correctly gets the highest possible membership in the "NORW2ii1" class. At .80 and .69, its memberships in NORW2ii2 and NORW2iii are also fairly high.

The degrees of belief that the experimenter wishes to assert in response to the various levels of fuzziness remain to be determined—by the experimenter. In this case, it is clear that, if a single choice needs to be made, the best bet is to classify the unknown signal as being from NORW2ii1.

TABLE 11-1   FUZZY MEMBERSHIPS

Training Signal	Activation Sum	Certainty Ratio	Fuzzy Membership
NORW2ii1	15.4	0.248	1.00
NORW2112	12.3	0.198	.80
NORW2iii	10.7	0.173	.69
NORW2iv1	9.1	0.147	.59
NORW3i4	6.6	0.106	.43
NORW21v3	6.3	0.102	.41
ANTARCTIC	1.1	0.018	.07
ALASKA	.5	0.008	.03
ICELAND	0	0	0
CANADIAN	0	0	0

If, on the other hand, there are appropriate responses to be made in response to various classifications, and these responses are not mutually exclusive, you can believe more than one of these fuzzy levels.

Suppose that, instead of orca calls, an analyst is looking at a stock market indicator, whose behavior indicates a predicted rise in the worth of certain stocks. In fact, let's give Table 11-1 a whole new context and suppose that the names Alaska, NORW2iii, and so forth are the names of stocks rather than of orca species. The question, instead of "Which orca class does the signal belong to?" becomes "Which stock purchase does the indicator belong to?"

If the analyst decides to believe only fuzzy memberships of .60 or greater, then he or she will believe NORW2ii1, 2ii2, and 2iii, and will invest in these three stocks but in none of the others.

An open question is why to use fuzzy logic as a criterion in these situations, rather than probability theory. The answer is that there is not enough information available to use probabilities. In the orca example, a particular pattern may represent an aberrant variation on a class of orca calls whose pattern has been stored. Or an orca may be sick or injured, dramatically changing its sound spectrum. (As for the second scenario, the stock market is undoubtedly even more whimsical than the world of orcas.) There is no way to estimate probabilities in the face of so much unknown data.

It is in this kind of hard-to-formulate problem that fuzzy logic becomes appropriate. Instinctive measures of similitude are needed to determine the degree of membership of sample data within a preestablished class. Fuzzy logic does that.

Rod Taber, who later left General Dynamics for the University of Alabama at Huntsville, has some added remarks on these subjects. He makes the point that a neural ring is readily embodied in a silicon chip. A chip that included an n-element ring in its lower half could contain photocells in its upper half. Because all neurons

in the ring receive common inputs at the same time, the input data could be transmitted optically, activating photocells, which, in turn, would provide electronic
input signals to the neurons.

A Fuzzy Truck Driver

In an article by Seong-Gon Kong and Bart Kosko, a fuzzy logic neural "truck
backer-upper control system" is compared with a neural system that does the same
task using backpropagation. Here we see fuzzy and neural systems in contrast,
although the authors discuss the possibility of using them in combination.

Whether they are viewed as competitive or complementary approaches, the
juxtaposition is significant. We are probably not facing a mere dual era, in which
our machines are divided between classical computers and neural networks, but a
triple era, with fuzzy logic as the third pervasive discipline.

Apart from the contrast with the backprop network, the description of the
fuzzy "truck driver" in the Kong/Kosko article is enlightening with regard to the
powers of the fuzzy process.

Figure 11-3 diagrams a simulated truck and loading zone, with the latter represented as an x,y plane. The position of the truck is defined by two input variables.
One of these is ϕ, the angle between the fore-to-aft axis of the truck and the abscissa; it ranges from -90 through 270 degrees. The second input variable is x, the
left–right position of the midpoint of the truck's rear end; x is defined on a scale
from 0 to 100. The y coordinate of the truck is treated as insignificant, under the
assumption that it is sufficiently large so that the truck does not prematurely contact the dock.

The loading dock is the horizontal line at the top of the diagram, $y = 100$.
The target point on the dock is the x,y point 50,100. As the goal of the simulation,
the fuzzy truck driver is to back the truck into this goal point at right angles to the
dock. The reaching of the goal corresponds to the ϕ, x pair 90°, 50.

The beauty of working with fuzzy concepts appears in the way that the

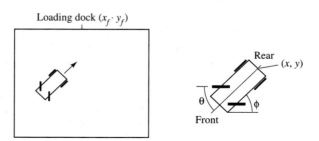

Figure 11-3:   Diagram of simulated truck and loading zone. [From Seong-Gon Kong
and Bart Kosko, "Adaptive Fuzzy Systems for Backing Up a Truck-and-Trailer," *IEEE
Transactions on Neural Networks*, Vol. 3, No. 2, March 1992.]

Angle φ		x-position x		Steering-angle signal θ	
RB:	Right below	LE:	Left	NB:	Negative big
RU:	Right upper	LC:	Left center	NM:	Negative medium
RV:	Right vertical	CE:	Center	NS:	Negative small
VE:	Vertical	RC:	Right center	ZE:	Zero
LV:	Left vertical	RI:	Right	PS:	Positive small
LU:	Left upper			PM:	Positive medium
LB:	Left below			PB:	Positive big

Figure 11-4: Fuzzy variable for truck steering. [From Seong-Gon Kong and Bart Kosko, "Adaptive Fuzzy Systems for Backing Up a Truck-and-Trailer," *IEEE Transactions on Neural Networks*, Vol. 3, No. 2, March 1992.]

inputs and outputs of the problem are defined. The table in Figure 11-4 lists these. They have the nice property of being qualitative. "Right below" (RB) means that the rear end of the truck is pointed downward to the right in the diagram, whereas "vertical" (VE) means that it is pointed straight upward in the diagram, toward the dock. Similarly, "left" (LE) says that the x coordinate of the truck is to the far left, whereas "left center" (LC) says that it is somewhat to the left.

The fuzzy truck driver's responses have the same casual structure. With the steering signal, θ, ranging from −30 (counterclockwise rotation) to +30 (clockwise rotation), the steering signal says to make a "positive small" (PS) turn, a negative big (NB) turn, and so forth.

Figure 11-5 shows some common sense assignments of fuzzy ranges for each of the three key variables. These fuzzy sets are narrower for conditions that correspond to proximity to the target, allowing for precision control in those stages.

In Figure 11-6, a fuzzy associative memory (FAM) matrix is established, showing the steering signals that result from various mixes of the two input signals. For instance, FAM rule number 18 says that if φ is VE and x is CE, then θ is ZE.

At some point, it becomes necessary to make the various parameters crisp. How does the system know whether its x input is RC or RI if it falls in the fuzzy crossover region between the two? A fuzzy union rule could be invoked, telling it to take the larger value—that is, the higher of the two graphs. Or, given that the steering angle is NB, what steering angle does the fuzzy truck driver set over the range of angles within NB? The authors discuss some possible rules for this, settling (in this case) on the use of the centroid of the NB set.

The result of finally pinning things down in this way is that the fuzziness goes away, leaving a crisp lookup table. It might seem, at this point, that a crisp lookup table could have been used in the first place. What good was the fuzziness?

But when you stop to think about it, this process (which leads to an efficient, accurate solution) never requires an analytical representation. No involved function of the three variables ever had to be concocted. And that is exactly where the

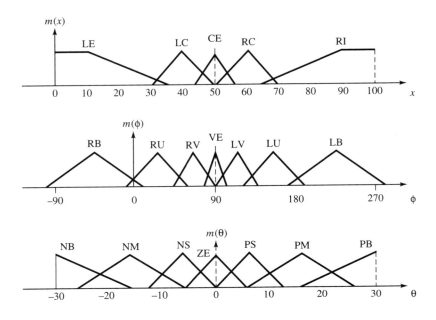

Figure 11-5: Fuzzy membership functions for each linguistic fuzzy-set value. [From Seong-Gon Kong and Bart Kosko, "Adaptive Fuzzy Systems for Backing Up a Truck-and-Trailer," *IEEE Transactions on Neural Networks*, Vol. 3, No. 2, March 1992.]

power of the fuzziness appears. Simple, instinctive, qualitative commands, based on simple, instinctive, qualitative inputs are sufficient.

Figures 11-7 and 11-8 show the paths of the truck under fuzzy and neural control, with the fuzzy controller doing a better job. This doesn't mean that the fuzzy solution is always better than the neural one. As the authors of the paper

	x				
	LE	LC	CE	RC	RI
RB	1 PS	2 PM	3 PM	4 PB	5 PB
RU	6 NS	7 PS	PM	PB	PB
RV	NM	NS	PS	PM	PB
VE	NM	NM	18 ZE	PM	PM
LV	NB	NM	NS	PS	PM
LU	NB	NB	NM	NS	PS
LB	NB	NB	NM	NM	35 NS

ϕ labels the VE row.

Figure 11.6: FAM-bank matrix for the fuzzy truck backer-upper controller. [From Seong-Gon Kong and Bart Kosko, "Adaptive Fuzzy Systems for Backing Up a Truck-and-Trailer," *IEEE Transactions on Neural Networks*, Vol. 3, No. 2, March 1992.]

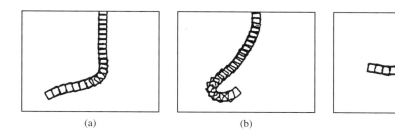

Figure 11-7: Sample truck trajectories of the fuzzy controller for initial positions (x, y, ϕ): (a) (20,20,30), (b) (30,10,220), and (c) (30,40,−10). [From Seong-Gon Kong and Bart Kosko, "Adaptive Fuzzy Systems for Backing Up a Truck-and-Trailer," *IEEE Transactions on Neural Networks,* Vol. 3, No. 2, March 1992.]

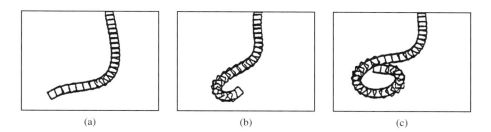

Figure 11-8: Sample truck trajectories of the neural controller for initial positions (x, y, ϕ): (a) (20,20,30), (b) (30,10,220), and (c) (30,40,−10). [From Seong-Gon Kong and Bart Kosko, "Adaptive Fuzzy Systems for Backing Up a Truck-and-Trailer," *IEEE Transactions on Neural Networks*, Vol. 3, No. 2, March 1992.]

point out, when structured knowledge of the control process is available, the fuzzy approach is simpler. When that knowledge is not available, the neural approach is indicated. In relation to traditional control systems, both the fuzzy and neural controls have the advantage of providing model-free estimation. The user does not have to formulate a mathematical model relating the inputs to the outputs.

The combination of fuzzy logic and neural networks is discussed in a 1990 paper (Langheld and Goser). The authors consider replacing the sum-of-products rule used in determining neuron activations with a fuzzy Boolean function of the inputs and the synaptic weights. Symbolically, they are asking whether the activation expression $S_j = \sum_i x_i w_{ij}$ can be replaced by the more general fuzzy expression

$$S_j = f(x_i, w_{ij}).$$

Langheld and Goser argue that the sum-of-products formula, in the very action of performing a sum is equivalent to an averaging of the inputs. Local deviations are washed out in the summing process. They also note that the adaptation of weights in a fuzzy synapse shows evidence of following a natural learning curve, and therefore appears closer to representation of neural processes.

Their paper provides several examples of fuzzy synaptic logic functions that might be employed. One of these is:

$$u_j = \max(\min(x_i, w_{ij})).$$

This expression calls for updating the activation of only that node whose synaptic weight vector has the largest fuzzy intersect with the input data vector. In other words, it is an indicator of similarity.

12

INTEGRATED CIRCUITS

The implementation of neural networks in the form of integrated circuits has been emerging from a research and development phase and moving into a phase in which neural chips are available in the electronic marketplace. Perhaps it is most accurate to say that the two activities are now overlapped: the exploratory research continues while, at the same time, early generations of working chips have been produced.

What were some of the technical issues that the pilot programs had to face in order to put ANNs on chips?

Putting a neural network architecture into silicon is like trying to map a three-dimensional space onto a plane. The multiple interconnectivity of neurons in a network demands a three-dimensional geometry to avoid an impossible multiplicity of crisscrossing synapses, rapidly rising as a function of neuron population (see Figure 12-1). But semiconductor technology restricts us to work within an essentially planar arena.

Another geometric constraint involves the number of input/output lines that are needed. The numbers of I/O nodes that a single chip can contain is limited by the pinout counts that can be provided for integrated circuits—and the pinout count is limited, in turn, by the sizes of the bonding pads and of the leads from the pads to the macroscopic outer world of switches and power supplies.

Therefore, it was necessary to develop physical arrangements that could preserve the three-dimensional requirements of the network, as well as the needed multiplicity of connections to the outer world. Various ways of contending with this problem have been generated.

One approach has been to utilize thin juxtaposed layers, in which each layer

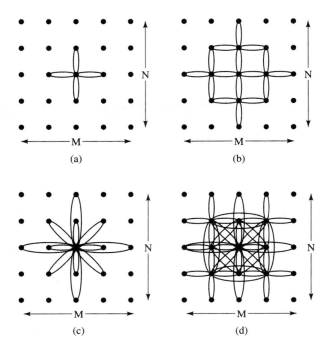

Figure 12-1: Multiplicity of interconnections in a silicon neural network:
(a) Single neuron connected through a pair of lines to its nearest neighbors
(b) Same as (a), but with each of the original neuron's four nearest neighbors also connected to each of *its* four nearest neighbors
(c) Corresponds to (a) with eight nearest neighbors
(d) Corresponds to (b) with eight nearest neighbors.
[DARPA Neural Network Study, October 1987–February 1988, AFCEA International Press, 1988.]

is a substrate containing planar elements. When these layers are vertically stacked, interconnected, and bonded together, a three-dimensional geometry results.

Alternatively, a building block approach can be used, in which the neural network is put together from multiple subnetworks, each on a different chip. This approach sacrifices speed because signals are led on and off chips, but it has the advantage of design flexibility because the chips can be stacked and interconnected in diverse arrangements.

Building Block and Thin-Film Approaches

An example of a building block approach can be seen in work carried out at the Jet Propulsion Laboratory (JPL) of the California Institute of Technology. A precursor to the integrated circuit models at JPL was a neural network built in 1986 from discrete components (Thakoor, 1986). The synaptic board contained 32 neurons and

1,024 programmable binary synaptic connections to implement the Hopfield network. A small personal computer interfaced with the board for encoding and decoding data in and out of the matrix.

Experiments with this board convinced the JPL researchers of the importance of sparse or dilute coding. Also, they used this phase of development to study the creation of induced stable states.

Within a few years of this pilot program, JPL had developed several neural network implementations based on integrated circuits. In one of these, three types of CMOS mixed analog–digital ICs were used as building blocks (Eberhardt, Duong, and Thakoor, 1989). These included a 64-channel multiplexing input chip to store and buffer the input charges; a hidden or output layer chip that applied a variable-slope sigmoidal function to internal activation levels in 32 on-chip neurons; and a connection or synapse chip containing 32 summed outputs fully connected to 32 inputs, for a total of 1,024 on-chip synapse cells. Interconnecting multiple numbers of these chips made it possible to construct a variety of neural networks.

The *on* state of each device on a binary synaptic chip must be weak in order to keep overall power dissipation low, in view of the multiple operations taking place in parallel. And to attain the needed thresholding accuracies, the *on* resistance must be accurate within relatively narrow limits. For chips with a thousand synapses, the *on* state resistance needs to be above 10^5 ohms and should vary on a single chip (as well as between chips) by no more than about 5% (Moopenn and Thakoor, 1989).

As Moopenn and Thakoor point out, these combined requirements were hard to meet. Among the approaches that they describe as having been explored were various thin-film implementations. One of these involved the development of an ultra-high density matrix capable of approximately 10^9 binary connections per cm^2.

Another thin-film approach that was taken was the fabrication of a 40×40 synaptic array using a write-once logic, based on memory switching in hydrogenated amorphous silicon (a-Si:H). A voltage pulse was used to switch a normally *off* microswitch to a permanent *on* state. The pulse width used was in the 100-μs range and dissipated only 200 to 300 nJ. A synaptic weight variation as low as ±2% was attained over the entire 1600-synapse array.

Although the synapses in this array were binary, synapses having multiple levels could be attained by combining several such arrays. The write-once limitation was an interim proviso, capable of being eliminated in later designs, as more advanced thin-film technologies became available.

Adaptive Synapses Based on MNOS and CCD Technologies

At the Lincoln Laboratory of the Massachusetts Institute of Technology, research concentrated on adaptive synapse design. In the conceptual work of Jay Sage and his colleagues at Lincoln Laboratory (Sage, Thompson, and Withers, 1986) metal-nitride-oxide-semiconductor (MNOS) devices were used to represent changeable analog synapse weights.

These circuits have been used to perform the dot products between input vectors and the synaptic weights, then to carry out a threshold operation on the results:

$$y_j = \text{sgn}\Big(\sum_i w_{ij} x_i\Big).$$

Also, changes in the synapses were carried out according to the Hebbian signal law:

$$\dot{w}_{ij} = -w_{ij} + S_i S_j$$

The MNOS chips that were used to do all this are nonvolatile (yet alterable) memory chips, on which electrical charges can be trapped in an insulating layer for an indefinitely long period. The source-to-drain current of the device is modulated as a function of the amount of charge that is present (see Figure 12-2.) Therefore, the amount of trapped charge is measurable and can serve as the analog representation of a synaptic weight.

These weights are neither built into the MNOS transistors at fabrication, nor preset to fixed values. Rather, they can change during the operation of an adaptive paradigm.

The MNOS devices are implemented as regions within a charge-coupled device (CCD). Other gates located in the same CCD provide the mechanism by which charge packets are moved in and out of the MNOS synapse, sometimes representing input vector multiplication of the weights, at other times adaptation of the weights. The motion of these packets is illustrated in Figure 12-3, which shows

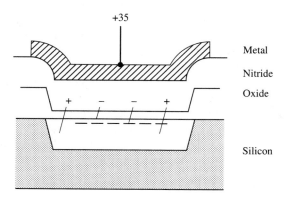

Figure 12-2: Charges trapped in the nitride layer of an MNOS chip serve as an analog representation of synaptic weight. [From J. P. Sage, K. Thompson, and R. S. Withers, "An Artificial Neural Network Integrated Circuit Based on MNOS/CCD Principles," *AIP Conference Proceedings 151: Neural Networks for Computing*, J. Denker (ed.), 1986.]

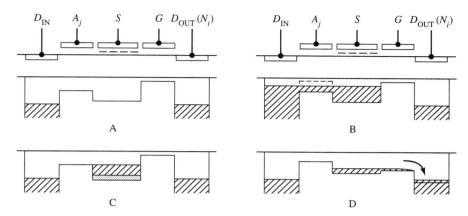

Figure 12-3: CCD clocking sequence during readout of MNOS synapse. Dashes under gate S represent trapped charge stored in nitride layer. In the readout sequence (A through D), a charge packet is moved along like water going through canal locks.

A: Initial condition
B: Voltage on D_{in} pulsed low, filling synaptic region with charge
C: Excess charge flows back to D_{in}, packet left under gate
D: Charge packet transferred to neuron (D_{out})

[From J. P. Sage, K. Thompson, and R. S. Withers, "An Artificial Neural Network Integrated Circuit Based on MNOS/CCD Principles," *AIP Conference Proceedings 151: Neural Networks for Computing*, J. Denker (ed.), 1986.]

how the CCD clocking sequence transfers an input through the MNOS synapse into a neuron.

Commenting on analog implementations of neural networks such as this one, Sage points out an advantage to analog over digital. To multiply signals by weights and then summarize hundreds of such products would require tens of thousands of digital gates. But a single analog device occupying less area than the power supply line for the digital circuit can fulfill the requirement.

In a document summarizing the results of the DARPA Neural Network Study (*DARPA Neural Network Study*, 1988), conducted from October 1987 through February 1988, tradeoffs between digital and analog approaches are posed in further detail. An argument that is given on the side of digital neural networks is that a 100% improvement of accuracy in the analog case generally means doubling the size of the analog device or group of analog devices. On the other hand, a 100% accuracy improvement in a digital implementation merely requires one additional bit of capability. Therefore, an escalating need for accuracy could eventually swing the balance sharply toward the digital side.

However, as is argued in the DARPA document, the efficiency of the analog approach may depend, not on the physical accuracy of a circuit, but rather on the degree of precision with which multiple synaptic levels can be set and resolved. Given these resolvable levels, the network paradigm can converge to the required accuracy.

The recent trend in the field is more toward the analog—which, incidentally, has the added advantage of apparently being a more accurate representation of biological processes. However, research into digital techniques remains important in a neural context and is supported by the existence of single-chip digital signal processors, as well as high-performance standard digital building blocks.

An All-Digital Neural Network

The design of a fully pipelined bit-serial classifier chip from AT&T Bell Labs focused on pattern recognition applications such as image processing and speech recognition. Developed by Stuart Mackie and John Denker of Bell Labs, it made use of exemplars stored on-chip to output a list of the five best matches to an input vector. The chip, specifically built in order to investigate the relative merits of analog and digital approaches to neural networks, calculated the dot product of the input vector and a series of stored synaptic vectors:

$$\mathbf{V} \cdot \mathbf{F}(i) = \sum_j V_j f_{ij},$$

where $\mathbf{V}$ is the input vector and $\mathbf{F}(i)$ is the ith stored vector. Then it performed various comparisons using this dot product. For instance, in feature detection, it identified all stored vectors whose dot products exceeded a threshold, T:

$$\mathbf{V} \cdot \mathbf{F}(i) > T.$$

A different calculation is needed for pattern classification, in which the stored vector closest to the input vector is to be identified:

$$\mathbf{V} \cdot \mathbf{F}(k) > \mathbf{V} \cdot \mathbf{F}(i), \text{ for } i \neq k$$

This calculation plays a part in several of the paradigms that we have looked at, starting with Kohonen's self-organizing map (Chapter 5).

Another alternative for classification is to select not only a single best match, but the k best matches. As an example of this approach (Mackie and Denker, 1988), 50 processors are implemented on a single chip. In order to maintain a high throughput, each processor stores a single exemplar, and the processors run in parallel. Whenever more stored vectors are needed, chips can be connected together to extend the pipeline.

To perform their bit-serial calculations, the processors on a chip are chained together along a one-bit-wide data pipeline, a one-bit-wide match pipeline, and twelve one-bit-wide control pipelines. Associated with each processor is a 128-bit ring register containing the stored vector.

The Hamming distance between the input vector and a stored vector is summed in an accumulator. The distances that each of the processors calculates in this way are then compared in an on-chip comparator, and the closest five matches are selected for output.

The chip was designed to operate at a clock frequency of at least 100 MHz, using nonoverlapping two-phase clocks. Following a latency of 2.5 ms, the five best distances and tag strings were issued every 1.3 ms. Based on 1.25-μm CMOS technology, each chip design included 300,000 transistors. A string of 1,000 such chips, containing 50,000 stored vectors, had the same latency as the single chip: 2.5 ms.

This implementation illustrates the specific areas in which digital techniques are favorable for neural network applications. The use of standard building blocks, modularity in extending the capabilities of a configuration, and high-speed operation are among the advantages inherent in this design.

Benefiting from the research efforts that had been going on, a diversity of neural and fuzzy chips went into production in 1989, marking a shift away from the pure R&D phase. Since some years have passed since then, the following descriptions of a few of those ICs are intended as a historical lookback. No attempt is made here to represent the entire 1989 marketplace, much less to summarize the changing semiconductor neural and fuzzy chip markets since that time—especially since it is impossible to remain current in the time frame of the reader.

Intel (Santa Clara, California) announced its 80172 (initially called the N64), an analog chip that contained 64 fully interconnected neurons, each one of which was also fully connected to each of 64 inputs. This meant a total of $2(64)^2$ synapses. There were also an additional 2,048 synapses, with fixed positive biases, that were used to establish thresholds for the neurons. The fact that there were 32 of these fixed synapses per neuron means that any one of 32 levels of threshold could be selected for each neuron.

The 80170, designated by Intel as an Electrically Trainable Artificial Neural Network (ETANN), and sponsored by the Naval Weapons Center at China Lake, California, was designed around electrically erasable programmable read-only memories (EEPROMS). In fact, each synapse was constructed from a pair of EEPROM cells (Figure 12-4), whose differential voltage represented the weight to be stored or adjusted.

An EEPROM has a *floating gate* on which charge is stored—traditionally in a discrete binary quantity, to represent a 0 or 1 in a memory location. The floating gate is charged or discharged through the quantum mechanical tunneling of electrons between the floating gate and the diffusions (Holler, Tam, Castro, and Benson, 1989). In the 80170, the gate was used in analog fashion to store varying amounts of charge. This synaptic design was influenced by work carried out by J. Alspector et al. at Belcore, who proposed a floating gate approach (Alspector and Allen, 1987).

Intel claimed an industry-leading speed of more than a billion interconnec-

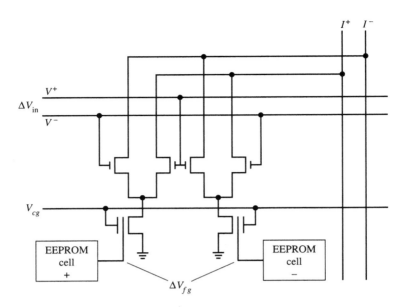

Figure 12-4: The Intel 80170 chip employs a differential "floating gate" synapse. The differential voltage between EEPROM cells represents the weight to be stored or adjusted. [From "An Electrically Trainable Artificial Neural Network (ETANN) with 10240 'Floating Gate' Synapses" by Mark Holler, Simon Tam, Hernan Castro, and Ronald Benson, Intel Corporation.]

tions per second for the 90170. The chip was still active in the marketplace as of September 1992, with Intel expected to announce second-generation neural chips in 1993 (a prediction whose accuracy the reader may be able to verify).

In contrast to Intel's analog approach, Micro Devices in Orlando, Florida, announced and made available an all-digital neural chip. The MD1210 combined fuzzy and neural concepts. Its builders called it a Fuzzy Set Comparator (FSC) and used it to rank fuzzy data in groups by certain predetermined characteristics. It was oriented toward operating on noisy or incomplete data, and toward making real-time decisions in the imperfect signal environment.

Data comparisons were made using either linear or Hamming distance measurements. The CMOS integrated circuit could compare an unknown fuzzy input vector against eight stored reference vectors—or the other way around, comparing eight input fuzzy vectors with a single stored vector. Because the IC was cascadable (up to 32 chips), these capabilities could be expanded up to 1:256 comparisons.

The resulting comparisons, generated in the fuzzy part of the circuit, were then fed into a neural postprocessor for ranking. Here, the MD1210 employed a modified Hopfield paradigm, fully transparent to the user, to perform the ranking.

Micro Devices was subsequently dropped by its parent company, but its personnel reestablished the company and its product line as American Neurologics

(Sanford, Florida). Now, this successor to Micro Devices is producing a later generation of neural chips and fuzzy microcontrollers.

The MD1210 was not the first IC with fuzzy logic capabilities. In December 1985 AT&T Bell Laboratories had announced an expert system implemented on a chip and incorporating fuzzy logic. This was the world's first fuzzy logic chip. The IC was designed for applications requiring real-time response, such as missile command and control, robotics, and manufacturing operations. Aimed initially at in-house use only, it was put to experimental uses, controlling a robot arm.

In 1989, Togai InfraLogic, Inc. (Irvine, California), a company founded by Masai Togai, the co-developer of the AT&T chip, announced a chip called the FC110 DFP—a digital fuzzy processor. Designed to interface to a fuzzy logic knowledge base, it evaluated 100,000 fuzzy rules per second to produce 60,000 crisp outputs per second. In its repertoire of fuzzy operations, it included a fuzzy AND (FZAND), fuzzy OR (FZOR), and fuzzy NOT. It allowed up to 256 levels of fuzzy membership, with 8 bits of membership resolution.

More advanced versions of the FC110 have been developed since 1989.

Another neural IC announced in 1989 was the Dendros-1, a CMOS chip from Syntonic Systems (Portland, Oregon). This analog chip implemented Grossberg's ART-1 paradigm, processing 22-element input vectors. Synaptic weights were stored as charge levels on capacitors.

The designer of Dendros-1, Carlos C. Tapang (president of Syntonic Systems), developed a concept of "sleep" for a neural network, and introduced sleep and "deep sleep" modes into the design of the chip.

In his neural investigations, Tapang addressed the issue of how a neural system (whether biological or electronic) could retain its long-term memories while retaining its ability to adapt in the face of new data. In the biological case, he hypothesized that sleep is the means by which an animal or person preserves the stability of an adaptive (and therefore potentially unstable or amnesiac) nervous system. Tapang based his concept on various factors, including studies that imply a key role for sleep in helping the brain to retain long-term memory.

In the electronic case, Tapang observed that neural networks are composed of imperfect silicon transistors whose characteristics tend to drift over time. But the stability of a neural memory undoubtedly lies not within individual neurons or synapses, but within the network as a whole. So, as Tapang concluded, why not provide a restoration or healing phase for a neural network, in which the network itself corrects its drifting components? In other words: sleep.

Since top-level ART-1 neurons are competitive, they take irregular turns in becoming the "winning" node. Tapang observed, however, that some neurons would tend to lock into dominant modes, thereby distorting the operation of the network.

In Dendros-1, excessive activity by a dominant neuron would trigger the sleep phase. In this phase, the network was isolated from the outer world by I/O switches, as in Figure 12-5. It would receive a constant, nonspecific stimulus, activating all its bottom-layer nodes (see Chapter 8). This resulted in oscillations

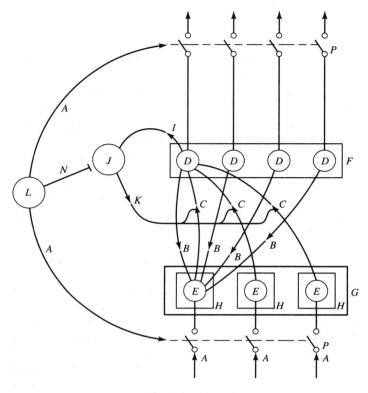

Syntonic systems

Figure 12-5: Dendros architecture implementing ART paradigm with sleep feature.
  G = comparison layer
  F = recognition layer
  C = bottom-up synapses
  D = top-down synapses
Sleep control node, L, fires when system is awake, turning on switches P, connecting
chip to environment, and inhibiting deep sleep nodes such as J. The sleep mode is initiated when any top-level node becomes excessively dominant. In the sleep state, discon-
nected from its external connections, the chip recovers, reversing the learning that created the aberrant node. [From Syntonic Systems, Beaverton, Oregon.]

between the top and bottom layers of the ART network, letting the system "meander in its state space."

   While it was in this sleeping condition, the network would reverse the learning patterns that had led to the excessive dominance. The over-favored node would
be restored to a more restrained level, while less aberrant levels of memory would
be maintained, and the network would "awaken" to reconnect to its outer world
inputs.

   Further development work on Dendros moved in the direction of higher integration and an application-specific architecture, dedicated to written character recognition.

The anthropomorphic connotations of a chip that "sleeps" are echoed in a project that was initiated by Motorola Inc. (Phoenix, Arizona) and Odin Corporation (Manhattan, Kansas). Based on the concepts of Willard Olson, president and founder of Odin, whose earlier background was in neurophysiology, the chip set was intended to represent several parts of a human (or, more generally, mammalian) brain. This contrasts with a strict concentration on modeling the cerebral cortex, which Olson saw as the implicit focus of previous neural models.

The cerebral cortex, a relatively late development in vertebrate evolution, is the apparent site of our conscious thoughts. But the functioning of the cortex involves information exchanges with key lower brain centers. The thalamus seems to act as a switching center or preprocessor for signals to the cortex from many of our physical senses, including vision, touch, hearing, pain, and temperature. There are not only paths from the thalamus to the cortex, but also reverse paths, providing feedback or perhaps templates of what the thalamus should "expect" in the sensory patterns that it receives. (This is not true for the sense of smell; smell sensations have a direct route to the olfactory lobes, not mediated by the thalamus.)

Other brain regions that play an interesting role in relation to the cortex include the hypothalamus and the hippocampus. The hypothalamus, located just beneath the thalamus, appears to be a reward center, sending signals of pleasure and pain to the cortex. The hippocampus seems to govern the emotional relevance of the events we experience, controlling the degree to which each is retained in memory.

These and other areas of the brain interact with the cortex in a complex of logical and motivational ways. The Odin approach was to design a chip set to represent this communication between differently organized neural elements, corresponding to these functional divisions of the brain.

Although the Odin-Motorola effort in this direction seems to have dissolved, Odin is still exploring the concept. It is a concept that probably sounds abstract to anyone not operating at the boundary between biology and semiconductor technology. Yet, some existing neural paradigms have features that would appear to fit aspects of the physiological model. Grossberg's adaptive resonance theory contains elements reminiscent of the transfer of "expected" patterns from the cortex to the thalamus. In Dendros, sleep "knits up the ravell'd sleeve of care," as Shakespeare put it. And the combination of different kinds of neural processes within the same system (connoted in the physiological case) appears in at least one form, in recurrent backpropagation.

A Silicon Retina

If neural chips mapping regions of the brain ever emerge into the world, they will find neural networks simulating the operations of sensory organs already in existence. An eventual linking of these two lines of development would then seem likely.

Prominent among researchers who have been implementing sensory capabilities in silicon are Carver Mead and his colleagues at the California Institute of Technology. Much of their work has involved the visual retina (Mahowald and Mead, 1988; Sivilotti, Mahowald, and Mead, 1987; Mead, 1989). The cells of the retina, even though their function is sensory, are made of neural tissue. Mahowald and Mead refer to the retina as "a tiny outpost of the central nervous system."

The retina simulation uses an hexagonal array of cells, each featuring a photoreceptor and associated circuitry. Each cell is linked to its six neighbors by resistors. Wide-range amplifiers, fed by the photoreceptor outputs, drive the network through these resistors.

This gives every cell the ability to measure the overall excitation field created by one or more light stimuli impinging on the array. By varying the gain of the amplifiers or the value of the resistances, the experimenter can vary the area of the array over which excitations are propagated. The excitation is attenuated as it propagates, so that the voltage at points relatively far from light stimuli is relatively small.

Each cell has a second amplifier, which generates a voltage proportional to the difference between its own photoreceptor and the network potential at that point. This is a measure of the difference between the light intensity at that cell and the time-space average among its neighbors. The intensity of this difference–function at each point represents the sensing of a contrast in the visual field—a strong gradient between adjacent areas of very different brightness.

Additional logic circuitry in each cell measures the rate of change of the excitation within any cell. A high measurement indicates the motion of a visual edge or vertex through the cell.

The motion sensitivity of the retina was demonstrated in an experiment with a dark cross rotating at about 10 rpm. When the stationary cross was presented to the retina, response was insignificant. When the cross rotated, however, a strong response took place, mapping the position of the cross on a display screen.

Since a biological retina employs an on-center, off-surround logic, it is natural that those designing a silicon retina should have set out to do the same thing. There are good reasons for this competitive structure of a retina. The range of light intensity in the visual field would make it impossible for the eye to detect contrasts in both bright and dim parts of the field—if absolute intensity were the only governing factor. Under high levels of illumination, the brighter parts of the field would be saturated; under low levels, the dimmer parts would be lost in the noise.

However, when each cell of the retina reacts to the differences between the signal that it receives and the average received by cells in its immediate vicinity, it remains contrast-sensitive over a wide range of illumination. This competitive strategy gives the retina (whether living or silicon) sensitivity to contrast.

A silicon cochlea developed in the same laboratory (Lyon and Mead, 1989) processes auditory signals. Sound frequencies are converted to electrical frequencies and propagated along a delay line designed to be a low-pass filter. The cells of the silicon cochlea are frequency-sensitive elements that act as taps along the delay line. Taps at the starting end of the line are tuned to high frequencies, those at the destination end are tuned to low frequencies, and the whole spectrum of auditory frequencies is represented by gradations along the way. However, this is a classical electronic implementation, not a neural one.

On the other hand, the silicon retina, in which each cell in the array has reciprocal competitive communications with its neighbors, is a neural network.

13

OPTICAL NEURAL NETS

There are a few good reasons for using optics—either instead of, or along with electronics—to implement neural nets. Foremost among these is the fact that light rays do not suffer, as electrical wires do, from cross-talk. No matter how closely you pack the optical paths in and out of a processing element, or even if they cross, they do not perturb one another. Ultimately, this stems from the fact that light particles obey Bose-Einstein statistics, in which there is no exclusion principle. That is, the number of photons that can dance on the point of a needle is infinite. Electrons obey Fermi-Boltzmann statistics, and along with that, they obey the Pauli exclusion principle. They want to be as far away from each other in space or in quantum states as they can get.

Thus, optics allows very large fan-ins and fanouts among processors. This is an ideal attribute for neural processing elements in a multiply connected network.

In addition to the lack of cross-talk, optical paths are physically easier to pack together than electronic paths. The electronic paths leading in and out of a processor are wire leads, which need to be bonded to bonding pads in the package that contains a processing chip, and need to come out of the package in the form of pins that can be connected to sockets or traces on a pc board. The constraints on implementing these I/O connections are rapidly becoming the governing factor in how small you can make an electronic chip.

Optically, the I/O leads can be a tightly packed bundle of hair-thin light-conducting fibers—or, better yet, mere paths through the air between optical processors. The light must be brought to a photosensitive area, but it need not (and cannot) be bonded to it. Making and breaking connections, difficult in electronics, is trivial in optics.

Low power consumption is another benefit of optics. The ratio of energy dissipation for an electronic system versus that for an equivalent optical system is very large.

In summary, because neural networks are characterized by large numbers of processing elements, with a large multiplicity of interconnections, it is a good idea to implement them in a technology that not only allows large fan-ins and fanouts but also keeps power dissipation low, even when all this is happening in a small volume. Optics does all this.

At the same time, electronics is much further along in terms of having been practically implemented and perfected over decades of computer technology. For the time being, then, it remains the principal way in which ANNs are built, despite the theoretical advantages of optics.

Optical Techniques

One approach is to compromise and use electronic processors with optical inter-connections. Consider a hybrid electronic package containing silicon chips along with photocells and light-emitting diodes (LEDs) for I/O. The processors in these packages can exchange optical signals with each other via fiber optical paths or along free-form paths through air or space.

In a purely optical ANN, the light-emitting and light-receiving elements are not mere adjuncts to the processors; they *are* the processors. In between them, however, along the paths of the light rays, you need something that acts as a synapse—something that modulates the transmitted light. The things that do this are known as spatial light modulators, or SLMs. The optical implementation of the Hopfield paradigm, mentioned in Chapter 4 (Farhat et al., 1985), is a classical example of this approach.

One way to make an SLM is to put an optical filter in the path of a light ray. The light ray corresponds to an input signal. The transformations that occur to it in passing through the SLM (variations in phase, polarization, or amplitude of the transmitted light) correspond to the action of weighted synapses.

An issue that arises is: How do you represent a negative synaptic weight on such a scale? Solutions to this are not hard to find. Two orthogonal polarization planes can be used to represent positive and negative signals. A synapse with a negative weight is then made from a filter that rotates the plane of polarization through 90 degrees—thus switching the polarization plane of incident signals, changing positive values to negative and vice versa. Modulations of phase or amplitude would continue to provide the absolute values of the synaptic weights.

On the other hand, in place of transmissive filters, reflectance can be used, in which each element of the SLM has a level of reflectance that represents a synaptic weight. Reflective spatial light modulators also can rotate polarization vectors, so the techniques used in transmissive synapses are carried over into reflection.

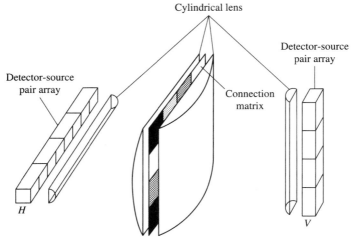

Optical BAM matrix-vector multiplier

Figure 13-1: Optical BAM matrix-vector multiplier. The spatial light modulator (SLM) is sandwiched between the two cylindrical lenses. It provides the synaptic connections between optical neural layers *H* and *V*. [From Bart Kosko and Clark Guest, "Optical Bidirectional Associative Memories," *Proceedings of the Society for Photo-optical Instrumentation Engineers (SPIE)*, Vol. 758, p. 11, 1987.]

Research and development efforts are active in both refractive and reflective neural networks.

Figure 13-1 shows the implementation of an optical BAM (Kosko and Guest, 1987). A cylindrical lens projects an input vector from array *H* onto a horizontal row of synapses in the SLM, where the vector components are "weighted" by the transmissive properties of the synaptic elements; a second cylindrical lens projects the weighted vector onto array *V*. Then the process reverses, in BAM fashion, as the input from *V* is projected onto a vertical column of the SLM, weighted, and so forth. The reverberation, as with any BAM, stabilizes when the I/O vectors at *H* and *V* stabilize.

Holograms

Holograms are very compact media for the storage of optical information. A hologram is formed when a photographic plate is illuminated by two coherent light beams. One of these beams, reflected from an object or scene, is called the *object beam*. The other, shined directly onto the plate, is the *reference beam*.

In creating a hologram, it is essential that the two light beams be able to form a stable interference pattern. This property is called *mutual coherence*. The object and reference beams must be derived from the same laser. Lasers have a very sharply defined wavelength and can be focused to a very small spot. These are the properties required for high coherence.

The two beams create an interference pattern across their common target, the photographic plate. As a result, the information recorded on the plate implicitly contains both phase and amplitude information. In other words, the hologram contains more information than can be detected in an ordinary photograph or visual view of the object or scene. In particular, the phase information preserves data on the direction of travel of light beams. This, in turn, relates to the depths and orientations of the various reflective surfaces that make up the scene.

After the plate is developed and fixed, it is illuminated by a reference beam of the same wavelength as the original reference beam. An optical pattern is formed that is a reconstruction of the original illuminated scene. As a result of the three-dimensional information that was abstracted from the original phase and amplitude data, the hologram produces a three-dimensional image. You can see the scene differently when you look at it from different angles.

The fact that a great amount of information can be stored, and that it can be simply recalled, immediately suggests that a hologram is a natural medium for neural applications. And, in fact, most of the R&D efforts in optical neurocomputing are hologram-based. In most neural applications, the hologram is not storing pictorial elements, as it does in conventional holography. Instead, it is storing optically coded information representing the neural interconnection weights.

There are two general ways in which to make a holographic neural network. One is to use a page-oriented holographic memory (POHM). In a POHM, a hologram array stores the synpatic information. Each element in the array is an optical point source whose image is projected onto the plane of a refractive or reflective SLM—the reflective case being illustrated in Figure 13-2 (Caulfield, Kinser, and Rogers, 1989).

Notice that the SLM, which was used to store the synapses in the geometry of Figure 13-1, is now the source of inputs to the network. The reflectance of each SLM element in Figure 13-2 is an input level. And the synapses, rather than lying between the input and output planes, are projected onto the input plane along with the incident light.

Also, it is important to realize that a single point source in the synaptic hologram array projects a different intensity of light upon each element, k,l, of the SLM array. If the synapses were merely transmissive, that would not be so. But the phase information stored in each point of the hologram array projects a diverse set of intensities onto the SLM input plane. Each such projected point is, in effect, a synaptic weight multiplying the corresponding input element of the SLM.

Thus, if the SLM measures $M \times M$, then each point in the hologram array provides M^2 synapses.

The projections of hologram array element i,j on the SLM are focused by the lens (Figure 13-2) onto a single point, i,j, of the output plane. That is, the output point i,j receives the sum of all the M^2 weighted inputs corresponding to the synaptic set i,j.

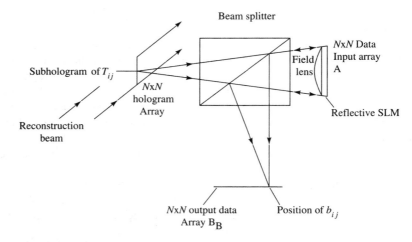

Figure 13-2: Page-oriented holographic memory (POHM) using a reflective spatial light modulator (SLM) can store a vast number of exemplar patterns and recall them at an extremely high rate. [From "Optical Neural Networks" by H. John Caulfield, Jason Kinser, and Steven K. Rogers, *Proceedings of the IEEE*, Vol. 77, No. 10, October 1989.]

The intensity, y, of the output signal at i, j is:

$$y_{ij} = \sum_{kl} w_{ijkl} x_{kl},$$ (13.1)

where w_{ijkl} is the synaptic weight projected from hologram element i, j, via modulator input elements k, l, onto output element i, j. The factor x_{kl} is the input level associated with element k, l of the SLM—in this case, the reflectivity of that element.

Equation (13.1) corresponds to the usual expression for the output of a neuron as the sum of its weighted inputs.

The description of i, j as a point source and as the corresponding point output does not reduce these to mathematical points. Instead, it is the resolution of the detector elements in the output plane that ultimately determines what is a *point*. The small output region i, j that is summed as a light intensity by the i, j detector is an effective optical point in the output plane, and it implicitly defines the corresponding optical point in the synaptic plane. If the output detectors were smaller, we would need bigger holograms to resolve them. Then we could fit fewer of those holograms into a unit area. In general, it is desirable to have the holograms and the detectors about the same size.

We have traced the history of one point in the synaptic plane, involving the sum of the products of a large number of inputs and weights. However, every source point in the synaptic plane is simultaneously illuminating the entire input plane. Each of these points is projected, via the input plane, onto a corresponding point in the output plane.

Thus, each of the N^2 optical points in the matrix produces N^2 synapses, for a total of N^4 synapses or interconnects. Values of N can approach 1,000, so 10^{12} independent synapses can be active at the same time: a million inputs, each individually connected to a million outputs.

POHMs have the capability of storing enormous numbers of exemplar patterns and recalling these at an extremely high rate. However, the stored patterns are fixed, so this geometry is not usable for a neural network that is undergoing learning.

The principal other way in which to use holograms in neural networks is to employ three-dimensional or volume holography. For example, image patterns can be stored as holograms in a photorefractive crystal. This is a crystal that develops an interior pattern of electrical charge corresponding to the pattern of light intensity throughout its volume. The charge pattern, in turn, determines the index of refraction of the crystal at each point.

All of this adds up to the fact that the photorefractive crystal can replace the photographic plate as a storage medium for holograms (Wagner and Psaltis, 1987; Caulfield et al., 1989). But it has a capacity and flexibility beyond anything that a photographic plate can provide. To begin with, a crystal with a volume of 1 cm^3 can store enough information to specify 10^{12} interconnections. This brings it into the biological range. Furthermore, it can store multiple holograms concurrently. Moreover, it is changeable; new holographic images can be learned. However, there is a penalty for this capability—old patterns can be forgotten.

A complementary pair of laser wavefronts form an interference pattern within the crystal to store an initial set of synapses. Subsequent illumination of the crystal with either member of the laser pair will evoke the other. This means that the stored pattern automatically acts as a bidirectional associative memory (BAM).

When a second pair of wavefronts go through interference within the crystal, another BAM pattern is stored. The first set of associations remains essentially intact—but, as synaptic patterns representing many complementary I/O pairs are stored in the crystal, the older associations start to attenuate.

The ability of the three-dimensional holographic network to learn new associations makes it not just a BAM, but an ABAM—an adaptive bidirectional associative memory, which is described in Chapter 9. The tendency of optical or electronic ABAMs to saturate remains a problem in the evolution of this form of intelligence.

On the other hand, saturation at an extremely large number of stored patterns may not be a real obstacle. Biological memories—even our own—undoubtedly have upper limits on how much information they can retain. The problem in approximating biological memories is not that artificial neural memories saturate; the problem is to construct them in such a way that they do not saturate until they have stored an astronomically vast number of associations.

Optical neural networks have the advantage mentioned earlier in this chapter of being able to operate on extremely large data sets with a minimum of energy expenditure. Researchers at the University of Alabama in Huntsville (Caulfield and

Shamir, 1988) compare the process of recall in an optical ANN to wave-particle phenomena in quantum physics.

Caulfield and Shamir note the quantum mechanical concept of fundamental entities such as light photons propagating as wave groups, and manifesting themselves as particles only upon the event of detection by a detector such as a photocell. Prior to the detection of the photon as a particle, the observer has no information regarding its location or momentum—only information relating to its wave properties, such as wavelength and energy. Only when the wave function is "collapsed" by a measurement do we obtain this information, and only then do we pay an energy price for it.

Analogous to these relationships, an optical neural network provides the observer with no initial information with respect to an output vector—only the totality of the array of stored wave patterns. The interaction of an input pattern with a stored pattern results in detection by one of many photocells—analogous to the transition from wave group to particle.

Caulfield and Shamir use the wave-particle model as more than a metaphor. Their calculations show that the energy used by the optical neural network to make an output decision approaches the frugal quantum theoretical limits:

$$e = mh\nu/w,$$

where m is the number of photons that must be detected by a photocell in order to sufficiently exceed the inherent random noise level, h is Planck's constant, ν is the frequency of the impinging light, and w is the number of weights or synapses leading into that detector.

Using $m = 10^3$ and $w = 10^6$ as representative values, Caulfield points out (in a separate communication) that this means about 1/1,000 of a photon per input line. "If we used optical fibers," he adds, "we would need 10^3 or more photons per fiber, or 10^9 photons to make the same calculation. For visible light at room temperature, $h\nu$ is about 100 times the average energy of atoms in the room. That thermal energy is usually considered the minimum possible energy per calculation. Most electronic computers spend a hundred million times as much energy. By operating at 1/1,000 of $h\nu$, an optical neural network can actually operate below the thermal energy level."

14

THE EVOLUTION OF INTELLIGENCE

A number of investigators are looking into the evolution of intelligence in neural networks. So far, efforts are underway on the genetic front, in which neural networks undergo symbolic matings, mutations, and the transmission of genetic codes through successive generations. There are also efforts on the individual front, as an individual network learns and adapts.

Of course, the latter case pervades much of neural network research, as has been shown here in earlier chapters, in paradigms such as backpropagation that undergo supervised learning or those such as ART or the ABAM, where the learning is unsupervised. Some researchers, rather than focusing on the nature of paradigms that exhibit learning, are studying the behavior of neural networks as they learn, much as a biologist would study the behavior of an animal as it learns from its experiences. At least one example of this emphasis has been seen in the drive reinforcement model of Chapter 10.

Genetics

Research into the biological evolution of logical entities did not begin in neural network research. Rather, it began in a classical computer environment, oriented toward machine learning and the development of search and optimization procedures.

The field was founded by John Holland, a professor at the University of Michigan (Holland, 1975). Holland, along with his colleagues and students, developed processes called *genetic algorithms*, in which binary strings of numbers go through processes of competition, reproduction, and the struggle for survival.

David Goldberg, a former student of Holland's who has become a major contributor to the field, describes these processes (Goldberg, 1989). In an introductory chapter, he illustrates genetic algorithms with a group of four 5-bit binary strings. There are endless ways to establish algorithms of this kind. What follows, in a variation on Goldberg's procedures, is one way.

Table 14-1 presents an initial set of four 5-bit strings, representing the population of a culture of such strings. The names, M, N, X, and Y, are arbitrary.

TABLE 14-1   A POPULATION OF STRINGS

Name	String	Fitness	Probability
M	11111	3	.30
N	10111	4	.40
X	11000	2	.20
Y	01011	1	.10
		Sum: 10	

An arbitrary fitness has been assigned to each string by evaluating the expression $(O - E + 2)$, where O is the algebraic sum of all bits in odd positions in the string and E is the sum of all bits in even positions. The fittest possible string, $A = 10101$, would have a fitness of 5; the least fit of all possible strings, $Z = 01010$, would have a fitness of 0. Between these extremes are 30 examples of strings with fitnesses in the 1–4 range, four of which have been used in the initial population of Table 14-1.

The ability of each string to reproduce is assumed to be directly proportional to its fitness—by analogy to an organism being able to survive the hazards of its environment to reproduce. The sum of the fitnesses in Table 14-1 is 10. String N, with a fitness of 4, is therefore assigned 4/10 of the probability pie, for a probability of .4—and, in this way, each string gets a probability, as shown in the table.

A random process is performed, involving use of a random-number generator, dice, coins, or (as Goldberg assumes in his introduction) a roulette wheel. This process duplicates strings from the initial culture and places them in a "mating pool." The probability that any particular string is the one selected for the pool, on a single random trial, is the value from the table. With repeated trials, the mating pool gradually becomes populated with strings, with those having the higher levels of fitness tending to be the more prevalent.

In the next phase of the algorithm, a pair of strings is randomly selected from the mating pool. This is a uniform random selection, like drawing lottery tickets from a bowl; the only thing that favors the fittest strings at this stage is that there tend to be more of them in the mating pool in the first place.

The two strings that are selected for mating (the "happy couple," as Goldberg calls them) are split at a common crossover point, which also is selected at random, and then they trade split-off segments. The crossover occurs between bits, so, in the 5-bit strings, there are four possible choices. If strings N and X are selected for mating, here is what would happen during this mating process, if the split occurred between positions 3 and 4:

Before	After
N: 101 11	NX: 101 00
X: 110 00	XN: 110 11

Of course, the mating would produce different types of offspring if the random split point had occurred at a different common point in the two strings.

When $P = NX$ and $Q = XN$ are added to the culture, the population table will look like Table 14-2:

TABLE 14-2 NEW POPULATION OF STRINGS

Name	String	Fitness	Probability
M	11111	3	.165
N	10111	4	.220
X	11000	2	.110
Y	01011	1	.055
P	10100	4	.220
Q	10111	4	.220
		Sum: 18	

As successive tables show the expanding population, there will be a comparative buildup in the fitter strings and in the descendants that they generate. More persistent than the strings themselves (for long strings) are templates called *schemata* that describe the strings. A schema contains an asterisk (*) as a "don't care" symbol at string positions of no significance in the context of that particular schema. At positions of significance, the schema has either a 1 or a 0.

Thus, the schema *011* will match any 5-bit string whose central three bits are 011. For instance, it describes strings N and Q from Table 14-2.

A schema can be used to define classes of strings, or to define substrings within the strings. A schema that correlates closely with a substring conducive to survival will tend to be more durable than the strongly surviving string itself. Thus, the schema 101** correlates well with strings having high fitness, and will occur often (like the genes or alleles of a positive biological survival trait) throughout successive generations.

It happens that the fittest possible string, $A = 10101$, cannot be generated from the initial population in the preceding example (Table 14-1). However, it becomes possible from the second population (Table 14-2) if P mates with anything other than X and splits after the fourth bit. The fact that A is composed of schemata that contribute strongly to fitness, such as 101** contributing +2 or 1*1*1 contributing +3, makes the eventual appearance and abundant survival of A inevitable.

It should also be noted that the mating of a string with its own type is an invisible event, since no new string type is generated by the process. Therefore, such matings must to be ignored as frivolous.

Another operation that can occur within any string is a random single-bit mutation, in which a 1 turns to a 0 or vice versa. These are assigned low probabilities in genetic algorithms, because if they occurred with great frequency, the algorithm would be washed out in noise. Goldberg assigns a mutation probability of .001 per bit per generation.

This kind of process is more than the casual game that it might appear at first glance. When various search operations are encoded into much longer strings of this kind and the fitness of a string is established in a way that facilitates the search, the genetic algorithm can be put to powerful uses.

The use of genetic algorithms in a neural context is a later development. Some examples of this are shown in the sections that follow.

Modular Neural Evolution

Hugo de Garis, involved in neural networks research at the University of Brussels, is one of those who has been applying the genetic algorithm (GA) to neural networks. In 1990, looking toward future integrated circuit densities on the order of 10^7 artificial neurons on a chip, he addressed the complex patterns of behavior that could be represented under such conditions.

At complexities of this order, it becomes implausible for the network designer to oversee the logic of interconnections or to specify the paradigms of learning and recall. What de Garis hypothesizes is a genetic algorithm by which the neural populations evolve. Concluding that crossovers would be an unnecessary complicating factor in the nonlinear neural environment, and that mutations are sufficient—since a change in any synaptic weight affects the behavior of a network as a whole—he bases the evolutionary process on mutation alone. This is analogous to evolution in the context of asexual reproduction.

Implemented in the algorithm would be a large population of competing neural modules—each one an independent network. Fitness would be the degree to which a module approached the behavior established in the design goal.

A simple example of how the evolutionary process would operate involves the evolution of robot arm control modules (de Garis, 1990). The arm itself is assumed to be two-jointed (having a shoulder and an elbow) and is confined to motions in a plane.

Three modules need to evolve. Two of these are joint modules directly controlling the two joints. The other is a control module, which receives inputs from a pair of eyes. On the basis of the visual inputs and a specified destination point for the arm, the control module provides inputs to the joint modules. Each of the modules is a fully connected neural network, with six neurons in a control module and four in each of the joint modules.

The synaptic weights between the N neurons within a module contain $6N^2$ bit positions. The N^2 factor allows the random selection of two of the neurons (implying, also, the possibility of feedback from a neuron to itself). The synaptic weight between the selected input and output neurons (or in a neuron's self feedback) is defined by a 6-bit binary string. The first of these six bits specifies that the weight is negative/inhibitory (1) or positive/excitatory (0). The remaining randomly selected bits specify a binary number to the right of the binary point, thus producing a weight that ranges, in decimal terms, from 0 to .999 . . . For example, a weight of 101101 would convert to -0.40625. Activation within each neuron is provided by the usual summation process, and a sigmoidal function of activation determines signal output.

The statistically formed codes or "chromosomes" act as synaptic weight generators. A population of chromosomes compete in software for the robotic arm job. All synaptic weights are set to random initial values, and are allowed to evolve through mutation. The initial weights produce nothing at all like the required behavior of the arm. But, as the evolution proceeds, those modules whose outputs furnish approximate arm-controlling signals are selected as *survivors*—as are the chromosomes that evolved to generate its synapses. Surviving modules (and their chromosomes) are used as the entry populations to the next level of evolution in arm control.

De Garis describes a particular result: With the synapses set to their initial random values, the mutation process was initiated with the two joint modules being evolved first. The fitness of a module was measured at each stage by the inverse of the sum of the squares of the distances between the sets of position coordinates output by the module and the real positions desired for the arm. After about 100 generations, the output values differed from the desired values by less than 1%.

After the joints were defined, a similar process was used to evolve the control modules.

Although this demonstration used relatively small populations of competing chromosomes to evolve the robotic controls, the full-scale application would involve competition for far more sophisticated tasks among large populations of competing chromosomes—perhaps implemented in hardware. The experimenter would feed the requirements of the task into the tutorial circuitry, and the vast populations on the neural chips would evolve to carry out that task. The experimenter would not need to know just how the evolution was being carried out, and would merely reap the results, as the fittest modules evolved and then went about doing the thing that was wanted.

Natural Selection

The genetic algorithm leads naturally to simulations of evolving symbolic neural entities struggling for survival in an environment of hazards. The motivation for generating scenarios of this kind is at least twofold. First, by pitting evolving entities against a rich environment, the resulting adaptations may develop in more creative directions than they otherwise would. Second, such simulations serve as useful parallels for biological and societal evolutionary processes, and can aid in our understanding of these processes.

De Garis has developed stick figures that evolve increasingly agile walking modes across the display screen. And he has also developed a population of displayed electronic lizards that cope with dangers (such as electronic snakes) as they evolve survival traits.

Another study, conducted by David Ackley and Michael Littman of Bellcore, combines both evolution and learning. It describes the struggle for survival among a population of fictitious neural creatures moving about on a display screen. In this research, the creatures undergoing evolution and learning are called "agents." They live in an artificial life (AL) environment that includes trees in which they can obtain shelter, plants that they can eat, carnivores that can damage or kill them, and walls that delimit their motions and also cause them damage when the agent bumps into one. An evolutionary reinforcement learning (ERL) strategy enables them to adapt to AL—which, the authors point out, is "not a very kind world."

Each agent consists of two neural networks. One of these accepts inputs descriptive of the agent's nearby surroundings (locations of carnivores, trees, food, and walls) and its own internal state (its levels of damage and hunger and whether or not it is in a tree) and uses these to determine the direction of its next move across the simulated landscape. That is, it accepts an environmental input vector, $I(t)$, and produces an output action vector, $X(t)$, both of which are functions of time.

The agent's second neural network evaluates the agent's latest move, giving it a correction signal (punishment) if the move worsened its condition. The evaluation rules, however, are themselves evolving from random beginnings. The evaluation rules that survive are those whose agents have survived and reproduced. ERL also contains fixed rules governing the mating and reproduction cycles in the agents, including the processes of mutation and crossover.

When an agent, A, gives birth to an offspring, O, several possibilities exist. A's genetic code can simply be copied to O, creating a clone—or, O's genetic code can be modified by flipping random bits. But if there are other agents within a specified distance of A, the nearest such agent (B) is selected as a mate for A, and O is generated through crossover of A and B codes.

An agent's behavior is a function of the environmental input vector $I(t)$ at time t, and the agent's bit pattern—which establishes its response. This internal pattern is its genetic code, modified by what it has learned in evaluations of its past actions.

Altogether it takes more than 280 bits to define an agent, including both its action and evaluation neural networks. The move of an agent (the output vector from its action network) is only two bits in magnitude, telling it whether to move east, west, north, or south. However, the input vectors are 8-dimensional. The evolving synaptic weights of the action network mediate between these inputs and outputs.

A simple development contributing favorably to the survival of an agent might be to move toward food, but away from carnivores.

Like the agents, the carnivores can see up to a certain range (generally a greater range than the visual range of the agents) and can move through the environment. However, the carnivores are simpler entities that neither learn nor evolve.

Ackley and Littman compared several different strategies. A partial list of these includes:

- B (Brownian): Nonevolving, nonlearning agents with uniform random actions.

- E (Evolve) Nonlearning agents with evolution of action networks (since these agents do not learn, their evaluation networks are useless, and thus do not evolve).

- L (Learn): Nonevolving agents with learning based on a fixed random evaluation network.

- ERL agents with learning in the action network and evolution of both networks.

The authors ran each strategy 100 times to determine how each affected agent survival. Most initial agent populations died out early, although some survived so long that truncation had to be performed after a preestablished upper limit of one million steps.

Mean population survival times were:

Agent Type		Number Surviving
B	(Brownian motion)	6,560
E	(evolution, no learning)	1,564
L	(learning, no evolution)	47,529
ERL	(evolution and learning)	80,707

The authors account for the high survival under uniform random strategy B because, in scattering agents in a uniform distribution over the AL landscape, it prevented clusterings of agents that (in other strategies) led to "spot famines" due to local overgrazing and other liabilities of overcrowding.

They were surprised, however, at the weakness of evolution without learning, versus the strength of learning without evolution. A tentative conclusion was that the rigors of the environment, in which so many agents died very early, left few genetic strains. Most viable populations would descend from a single agent, so that crossover would have little effect.

Clearly, these results leave room for more experimental variations. Pursued through environments of varying harshness and various assumptions regarding the logic governing agents, predators, and other elements, this model would undoubtedly produce a rich data bank of cause and effect in both learning and evolution.

Simulated Imagination

Three researchers at Johns Hopkins University performed a series of experiments involving the internal representations (cognitive map) that a neural network formed during its training. (Hutton, Sigillito, and Egeth, 1990). Their approach was to observe the behavior of the network as it attempted to apply its cognitive map to a changing environment.

To do this, they constructed a network that they named "HMS, a homuncular system." It had 3 input nodes, 10 hidden nodes, and 3 output nodes. Then, using backpropagation, they taught the HMS to follow seven fixed paths to a destination. Its starting point was any one of seven points along the top edge of a planar region. (A specific terrain that was used in the quest was a Lotus 1-2-3 spreadsheet.) As shown in the conceptual diagram (Figure 14-1), the region contained three specified subregions: primary and secondary goals and a forbidden zone that the homuncular system was discouraged from traversing.

In the training of HMS, its locations in the field of operation were described by vectors whose two components were normalized over a range from 0 to 1. The

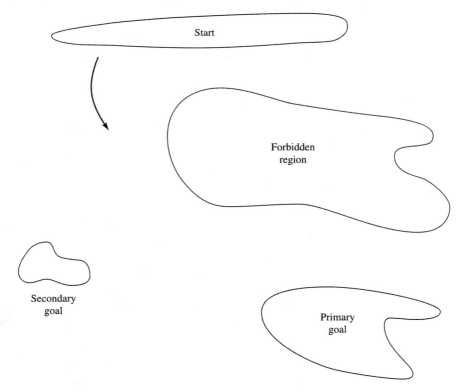

Figure 14-1: Quest of a homuncular system (HMS). The system is trained to navigate through a plane, avoiding a forbidden region to arrive at successive goals.

three-node input consisted of the two components of HMS's present location in the field, and a third input—a context—that was not always used. (Since the context was initially set to 0 or 1, it is sometimes referred to here as a bit. However, it too was allowed to move over a decimal range from 0 to 1.)

Similar to the input, the three-node output consisted of the two components of HMS's *next* location, and an optional context output. There was full connection between input and hidden layers and between hidden and output layers.

HMS was trained using backpropagation. For any given input vector, representing a particular point along one of the seven paths, the target vector was the next point along that predefined path. To the degree that the output vector differed from the target vector, corrections were propagated through the network in the usual backprop fashion. In this well-established way, HMS was taught the seven paths, taking an average of between 40 and 50 steps between the starting point and the goal.

In some versions of the training, it was given "anticipatory" target vectors three steps ahead of its present location. This amounted only to a changed metric for the terrain.

The system was never placed in the deep interior of the forbidden zone, but it was placed just within the perimeter of that zone and given target vectors to lead it immediately back out.

Having been trained to wend its way to its primary goal, it was taught to reach the second one. With the system inside the first goal area, the context bit was turned on manually, and target vectors were used that trained it, via backpropagation, to go from the first goal to the second one.

Through these methods, the cognitive map of the field was built.

The recall phase for the homuncular system is deliberately set up so that it receives no input from its environment other than one initial vector—not necessarily one of the seven starting points from its training paths. While it traverses the region, it gets no inputs at all from the environment. This unusual setup was designed in order to study the homuncular system's purely internal representation of the field. The experimenters call the process "daydreaming." The question is: How does HMS navigate in the field, based only on its own internalized model?

The technique used in recall is this: the first vector input to the system during recall is its starting point, somewhere in the field. But then the output (its next location) is fed back to the corresponding nodes of the input. Thus, the output and next input vectors become identical.

The accuracy with which the system traces the trained path toward its primary goal is subject to error, just as any backpropagation paradigm is during recall. This is particularly true when it is placed at a point that was not included in its training path. To the degree that the new input vector is relatively near one of the vectors that it was trained on, the error remains within predictable bounds.

Even though the past training leaves backpropagation features in the system, the network is no longer a backprop network.

Now (after the feeding in of the starting point) the outputs and inputs are identical. Each output node and the input node that it talks to are logically the same node (Figure 14-2). Thus the I/O layers join into a single logical layer during recall, and the network becomes a modified BAM, with the I/O layer at one end of the reverberation and the previous hidden layer at the other.

During recall, the HMS exhibited "resourceful" behavior, usually arriving at its primary goal. It tended to avoid the forbidden zone but sometimes took short-cuts through it to reach its destination. Even when placed at a starting point that it had never seen before, it went to the goal. And, once in the goal area, it did not meander back out, but stayed there.

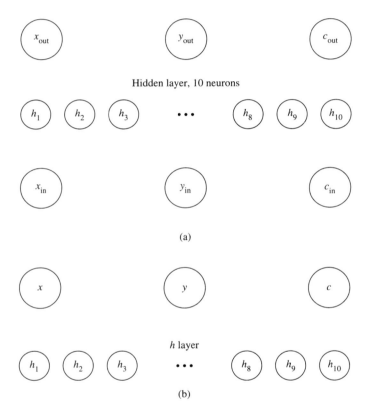

Figure 14-2: (a) HMS is trained as a three-layer backpropagation network with 3 input nodes, 10 hidden nodes, and 3 ouput nodes, all layers fully connected. Inputs to x_{in} and y_{in} specify the system's current location, and outputs x_{out} and y_{out} specify its next location. I/O levels at C_{in} and C_{out} provide a context selecting either the primary or the secondary goal. (b) During recall, the output nodes feed back into the input nodes, with the x_{out} signal dedicated to x_{in}, y_{out} to y_{in}, and C_{out} to C_{in}. This makes the input and output layers into a single logical layer, fully connected to the h layer. The h layer is no longer hidden but now becomes one of the two layers of a BAM, while the x, y, and c nodes form the other BAM layer. The synaptic weights learned via backpropagation become the stored vectors of the BAM.

Following training in the anticipatory mode, it usually converged more rapidly on the goal. However, there was a tradeoff, because its larger steps made it more susceptible to error. In one such case, it went deep into the forbidden zone, winding inward in a spiral path toward what appeared to be a spontaneously formed attractor state. In this, it was probably reflecting its BAM-like operation, as the reciprocal exchange of vectors between the two effective layers converged toward a potential well.

A starting point very slightly displaced from the one that led to the spiral resulted in a direct descent from the forbidden zone into the goal. The emergence of a large variation from a small initial displacement reminded the experimenters of the behavior of chaotic systems.

A manual switch added to the system corresponded to the third input and output nodes—those reserved for "context." When context was switched *on* during training, the homuncular system, having reached its first goal, was trained to go from there to the second goal. That is, vectors that included the context were associated with output loci in the direction from the first to the second goal.

It then occurred to the experimenters to see whether the system would change its context switch internally during recall.

To test that possibility, they trained the system with context switch *off*—but, as soon as it entered the first goal, gave it one additional input—its own output vector (exactly what it would see in recall test) *plus* the context node switched to *on*. Thus, the system was trained so that, after reaching goal 1, it would output a vector containing the context bit.

During subsequent recall runs, the system turned on its context as soon as it

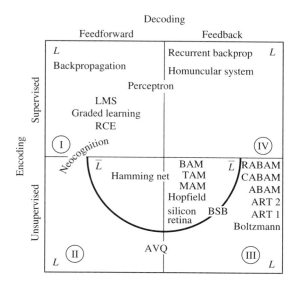

Figure 14-3:   Taxonomy update. (Modified from Kosko.)

reached the first goal, and proceeded to the second goal. An effort was made to confuse the homunculus by putting it in a region where it had been trained to go only to the first goal—but switching on the context at the start of the recall to signal that it should go to the second goal.

This led to a number of different responses during recall. In one of these, HMS went into the forbidden zone, where it spontaneously reversed the context switch, left the zone, and went to the first goal. As soon as it had reached the first goal, it reversed the context switch again and went to the second goal.

The ability of the system to navigate a terrain without new inputs is understandable in terms of the dynamics of a BAM. The weight matrix stored by backpropagation becomes the stored vectors of the BAM, which uses those as a map of the environment to reverberate to a solution.

The homuncular system shares the upper right quadrant of the updated taxonomy (Figure 14-3) with recurrent backpropagation. One of the contrasts between the two paradigms is that the feedforward and feedback phases are separated in HMS, but interleafed in recurrent backprop.

It is interesting to observe the degree to which the homuncular system's behavior simulates attributes of imagination and resourcefulness. Whether a two-phased mixture of backpropagation and BAM paradigms is generally a powerful source of innovative behavior remains to be determined.

APPENDIX:
MATHEMATICAL NOTATION

1. MATRICES: Any relationship between the ith and jth neurons in a network is represented by a term with an ij subscript. Thus, a signal sent from the ith neuron to the jth can be represented as x_{ij}, and the synaptic weight on the corresponding input line can be represented as w_{ij}. This is consistent with an array of interconnected neurons, $N1, N2, N3, \ldots$, as in this diagram:

	$N1$	$N2$	$N3 \ldots$
$N1$	w_{11}	w_{12}	w_{13}
$N2$	w_{21}	w_{22}	w_{23}
$N3$	w_{31}	w_{32}	w_{33}

Thus, the interconnects are described by a matrix, $\mathbf{w}$, whose elements are w_{ij}. A matrix with R rows and C columns is described as an R by C matrix.

2. VECTORS: A vector is a 1-by-n matrix, such as 1-by-3 matrix $\mathbf{A} = (1\ 0\ 2)$ otherwise known as a *row matrix*. Or, the vector can be transposed into an n-by-1 *column matrix*,

$$\mathbf{A}^T = \begin{matrix} 1 \\ 0 \\ 2 \end{matrix}$$

For the sake of compactness, this column matrix can be written as col(1 0 2).

Any scalar component of a vector $\mathbf{B}$ (whether it is a row or a column matrix) can be indicated by a subscript. Thus, in a generalized context, components of $\mathbf{B}$ appears in this text in the form B_i or B_j. Or, if a particular component of $\mathbf{B}$ is to be referenced—for instance, the third component—it can be designated as B_3.

On the other hand, if there are several vectors of class $\mathbf{B}$ under discussion, they are referenced (in this text) by superscripts—such as $\mathbf{B}^1$, $\mathbf{B}^2$, $\mathbf{B}^3$, . . . , or, in a generalized reference, through use of a variable superscript, such as in $\mathbf{B}^k$. Since the transpose function uses T as a superscript, the capital T symbol is reserved and is never used in this text as an identifying index. In some cases, the transpose of a vector requires a double superscript, as in the transpose of $\mathbf{x}^k$, which is written as $(\mathbf{x}^k)^T$.

The dimensionality of a vector is equal to its number of components. Thus, if a vector has four components, B_1, B_2, B_3, and B_4, it is a four-dimensional vector. In general, a vector having n components is n-dimensional. In a matrix context, an n-dimensional row vector is a 1-by-n matrix, and an n-dimensional column vector is an n-by-1 matrix.

The n components of an n-dimensional vector can be treated as its projections onto a set of n orthogonal axes. Thus, the components determine a direction as well as a magnitude for the vector that they generate.

The magnitude of a vector is a scalar number equal to the square root of the sum of the square of the vector's components. It is designated by double vertical bars on either side of the vector symbol. Thus, the magnitude of vector $\mathbf{V}$ is:

$$\|V\| = \left[\sum V_i^2\right]^{1/2}$$

Binary n-dimensional vectors (n-tuplets), having components equal to 0 or 1, are identified as belonging to the vector space $\{0, 1\}^n$. In similar notation, fuzzy n-dimensional vectors, having components drawn from the continuum between 0 and 1, are identified as belonging to the vector space $[0, 1]^n$.

Like vectors, matrices are distinguished from one another in the text by superscripts, in a list such as $\mathbf{M}^1$, $\mathbf{M}^2$, . . . , $\mathbf{M}^k$. Other mathematical functions using superscripts (such as powers of variables or the vector spaces of the preceding paragraph) are clearly distinguishable, by context, from these vector or matrix indices.

3. SCALAR NOTATION: Scalars usually appear without subscripts. However, they may appear with subscripts when they are understood to be components of vectors or matrices—or a scalar may have a subscript merely to associate it with an ith or jth node in a network.

In some cases, where the scalar output of a single neuron (for instance, the jth neuron) is being indicated, it may be *implicitly* treated as the jth component of the vector output from a group of neurons, and would then be subscripted; similarly, the input bias to the jth neuron may be implicitly treated as the jth component of a bias vector. This implicit convention is often used here in a context of a matrix of interconnections among neurons; see, e.g., equation (1.1) of Chapter 1.

Also, scalars from a class U of scalars can be distinguished from one another by a superscript, j, in the form U^j, without reference to their possible use as components of a vector or matrix.

4. MULTIPLICATION OF VECTORS—INNER PRODUCT: The inner (or "dot") product of two vectors is performed through a summation of paired products. If two-dimensional vector **A** has components A_1 and A_2, and two-dimensional vector **B** has components B_1 and B_2, then the inner product of **A** and **B** is $\mathbf{A} \cdot \mathbf{B} = A_1 B_1 + A_2 B_2$. Notice that products of corresponding components are multiplied together, so the vectors that enter into dot multiplication must be of equal dimensionality. Using variable indices and a summation sign, the dot product of vectors **A** and **B** becomes:

$$\mathbf{A} \cdot \mathbf{B} = \sum_i A_i B_i.$$

The result of the dot multiplication is a single number, a scalar.

The square root of a vector's dot product with itself equals the magnitude of the vector:

$$(\mathbf{V} \cdot \mathbf{V})^{1/2} = \sum_i V_i V_i = \|V\|.$$

5. MATRIX MULTIPLICATION: The multiplication of two matrices makes use of the dot product concept in the following way:

   a. Each row of the left-hand multiplier (LHM) forms a dot product with each column of the right-hand multiplier (RHM).

   b. When the ith row of the LHM forms a dot product with the jth column of the right-hand multiplier (RHM), the resulting scalar occupies position i, j in the product matrix.

   c. Clearly, matrix multiplication is not commutative. In general, **AB** $\neq$ **BA**.

   d. For the dot products to exist, each row of the LHM must have the same number of elements as each column of the RHM. This is equivalent to the LHM having a number of columns equal to the number of rows in the RHM.

   e. Thus, matrix multiplication involves the product of an $[R \times S]$ LHM and an $[S \times T]$ RHM to yield an $[R \times T]$ product matrix.

   f. The inner product of two vectors is a special case in which the LHM is a $[1 \times N]$ matrix, the RHM is an $[N \times 1]$ matrix, and their product is a $[1 \times 1]$ matrix—that is, a scalar.

6. MULTIPLICATION OF VECTORS—OUTER PRODUCT: The outer product of two vectors is another special case of matrix multiplication. In the outer product **AB** (of two vectors **A** and **B**), the left-hand multiplier, **A**, must be a column or m-by-1 vector, and the right-hand multiplier, **B**, must be a row or 1-by-n vector. Their product is an m-by-n matrix. Thus, the product of a column vector **A** = col(1 2 1) and row vector **B** = (3 −1) is:

$$
\begin{array}{cc}
& 3 \;\; -1 \\
\mathbf{1:} & 3 \;\; -1 \\
\mathbf{2:} & 6 \;\; -2 \\
\mathbf{1:} & 3 \;\; -1
\end{array}
$$

Each element in the matrix is the product of the vector row element A_i and the vector column element B_j.

Note that the outer product of a column vector and its transpose is $\mathbf{AA}^T$—of a row vector with its transpose is $\mathbf{A}^T\mathbf{A}$.

7. MULTIPLYING A MATRIX BY A VECTOR: When a row vector, $\mathbf{V}^L$, operating as a left multiplier, multiplies a matrix $\mathbf{M}$, it performs a dot product with each column of $\mathbf{M}$. Therefore, $\mathbf{V}^L$ must have the same dimensionality as do the columns of $\mathbf{M}$, each of which is itself a column vector. In matrix terminology, this is the product of a $[1 \times M]$ LHM and an $[M \times N]$ RHM, yielding a $[1 \times N]$ product matrix—that is, another row vector. Thus, if $\mathbf{V}^L$ is row$(1 \; -1 \; 1)$, and $\mathbf{M}$ is: then the product $\mathbf{V}^L\mathbf{M}$ is a row vector whose components are the consecutive scalar

$$
\begin{array}{cccc}
3 & 0 & -2 & 1 \\
1 & -1 & 0 & 3 \\
2 & -2 & 1 & -1
\end{array}
$$

dot products of $\mathbf{V}^L$ and the columns of $\mathbf{M}$:

$$\mathbf{V}^L\mathbf{M} = 4 \quad -1 \quad -1 \quad -3.$$

Similarly, in the product of a matrix $\mathbf{M}$ and a column vector, $\mathbf{V}^R$, operating as a right multiplier, the vector performs a dot product with each row of $\mathbf{M}$. Therefore, $\mathbf{V}^R$ must have the same dimensionality as do the rows of $\mathbf{M}$, each of which is itself a row vector. The product, $\mathbf{MV}^R$, is a column vector.

8. SUMMATION: Operations in this text that involve summation are:

   a. Dot products

   b. Matrix multiplication and its special cases of inner and outer products (all of which are based on dot products)

   c. Summing the weighted inputs to a neuron to determine its activation—also a dot product operation; see equation (1.1) of Chapter 1

   d. Adding matrices together, corresponding element to corresponding element

9. HAMMING DISTANCE: The "Hamming distance" between two binary vectors of equal dimensionality is the number of bit disagreements between them (Hamming, 1950). Thus, the Hamming distance between 0 1 0 1 1 and 1 1 0 0 1 is 2—since the vectors differ in bit positions 1 and 4.

REFERENCES
AND BIBLIOGRAPHY

ACKLEY, DAVID H., GEOFFREY E. HINTON, and TERRENCE J. SEJNOWSKI. "A Learning Algorithm for Boltzmann Machines." *Cognitive Science*, Vol. 9, pp. 147–169.

———, and MICHAEL S. LITTMAN. "Learning from Natural Selection in an Artificial Environment." *Proceedings of the International Joint Conference on Neural Networks*, Vol. 1, January 1990, pp. 189–193.

ALBUS, JAMES S. *Brains, Behavior, and Robotics.* Peterborough, NH: BYTE Books, McGraw-Hill, 1981.

ALKON, DANIEL L. "Memory Storage and Neural Systems." *Scientific American*, July 1989.

———, K. T. BLACKWELL, G. S. BARBOUR, A. K. RIGLER, and T. P. VOGL. "Pattern-Recognition by an Artificial Network Derived from Biologic Neuronal Systems." *Biological Cybernetics*, Vol. 62. Springer-Verlag, 1990, pp. 363–376.

ALMEIDA, L. B. "A Learning Rule for Asynchronous Perceptrons with Feedback in a Combinatorial Environment." *Proceedings of the IEEE First International Conference on Neural Networks*, Vol. II, 1987, pp. 609–618.

ALSPECTOR, J., and R. B. ALLEN. "A Neuromorphic VLSI Learning System." *Advanced Research in VLSI: Proceedings of the 1987 Stanford Conference*, P. Losleben (Ed.). MIT, Cambridge, MA: MIT Press, 1987, pp. 313–349.

AMARI, S. I. "Topographic Organization of Nerve Fields." *Bulletin of Mathematical Biology*, Vol. 42, 1980, pp. 339–364.

ANDERSON, JAMES A., and EDWARD ROSENFELD (Eds.). *Neurocomputing: Foundations of Research.* Cambridge, MA: MIT Press, 1988.

———, JACK W. SILVERSTEIN, STEPHEN A. RITZ, and RANDALL S. JONES. "Distinctive Features, Categorical Perception, and Probability Learning: Some

Applications of a Neural Model." *Psychological Review,* Vol. 84, 1977, pp. 413–451.

ANTOGNETTI, PAOLO, and VELJKO MILUTINOVIC (Eds.). *Neural Networks: Concepts, Applications, and Implementations.* Vols. I–IV. Englewood Cliffs, NJ: Prentice-Hall, 1991.

BAUM, ERIC B., JOHN MOODY, and FRANK WILCZEK. "Internal Representations for Associative Memory." *University of California (Santa Barbara) Preprint NSF-ITP-86-138,* Institute for Theoretical Physics, 1987.

BELEW, RICHARD K. "Evolution, Learning and Culture: Computational Metaphors for Adaptive Algorithms." Computer Science and Engineering Department, University of California at San Diego, CSE Technical Report #CS89-156, September 1989.

BLACK, MAX. "Vagueness: An Exercise in Logical Analysis." *Philosophy of Science,* Vol. 4, 1937, pp. 427–455.

BURR, DAVID J. "A Dynamic Model for Image Registration." *Proceedings, Computer Society Conference on Pattern Recognition and Image Processing, IEEE,* Chicago, August 6–8, 1979.

————. "Elastic Matching of Line Drawings." *IEEE Transactions on Pattern Analysis and Machine Intelligence,* PAMI-3, No. 6, November 1981, pp. 708–713.

————. "Matching Elastic Templates." *Proceedings of the Symposium on Physical and Biological Processing of Images,* O. J. Braddick and A. C. Sleigh (Eds.). New York: Springer-Verlag, 1983, pp. 260–270.

————. "A Neural Network Digit Recognizer." *Proceedings of the IEEE International Conference on Systems, Man, and Cybernetics,* Atlanta, Georgia, October 14–17, 1986.

————. "An Improved Elastic Net Method for the Traveling Salesman Problem." *IEEE International Conference on Neural Networks,* San Diego, July 1988.

CARPENTER, GAIL A., and STEPHEN GROSSBERG. "A Massively Parallel Architecture for a Self-Organizing Neural Pattern Recognition Machine." *Computer Vision, Graphics, and Image Processing,* Vol. 37, 1987, pp. 54–115.

————. "ART 2: Self-Organization of Stable Category Recognition Codes for Analog Input Patterns." *Applied Optics,* Vol. 26, No. 23, December 1987.

CAULFIELD, H. JOHN, JASON KINSER, and STEPHEN K. ROGERS. "Optical Neural Networks." *Proceedings of the IEEE,* Vol. 77, No. 10, October 1989, p. 1573.

————, and JOSEPH SHAMIR. "Wave-Particle Duality Considerations in Optical Computing." *Applied Optics,* Vol. 28, No. 12, Optical Society of America, June 15, 1989, pp. 2184–2186.

CAVIGLIA, D., G. BISIO, and F. CURATELLI. "Neural Algorithms for Cell Placement in VLSI Design." *Proceedings of the International Joint Conference on Neural Networks,* Vol. 1, 1989, pp. 573–580.

CHANG, ERIC I., and DAVID TONG. "Detecting Symmetry with a Hopfield Net." *Proceedings of the International Joint Conference on Neural Networks,* Vol. 2, January 1990, pp. 327–330.

COHEN, MICHAEL A., and STEPHEN GROSSBERG. "Absolute Stability of Global Pattern Formation and Parallel Memory Storage by Competitive Neural Networks." *IEEE Transaction on Systems, Man, and Cybernetics*, Vol. SMC-13, No. 5, September–October 1983.

CRUTCHFIELD, JAMES P., J. DOYNE FARMER, and NORMAN H. PACKARD. "Chaos." *Scientific American*, Vol. 255, December 1986, pp. 46–57.

DARPA NEURAL NETWORK STUDY. October 1987–February 1988. AFCEA International Press, 1988.

DE GARIS, HUGO. "Genetic Programming: Modular Neural Evolution for Darwin Machines." *Proceedings of the International Joint Conference on Neural Networks*, Vol. 1, Washington, DC, January 15–19, 1990.

DOMANY, E., and H. ORLAND. "A maximum overlap neural network for pattern recognition." *Physics Letters A*, Vol. 125, 1987, pp. 32–34.

DURBIN, RICHARD, and DAVID WILLSHAW. "An Analogue Approach to the Traveling Salesman Problem Using an Elastic Net Method." *Nature*, Vol. 326, No. 6114, April 16, 1987, pp. 689–691.

EBERHARDT, SILVIO, TUAN DUONG, and ANIL THAKOOR. "Design of Parallel Hardware Neural Network Systems from Custom Analog VLSI 'Building Block' Chips." *International Joint Conference on Neural Networks*, June 18–22, 1989.

ELSLEY, RICHARD. "Solution of Optimization Problems in Object-Level Vision." *DARPA Neural Network Study (Presentations to the Applications Panel)*. Fairfax, VA: AFCEA International Press, 1988, p. 508.

FARHAT, NABIL H., DEMETRI PSALTIS, ALUIZIO PRATA, and EUNG PACK. "Optical Implementation of the Hopfield Model." *Applied Optics*, Vol. 24, 1985, pp. 1469–1475.

FUKISHIMA, KUNIHIKO, and SEI MIYAKE. "Neocognitron: A new algorithm for pattern recognition tolerant of deformations and shifts in position." *Pattern Recognition*, Vol. 15, 1982.

———, SEI MIYAKE, and TAKAYUKI ITO. "Neocognitron: A Neural Network Model for a Mechanism of Visual Pattern Recognition." *IEEE Transactions on Systems, Man, and Cybernetics* 13 (5), September–October, 1983.

GÖDEL, KURT. "On Formally Undecidable Propositions of Principia Mathematica and Related Systems." *Monatshefte für Mathematik und Physik*, Vol. 38, 1931, pp. 173–198.

GOLDBERG, DAVID E. *Genetic Algorithms in Search, Optimization, and Machine Learning*. Reading, MA: Addison-Wesley, 1989.

GROSSBERG, STEPHEN. "Some networks that can learn, remember, and reproduce any number of complicated space-time patterns, I." *Journal of Mathematics and Mechanics*, 1969, Vol. 19, pp. 53–91.

———. "Some networks that can learn, remember, and reproduce any number of complicated space-time patterns, II." *Studies in Applied Mathematics*, Vol. 49, 1970, pp. 135–166.

———. "Embedding fields: underlying philosophy, mathematics, and applications to psychology, physiology, and anatomy." *Journal of Cybernetics*, Vol. 1, 1971.

————. "Pattern formation by the global limits of a nonlinear competitive interaction in *n* dimensions." *Journal of Mathematical Biology*, Vol. 4, 1977, pp. 237–256.

————. "Do all neural models really look alike?" *Psychological Review*, Vol. 85, 1978, pp. 592–596.

————. "How does a brain build a cognitive code?" *Psychological Review*, Vol. 87, 1980, pp. 1–51.

————. "Competitive Learning: from Interactive Activation to Adaptive Resonance." *Cognitive Science*, Vol. 11, 1987, pp. 23–63.

————. "Nonlinear Neural Networks: Principles, Mechanisms, and Architectures." *Neural Networks*, Vol. 1, 1988, pp. 17–61.

HAGIWARA, MASAFUMI. "Multidirectional Associative Memory." *Proceedings of the International Joint Conference on Neural Networks*, Vol. 1, January 1990, pp. 3–6.

HAINES, KAREN, and ROBERT HECHT-NIELSEN. "A BAM With Increased Information Storage Capacity." *IEEE International Conference on Neural Networks Proceedings*, San Diego, California, July 1988.

HAMMING, R. W. "Error Detecting and Error Correcting Codes." *Bell System Technical Journal*, Vol. 29, April 1950, pp. 147–160.

HANSON, STEPHEN JOSÉ, and DAVID J. BURR. "Knowledge Representation in Connectionist Networks." *Behavioral and Brain Sciences*, Vol. 13, No. 3, 1990.

HEBB, DONALD O. *The Organization of Behavior*. New York: Wiley, 1949.

HECHT-NIELSEN, ROBERT. "Nearest Matched Filter Classification of Spatiotemporal Patterns." *Applied Optics*, Vol. 26, May 15, 1987, p. 1892.

————. *Neurocomputing*. Reading, MA: Addison-Wesley, 1990.

HINTON, GEOFFREY E. "How Neural Networks Learn from Experience." *Scientific American*, September 1992, pp. 145–151.

HOLLAND, JOHN H. *Adaptation in Natural and Artificial Systems*. Ann Arbor: University of Michigan Press, 1975.

HOLLER, MARK, SIMON TAM, HERNAN CASTRO, and RONALD BENSON. "An Electrically Trainable Artificial Neural Network (ETANN) with 10240 'Floating Fate' Synapses." *Proceedings of the International Joint Conference on Neural Networks*, 1989.

HOPFIELD, J. J. "Neurons with Graded Response Have Collective Computational Responses like Those of Two-State Neurons." *Proceedings of the National Academy of Sciences*, Vol. 81, 1984, pp. 3088–3092.

————. "Neural Networks and Physical Systems with Emergent Collective Computational Abilities." *Proceedings of the National Academy of Sciences*, Vol. 79, 1982, pp. 2554–2558.

————, and D. W. TANK. "Neural Computation of Decisions in Optimization Problems." *Biological Cybernetics*, Vol. 52. New York: Springer-Verlag, 1985, pp. 141–152.

HUTTON, LARRIE, VINCENT SIGILLITO, and HOWARD EGETH. "Experiments on Constructing a Cognitive Map: A Neural Network Model of a Robot That

Daydreams." *Proceedings of the International Joint Conference on Neural Networks*, Vol. 1, January 1990, pp. 223–227.

ISRAEL, PEGGY, and CRIS KOUTSOUGERAS. "Associative recall based on abstract object descriptions learned from observation: the CBM neural network model." *International Journal of Pattern Recognition and Artificial Intelligence*, Vol. 4, No. 2, 1990, pp. 181–197.

JACOBS, R. A. "Increased rates of convergence through learning rate adaption." *Neural Networks*, Vol. 1, 1988, p. 295.

JOHNSON, R. COLIN. "Nakano's Positive Perceptron Perception." *Electronic Engineering Times*, April 17, 1989, p. 35.

———, and CHAPPELL BROWN. *Cognizers (Neural Networks and Machines That Think)*. New York: Wiley, 1988.

JORGENSEN, CHUCK C. "Robot Navigation." *DARPA Neural Network Study (Presentations to the Applications Panel)*. Fairfax, VA: AFCEA International Press, 1988, p. 540.

KLASSEN, M. S., Y. H. PAO, and V. CHEN. "Characteristics of the Functional Link Net: A Higher Order Delta Rule Set." *IEEE Annual Conference on Neural Networks*, San Diego, California, July 1988.

KLOPF, A. HARRY. "A Drive-Reinforcement Model of Single Neuron Function: An Alternative to the Hebbian Neuronal Model." Neural Networks for Computing Conference, Snowbird, Utah, April 13–16, 1986.

———. "A Neuronal Model of Classical Conditioning." *Psychobiology*, Vol. 16, 1988, pp. 85–125.

KOHONEN, TUEVO. "Self-Organized Formation of Topologically Correct Feature Maps." *Biological Cybernetics*, Vol. 43, 1982, pp. 59–69.

———. *Self-Organization and Associative Memory*, 2nd ed. Berlin: Springer-Verlag, 1987.

KONG, SEONG-GON, and BART KOSKO. "Comparison of Fuzzy and Neural Truck Backer-Upper Control Systems." *Proceedings of the International Joint Conference on Neural Networks*, June 1990.

———. "Adaptive Fuzzy Systems for Backing Up a Truck-and-Trailer." *IEEE Transactions on Neural Networks*, Vol. 3, No. 2, March 1992.

KOSKO, BART. "Bidirectional Associative Memories." *IEEE Transactions on Systems, Man, and Cybernetics*, Vol. 18, No. 1, January–February 1988, pp. 49–60.

———. "Feedback Stability and Unsupervised Learning." *Proceedings of the IEEE 1988 International Conference on Neural Networks*, Vol. 1, July 1988, pp. 141–152.

———. "Fuzziness vs. Probability." *International Journal of General Systems*, Vol. 17, No. 2, 1990a, pp. 211–240.

———. "Unsupervised Learning in Noise." *IEEE Transactions on Neural Networks*, Vol. 1, No. 11, March 1990b.

———. *Neural Networks: A Dynamical Systems Approach to Machine Intelligence*. Englewood Cliffs, NJ: Prentice-Hall, 1992.

————. "Fuzzy Systems as Universal Approximators." IEEE International Conference on Fuzzy Systems, San Diego, California, March 8–12, 1992.

————, and CLARK GUEST. "Optical Bidirectional Associative Memories," *Proceedings of the Society for Photo-optical and Instrumentation Engineers (SPIE)*, Vol. 758, 1987.

LANGHELD, ERWIN, and KARL GOSER. "Generalized Boolean Operations for Neural Networks." *Proceedings of the International Joint Conference on Neural Networks*, Vol. 2, Washington, DC, January 15–19, 1990, pp. 159–162.

LIPPMANN, RICHARD P. "An Introduction to Computing with Neural Nets." *IEEE ASP Magazine*, April 1987.

————, B. GOLD, and M. L. MALPASS. "A comparison of Hamming and Hopfield neural nets for pattern classification." *Technical Report 769*, Massachusetts Institute of Technology, Lexington, MA, 1987.

LYON, RICHARD F., and CARVER MEAD. "Electronic Cochlea." *Analog VLSI and Neural Systems*, edited by Carver Mead. Reading, MA: Addison-Wesley, 1989, pp. 279–302.

MACKIE, STUART, and JOHN S. DENKER. "A Digital Implementation of a Best Match Classifier." *Digest IEEE Custom Integrated Circuits Conference*, 1988.

MAHOWALD, M. A., and CARVER MEAD. "A Silicon Model of Early Visual Processing." *Neural Networks*, Vol. 1. New York: Pergamon Press, 1988.

MALSBURG, C. VON DER. "Self-Organization of Orientation Sensitive Cells in the Striate Cortex." *Kybernetik*, Vol. 14, 1973, pp. 85–100.

————, and D. J. WILLSHAW. "How to Label nerve Cells So That They Can Interconnect in an Ordered Fashion." *Proceedings of the National Academy of Science of the USA*, Vol. 74, 1977, pp. 5176–5178.

MATSUDA, S., and Y. AKIMOTO. "The Representation of Large Numbers in Neural Networks and Its Application to Economical Load Dispatching of Electrical Power." *Proceedings of the International Joint Conference on Neural Networks*, Vol. 1, 1989, pp. 587–592.

MCCULLOCH, WARREN S., and WALTER PITTS. "A Logical calculus of Ideas Immanent in Nervous Activity." *Bulletin of Mathematical Biophysics* Vol. 9, 1943, pp. 127–147.

MCELIECE, ROBERT J., EDWARD C. POSNER, EUGENE R. RODEMICH, and SANTOSH S. VENKATESH. "The Capacity of the Hopfield Associative Memory." *IEEE Transactions on Information Theory*, Vol. 33, No. 4, July 1987.

MEAD, CARVER. *Analog VLSI and Neural Systems*. Reading, MA: Addison-Wesley, 1989.

MINSKY, MARVIN, and SEYMOUR PAPERT. *Perceptrons*. Cambridge, MA: MIT Press, 1969.

MOOPENN, A., H. LANGENBACHER, A. P. THAKOOR, and S. K. KHANNA. "Programmable Synaptic Chip for Electronic Neural Networks." *Neural Information Processing Systems*, ed. D. Z. Anderson. New York: AIP, 1988.

————, and A. P. THAKOOR. "Custom VLSI and Thin Film Devices for Electronic Neural Nets." Third Annual Parallel Processing Symposium, Fullerton, California, March 29–31, 1989.

————, A. P. THAKOOR, and T. DUONG. "A Neural Network for Euclidean Distance Minimization." *Proceedings of the IEEE Second International Conference on Neural Networks*, Vol. 2, July 1988.

NAGEL, ERNEST, and JAMES R. NEWMAN. *Godel's Proof.* New York: New York University Press, 1958.

NEGOITA, CONSTANTIN VIRGIL. *Expert Systems and Fuzzy Systems.* Menlo Park, CA: Benjamin/Cummings, 1985.

NELSON, MARILYN MCCORD, and W. T. ILLINGWORTH. *A Practical Guide to Neural Nets.* Reading, MA: Addison-Wesley, 1990.

NEUMANN, ERIC K., DAVID A. WHEELER, JAMIE W. BURNSIDE, ADAM S. BERNSTEIN, and JEFFREY C. HALL. "A Technique for the Classification of Insect Courtship Song." *Proceedings of the International Joint Conference on Neural Networks*, Vol. 2, January 1990, pp. 257–262.

PALM, G. "On Associative Memory." *Biological Cybernetics,* Vol. 36, No. 19. New York: Springer-Verlag, 1980.

PAO, YO-HAN. "Adaptive Pattern Recognition and Neural Networks." *Systems Research Technical Report 88–105.* Reading, MA: Addison-Wesley, 1988.

————. "Functional Link Nets: Removing the Hidden Layer." *AI Expert*, April 1989, pp. 60–68.

————, and R. D. BEER. "The Functional Link Net: A Unifying Network Architecture Incorporating Higher Order Effects." *International Neural Networks Society First Annual Meeting*, Boston, September 1988.

PERLIS, SAM. *Theory of Matrices.* Cambridge, MA: Addison-Wesley, 1952.

PINEDA, FERNANDO J. "Recurrent Backpropagation and the Dynamical Approach to Adaptive Neural Computation." *Neural Computation*, Vol. 1, No. 2, pp. 161–171, Cambridge, MA: MIT Press, 1989.

POLANYI, MICHAEL. *"The Tacit Dimension."* Doubleday & Company, Inc., 1966.

ROSENBLATT, FRANK. "The Perceptron: A Probabilistic Model for Information Storage and Organization in the Brain." *Psychological Review*, Vol. 65, 1958, pp. 386–408.

RUMELHART, DAVID E., GEOFFREY E. HINTON, and RONALD J. WILLIAMS. "Learning Internal Representations by Error Propagation." *Parallel Distributed Processing: Explorations in the Microstructures of Cognition*, Vol. 1, D. E. Rumelhart and J. E. McClelland (Eds.). Cambridge, MA: MIT Press, 1986, pp. 318-362.

SAGE, J. P., K. THOMPSON, and R. S. WITHERS. "An Artificial Neural Network Integrated Circuit Based on MNOS/CCD Principles." *AIP Conference Proceedings*, Vol. 151, *Neural Networks for Computing*, J. Denker (Ed.), 1986.

SCHWARTZ, TOM J. (publisher). "Genetic Algorithms Made Easy." A videotape with Lawrence Davis and John Grefenstette as instructors. Mountain View, CA: The Schwartz Associates, 1992.

———— (publisher). "NeuroTapes." A videotape with Mark Jurik as instructor. Mountain View, CA: The Schwartz Associates, 1990.

———— (publisher). "FuzzyTapes." A videotape with Bart Kosko as instructor. Mountain View, CA: The Schwartz Associates, 1990.

SEJNOWSKI, TERRENCE J., and CHARLES R. ROSENBERG. "NETtalk: A Parallel Network That Learns to Read Aloud." *The Johns Hopkins University Electrical Engineering and Computer Science Technical Report* JHU/EECS-86/01, 1986.

SIVILOTTI, MASSIMO A., MICHELLE A. MAHOWALD, and CARVER A. MEAD. "Real-Time Visual Computations Using Analog CMOS Processing Arrays." *Advanced Research in VLSI: Proceedings of the 1987 Stanford Conference,* P. Losleben (Ed.). Cambridge, MA: MIT Press, pp. 295–312.

SOUCEK, BRANKO, and MARINA SOUCEK. *Neural and Massively Parallel Computers: The Sixth Generation.* New York: Wiley, 1988.

STEINBUCH, K. "Die Lernmatrix." *Kybernetik,* Vol. 1, 1961, pp. 36–45.

TABER, ROD. "Knowledge Processing with Fuzzy Cognitive Maps." *Expert System with Applications,* Vol. 2. New York: Pergamon Press, 1991, pp. 83–87.

TABER, W. R., and R. O. DEICH. "Fuzzy Sets and Neural Networks." *Proceedings, First Joint Technology Workshop on Neural Networks and Fuzzy Logic.* NASA/University of Houston, Houston: May 2–3, 1988.

————, R. O. DEICH, P. K. SIMPSON, and A. H. FAGG. "The Recognition of Orca Calls with a Neural Network." International Workshop on Fuzzy Applications, Iizuka, Japan, August 20–24, 1988.

TAPANG, CARLOS C. "The Significance of Sleep in Memory Retention and Internal Adaptation." *Journal of Neural Network Computing,* Vol. 1, No. 1, Summer 1989.

TAYLOR, W. "Cortico-Thalamic Organization and Memory." *Proceedings of the Royal Society of London, B,* Vol. 159, 1964, pp. 466–478.

THAKOOR, ANIL. "Electronic Neural Networks." *JPL Amplifier,* November 1986, p. 1.

————, A. MOOPENN, JOHN LAMBE, and S. K. KHANNA. "Electronic Hardware Implementations of Neural Networks." *Applied Optics,* Vol. 26, December 1, 1987, p. 5085.

WAGNER, K., AND D. PSALTIS. "Multilayer optical learning networks." *Applied Optics,* Vol. 26, 1987, pp. 5067–5076.

WAN, ERIC A., GREGORY T. A. KOVACS, JOSEPH M. ROSEN, and BERNARD WIDROW. "Development of Neural Network Interfaces for Direct Control of Neuroprostheses." *Proceedings of the International Joint Conference on Neural Networks,* Vol. 2, January 1990, pp. 3–21.

WASSERMAN, PHILLIP D. *Neural Computing: Theory and Practice.* New York: Van Nostrand Reinhold, 1989.

WILLIAMS, RONALD J., and DAVID ZIPSER. "Gradient-Based Learning Algorithms for Recurrent Connectionist Networks." *College of Computer Science Technical Report NU-CSS-90-9.* Boston: Northeastern University, April 1990.

————. "Experimental Analysis of the Real-Time Recurrent Learning Algorithm." *Connection Science,* Vol. 1, No. 1. Cambridge, MA: MIT Press, Summer 1989a, pp. 87–111.

————. "A Learning Algorithm for Continually Running Fully Recurrent Neural Networks." *Neural Computation,* Vol. 1. Boston: MIT Press, 1989b, pp. 270–280.

WILLSHAW, D. J. "Models of Distributed Associative Memory." Ph.D. Thesis, University of Edinburgh, 1971.

————, and H. C. LONGUET-HIGGINS. "Associative Memory Models." *Machine Intelligence*, B. Meltzer and O. Michie (Eds.). Edinburgh: Edinburgh University Press, 1970.

————, and C. VON DER MALSBURG. "A Marker Induction Mechanism for the Establishment of Ordered Neural Mappings: Its Application to the Retino-tectal Problem." *Philosophical Transactions of the Royal Society of London*, B287, 1979, pp. 203–243.

————. "How Patterned Neural Connections Can Be Set Up by Self-Organization." *Proc. Royal Society*, B194, 1976, pp. 431–435.

ZADEH, LOFTI. "Fuzzy Sets." *Information and Control*, Vol. 8, 1965, pp. 338–353.

INDEX